Excel at Business

Essential NLP and Coaching Skills for Business Success

Jimmy Petruzzi

Excel at Business

Essential NLP and Coaching Skills for Business Success

© 2014 Jimmy Petruzzi

Print: ISBN 978-1-908269-42-3
Digital: ISBN 978-1-908269-43-0
First Edition

Published by
DragonRising Publishing
The Starfields Network Ltd.
PO Box 3175
Eastbourne
BN21 9PG
United Kingdom
www.DragonRising.com

Printed and bound by CPI Group (UK) Ltd, Croydon, CR0 4YY

Excel at Business

Essential NLP and Coaching Skills for Business Success

Jimmy Petruzzi

Dedication

To Nieve and Luca

Praise for Excel at Business

"*I have known Jim personally & professionally for a number of years. I have seen how he delivers excellent training for sports people and know he has the same impact in the business world. He understands that whether relating NLP to sports people or business people, they are still just people! The same attitude and methodology of NLP principles apply.*

You will get a great deal out of his book Excel at Business, *which is a powerful insight into applying NLP in business.*"

—Mick Farrell
Culture & Performance Consultant to European Super League Champions
Wigan Warriors Rugby League & Wales Rugby League

"*I have known Jimmy for many years and attended several of his courses. I would go as far to say Jimmy has been an inspiration in my life through his coaching and mentoring. Jimmy has produced another good book and this time with a greater focus on skills for business.*"

—Martin Loynd
Business, Life and Sports Growth Coach, Inspiring Your Success Ltd.

"*Jimmy Petruzzi's NLP Programme has helped the Australasian Soccer Academy (ASA) become one of the most successful academies in Australia. I have learnt so many different techniques on how to communicate with players and prepare them mentally and physically. Without Jimmy's influence and technique, the academy would not be where it is today. The techniques and principles have also been transferred to the business side of running the academy with great success. We have become a power house, registering over 300 players. ASA has already produced 3 professional players in the past 6 years. Players including Mitchell Duke, a current Australian International socceroo, also undertook Jimmy's program. I know it works and I have excelled as a coach. For anyone that wants to improve as a person or coach, I highly recommend Jimmy's excellent work and new book,* Excel at Business.*"

—Tony Basha
Australasian Soccer Acadamey, Director Head Coach

v

Praise for Excel at Sports

"You need look no further than Jim's book, Excel at Sports, *when it comes to succeeding in sports or life."*

—Amdy Paschalidis
Sky Sports Radio

"This book is excellent. Throughout my 18-year playing career as a professional footballer I used all the techniques mentioned."

—Andy Hill
Former Professional Footballer, Manchester United FC, 1981–1984

"An excellent book! I highly recommend it to any coach looking to get the best out of his team. Jim has been a big part of the success of several teams I have coached."

—David Dias
Former Professional Footballer, Angolan National Football Team

"Brilliant book, would recommend to anyone studying NLP or indeed anyone who is just interested in the subject and wanting to learn more. Very informative, interesting and inspirational read. It's an incredibly useful book, not just for sports, but for business and life."

—Emma S.
Amazon.co.uk Customer

"Fantastic! I bought this book really to help with my mental attitude towards sport. I have never been the athletic type and last year I decided to take on the Great North Run. I was dreading it, BUT... I have to say I loved it and I have signed up once more. Getting hooked on that sense of achievement is something special. Who knows where this could lead to. Thank you!"

—S. Suthers
Amazon.co.uk Customer

Praise for Jimmy Petruzzi

"Jimmy is a dedicated professional who integrates NLP and psychological strategies with physical conditioning to excellent effect. Jimmy is extremely knowledgeable and a leader in his field."

—Tony Strudwick
Head of Fitness and Conditioning, Manchester United FC

"I was a student of Jimmy's for NLP Practitioner. He demonstrated an in-depth knowledge of his subject area and backed this up with real world examples where he had made a game-changing difference to people's lives. I enjoyed the course considerably and would highly recommend Jimmy and his company, the NLP Centre of Excellence."

—Jonathan Cleaver
Head of IT, Peninsula Business Services

"Jimmy is an excellent coach with a focussed yet laid back style that enables him to get his message across in a manner that produced a motivated response."

—Dave Edler
Chief Executive, Nelson Football Club Limited

"Jimmy is a true expert in his field. His teaching methods are extremely easy to follow and enjoyable to be a part of. Without exaggeration, the NLP course that Jimmy taught have changed all aspects of my life for the better. I have a much better understanding of myself and a clearer view of my future."

—Katie De-Mouilpied
Owner, Re-Activ8

"I attended an NLP Practitioners course held by Jimmy in January. Jimmy's knowledge on the subject is extensive however he can easily translate this into every day experiences making him an excellent teacher. I have already used a number of the strategies taught by Jimmy in my work place and seen great results."

—Vicky McDonough
Collections Operations Manager at Blemain Group

# Also by the Author

Excel at Sports: Be the Best at Sports, Business and Life with NLP Neuro Linguistic Programming

Available from DragonRising Publishing

ontents

Figures

Tables

Acknowledgements

There are many people to whom I would like to express my gratitude and appreciation for their support, guidance and suggestions in making this book possible. I would like to take this opportunity to thank all of my colleagues, clients, and students who have inspired me to write the book. My thanks to Sara Lou-Ann Jones for her contributions to the book, and her suggestions and efforts in assisting me to put the finishing touches to the book She continues to support and encourage my dreams and ambitions. Thank you.

To my family: Dario, my sisters, my cousin Tony, Aunty, Uncle, and my closest family and friends who are my inspiration and have always supported my dreams.

I feel privileged and honoured to have worked with a number of different businesses from all over the world, to have delivered staff training and had staff from many major businesses attend our training and completed one-to-one coaching.

I am grateful for the opportunity to have trained individual staff members who have attended our courses from hundreds of different companies, businesses and organisations, such as Manchester Metropolitan University, the Greater Manchester Police, Salford University, Mcdonalds, Astrazeneca, bmi health care, Barclays, Bury college, Easy fit, Momentum, National Health Service, Virgin Media, and many more over a number of years.

I am grateful to have had and have the opportunity to work with new business start-ups and watch them flourish, turn around struggling businesses and help them to drive forward to be successful businesses, and having had the opportunity to transfer NLP and elite sports principles and skills from sport to business.

I am honoured and privileged to have had an extensive background of working with some of the world's leading athletes and sports people.

I would especially like to thank Martin Loynd, Andy Paschalidis, Dr Tony Strudwick, Mark Hughes, Wyatt Woodsmall, Carlos Alberto Da Luz, Chris Casper, Amelia Harris, all the boys at Sky Sports Radio, Carlo Nash, Chris Butler, the guys at City Talk FM, BBC Radio, BBC Gmr, Ang, Andy Hill, David Dias, Lee Murphy, Colin Kazeem Richards, Tony Basha, the Welsh Girls Lacrosse team, the lads at Bury football club 2003 to 2006, Jeremy Lazarus, Ross Johnson, the lads at Accrington Stanley, Bacup FC, and Brent Peters. To everyone who ever supported my work.

Special thanks to my editor, Sheryl, and to everyone at Dragon-Rising Publishing for believing in me.

I would like to also especially thank the team at the NLP Centre of Excellence who are dedicated to working hard to getting a positive message out to the world.

Foreword

This is an easy-to-follow book that has been written for anyone who wants to get the best out of themselves and others in business, no matter what level of experience they have with NLP—beginner or experienced, NLP practitioner or a coach. This book also has powerful insights into how you can implement the techniques and strategies I provide.

For beginners, I have included a glossary at the back of the book filled with terms you will find throughout this book and when you are working with NLP.

NLP is an art, not a science. NLP is about having a box of tools you can use, rather than a prescriptive set of exercises. The key to NLP is about being creative and adapting the techniques to the situation.

Through my experience over many years in coaching I have come to realise that at times we all have personal problems in our life and those personal problems can affect our business life. I have worked with plenty of people who are experiencing difficulties and it doesn't matter who they are, the key to resolving these difficulties is to be able to manage their personal lives. All of us are going to have ups and downs in life and obviously our personal life can affect our business life. However, if you are very clear about the area in which the problem lies, even when you have difficulties in your personal life you will still be able to function in business at a level in which you can fulfil your potential.

The work I do in business is not only working with performance-related targets and measurements and business strategies, but it is also about helping people because people are *people* regardless of who they are and what they do. I have worked with some of the leading authorities in business and they all go through difficult situations in life, just like everybody else. I think the key to overcoming difficult situations is being able to manage emotions as much as anything else by developing emotional intelligence and emotional

1

muscle. One thing we all have in common as human beings is emotions and people who are emotionally fit tend to be the ones who fare the best in life. How we manage and channel those emotions is key. Sometimes people have the biggest setbacks you could ever imagine yet the way they respond is positive. I'm not saying to respond in an airy-fairy, "the grass is always greener" way because the reality in this world is that we do have difficult situations. I'm saying to respond in a positive way to achieve the best positive outcome. The skills in the book can be transferred to business life and sports.

Regardless of what level of NLP you have, whether you're new to the field or have experience, this book is highly interactive and has transcripts of sessions and stories that will help you even if you're a complete novice, or help you to develop extra awareness if you have a lot of experience. For those with experience, this book will help you to reinforce some of the work you already do and become aware of and have an open mind about other ways to deploy techniques.

The purpose of *Excel at Business* is for you to take away what works for you, helping you to focus on the results and outcomes you do want, and to minimise what you don't want. It provides you with a platform and information on NLP on which you can build to help you get the results you want in business, life or sports.

◢ HOW THIS BOOK IS STRUCTURED

The book provides you with the following chapters:

- ◢ Chapter 1: Understanding People and Behaviour
- ◢ Chapter 2: Asking Questions
- ◢ Chapter 3: Communication and Rapport
- ◢ Chapter 4: Meta-Programmes
- ◢ Chapter 5: Logical Levels
- ◢ Chapter 6: Emotional State Elicitation and Anchoring
- ◢ Chapter 7: Beliefs and Values
- ◢ Chapter 8: Goals
- ◢ Chapter 9: Modelling
- ◢ Chapter 10: Building Your Business

All of the chapters have exercises, tips, and examples of how the techniques have been used by people in business, sports, life/relationships, and education. Sometimes the names and gender of people referred to in examples have been changed in order to preserve confidentiality. However, where appropriate, I have used identifiable examples as a person that "walks his talk" so you can draw from their experience.

◢ HOW TO GET THE MOST OUT OF *EXCEL AT BUSINESS*

Excel at Business is a how-to book. There are numerous exercises and, in order to assist you in developing the skill to use the techniques effectively for yourself, the processes are explained step-by-step. The book can be used as a resource that you can reread and use to reapply the skills in different situations to assist you in achieving specific outcomes.

In my journey of learning NLP, I found that the more I read about and then practiced a particular NLP process, the better I was able to do it. It is recommended that you do and apply as many of the exercises as possible, especially those which may initially seem challenging to you, because these are the one you may find will benefit you the most.

I guarantee in business and life you will encounter challenges in your journey. This book has many powerful techniques you can use as a resource to help you tackle those challenges and achieve a positive outcome.

There are certain situations described in this book in which I have used NLP to help clients in medical situations. I want to stress that the techniques are **not** a substitute for medical advice, therapy or counselling if that is what someone needs. I strongly advise *anyone* who has a medical condition to consult their GP or clinical supervisor before deploying some of the processes.

I trust you will enjoy and benefit from reading the book and using the techniques as much as I have enjoyed and had the privilege to benefit from the skills personally and have used them to help many clients around the world.

◢ INTRODUCING NLP

SO WHAT EXACTLY IS THE DEFINITION OF NLP?

Neuro: The nervous system—the mind and the sensory organs with which we receive and filter information through our five senses.

Linguistic: The way we communicate and interpret experience through language, including body language, images, sounds, feelings, tastes and smells, as well as words.

Programming: The way we construct personal *programmes* (similar in some ways to computer programmes) of thought, communication and behaviour.

Beyond the definition, let's explore a bit about where NLP came from, how it has evolved and how it can benefit you.

Neuro-Linguistic Programming (NLP) is the study of how we think and communicate, with ourselves and with others, and of how we can use this to get the results we want. The heart of NLP is about modelling successful behaviour. The techniques that are commonly thought of as making up NLP are just the results of that modelling.

At the heart of NLP is the modelling of human excellence. This is the story of where NLP began during the early 1970s with the collaboration of Richard Bandler and John Grinder at the University of California.

Bandler was a student of mathematics with a particular interest in computer science. He got involved in transcribing some audio and video seminar tapes of Fritz Perls, the father of Gestalt Therapy, and Virginia Satir, the founder of Family Therapy. He found that by copying certain aspects of their behaviour and language he could achieve similar results, so he started running a Gestalt Therapy group on the campus at the University.

John Grinder, who as an associate professor of Linguistics at the University, was curious about Bandler's abilities. It was claimed that Grinder said to Bandler: "If you teach me how to do what you do, I'll tell you *what* you do."

It wasn't long before Grinder was achieving the same therapeutic results as Bandler and Perls simply by modelling what Bandler did and said. Grinder was able to determine what was essential and what was irrelevant by going through the process systematically and leaving various elements out.

The essence of NLP is that by studying, analysing and modelling experts in their field, you are able to copy the critical elements and achieve the same results. For example, if you want to be an expert golfer, leading sales person or manager, you first need to find a model of excellence; i.e., someone worth modelling. Observe what they do and say, and then ask specific questions about what is going on in their mind. This allows you to discover and create a template for success that you can use.

The critical findings in Bandler and Grinder's work was that our subjective experience of the world has a structure and that how we think about something affects how we experience it. This is illustrated by the work of Alfred Korzybski who wrote the book *Science and Sanity* in the 1930s. In NLP, we are making a clear distinction between the territory—the world itself—and the internal map we create of it. This is often referred to as "the map is not the territory," which we will explore in the first chapter of this book, "Understanding People and Behaviour".

In understanding NLP, John Grinder described it in the following terms: "NLP is an attitude and a methodology that leaves behind a trail of techniques." Attitude is important, but which kind of attitude should you adopt? The answer is one of *curiosity* because this will propel you to discover *how* people do what they do. What is going on inside their mind? You need to question, challenge and search for the structure rather than being interested purely in the content.

When it comes to the techniques, NLP provides us with the most powerful patterns ever devised for facilitating change in human beings. Some of the techniques are well known, like the Fast Phobia Model. However, as John Grinder states, the techniques are the product of NLP's attitude and methodology—the result of modelling and investigation.

Richard Bandler and John Grinder went on to model the work of Dr Milton H. Erickson, the world's foremost medical hypnotherapist. The result was a different set of language patterns that they called The Milton Model. This led to the publication of their second book, *Patterns of the Hypnotic Techniques of Milton H. Erickson MD.*

With others joining this field of inquiry and research, including Robert Dilts, Judith DeLozier, Leslie Cameron-Bandler, and Steve and Connirae Andreas, Bandler and Grinder developed many other NLP patterns including representational systems, submodalities and anchoring.

The Bandler and Grinder partnership came to an end in the late 1970s when they went their separate ways, although both remain active in the field of NLP today. NLP continues to evolve, with new models and techniques being added every year by a growing number of trainers and developers.

NLP AT WORK

The business world has come to strongly embrace NLP processes because the simple fact is that they increase results. When the tools and techniques that you are about to learn are put into action, they can enable individuals and teams to achieve their peak performance in areas as diverse as management, sales, communication, new product development and coaching.

THE BENEFITS YOU WILL GET FROM LEARNING NLP

You can expect many benefits from this book. It will:

- assist you to know what you want and how to get it,
- put you back in charge and in the driver's seat of your life,
- change limiting beliefs about yourself and the world,
- help you to build better and stronger relationships,
- improve your self esteem and confidence,
- assist you to control the way you think, feel and act,
- enable you to communicate in a more compelling way,
- assist you to perform at your best more and more often,
- enable you to consistently achieve your personal and professional goals,
- enhance your ability to connect with other people, and
- enable you to be even more creative

◢LET'S EXPLORE THE POWER OF THE MIND

In 1977, a grandmother named Laura Schultz heard screaming from the driveway. Her grandson had been playing with the car and accidentally released the emergency brake and the car rolled onto his arm. She was a petite woman and said she had never lifted a thing over 50 pounds in her life, yet she lifted a 2000-pound car off her grandson's arm to release him.

After the incident, she was reluctant to speak about it with anyone. Finally, she opened up. The reason she had never talked about it was because the event challenged her beliefs about what she could and could not do. She said, "If I was able to do this when I didn't think I could, what does that say about the rest of my life? Have I wasted it?"

When I first came across that story a few years ago, I was looking for inspirational stories on the internet to use with clients I was working with to demonstrate what we are capable of if we put our mind to it. That story has stayed with me ever since.

What amazes me most about the way people live their lives is the things that they don't attempt to do. The things that they don't even try. Most of us don't try because we have a fear of failure and that story demonstrates just how powerful the mind is. Just think of what you could do if you put your mind to it and really focused. Think of the things that you have done in your life so far when you've really focused.

The key is *focusing your mind*. Understanding your mind is one of the biggest and most important things you can ever do. We all spend a lot of time at school developing academically. Some people go on to more advanced education and university while others take various jobs or receive other training, yet rarely do any of us ever stop to think about how the mind actually works. We never take the time to tap into our most powerful resource. What do we know about the mind? How much do we know? How powerful is the mind? What can we do? If a 77-year-old woman can lift a car—and I'm sure you've came across a number of stories and seen a number of amazing feats—what could we do if we put our mind to it? What is possible?

If you think back to when you were younger and you first learned to ride a bike, to do a sport, or to do something you'd never done before, you probably thought it wasn't easy. Remember the first time on a bike? You may have fallen off and hurt yourself, but you kept getting back up and trying to ride that bike until you did. Eventually you could ride your bike with no hands, do a wheelie, do tricks, do all sorts of things. What was amazing is that you just kept trying until you got to where you wanted to be in the end.

If we think about it, some of the most powerful things we ever did in your lives, such as the first steps that we took as a baby, were nothing short of a miracle. Yet we often forget what we accomplished in the past and when we look to do new things, like running a marathon, starting a business, doing a course, finding a partner, or losing some weight, we say to ourselves, "I can't do that." We place limitations on ourselves in our own mind.

Believing in ourselves is extremely powerful. When we believe in ourselves and have the motivation to do something, we begin to build up momentum. It's like a train building up momentum, starting out slow and building speed as it goes from one destination to the next.

But, if we think, "I can't do that," it's just like a train hitting the emergency brake. What's stopping you from achieving what you want to achieve? What's stopping anyone from achieving what they want to achieve? What forms our reality? What shapes our thought processes? It could be that emergency brake. In order to get our train to go, we have to release the emergency brake.

We're born pretty much a clean slate. No one is really born optimistic or pessimistic, but along the way we pick up certain beliefs that push us toward one life or another. Those beliefs have a massive impact on our lives. Some of it might be nature, some of it might be nurture, but ultimately there's a point at which only we are in control and our mindset can help us to make the very most of any situation we're in. That mindset grows over time and it's never too late to start developing that mindset. Regardless of how old you are, what you do, where you've been, it's never too late. Just think, a 77-year-old woman lifted a car but she doesn't speak about this incredible feat because she thinks of all the things she could've done if she hadn't placed limitation on herself throughout her life.

Now, think about it for one minute. What's possible? What could you do if you put your mind to it?

I think it is important to have an open mind.

In 1997 I was employed as a conditioning coach in Oxted, Surrey, just outside London. Some of my clients were Ian Pearce, playing with West Ham, and Kevin Gallen, playing with the Queens Park Rangers. I was doing NLP-based exercises that caught the attention of other trainers at the centre. They would look on thinking, "What is all that about?"

At that time I started to work with football goal keeper Carlo Nash of Crystal Palace, predominately involving strength training. However, much of the work I did with Carlo while he was at Crystal Palace was always underpinned with NLP.

After working with Carlo for a few weeks, I began to understand that because he had been signed by Crystal Palace fc, which was in the premier league, from the non-league side, Clitheroe, which was around the 10th tier in English football, he had a lot of confidence in his abilities, though at times he may have lacked a bit of self-belief that he could maintain a position as keeper at that level. So much of the conditioning work I underpinned with NLP was about breaking that belief barrier.

Carlo went on to have a successful career and played with Stockport County, the Wolverhampton Wanderers, Manchester City, Middlesbrough, Preston North End, Wigan Athletic, Everton, and Stoke City.

I am not putting it all down to me, though I think certain things are about timing and the work we did together seemed to be at the right time in his career. However, it demonstrates how powerful NLP can be and how it can underpin conditioning work.

BEING MENTALLY RESILIENT

Mental toughness can make a huge difference in performance. I remember being interviewed by TalkSport radio when I released my last book. The presenters got on the subject about the tennis player Andy Murray and whether he had the mental toughness to win a major open. This was prior to Andy Murray winning a major open.

Although I had heard Murray had not come through the Lawn Tennis Associations program, I didn't comment because I didn't know much more than that about Murray's background. However, after watching his career, it comes as no surprise he has done well. During the interviews I have seen of him on TV, he seemed very focused and determined.

After watching Murray, it prompted me to think back to when the Lawn Tennis Association, based at Weybridge, Surrey, brought me in as a conditioning coach to do some work with the nation's young elite players. I was underpinning my tough fitness regime with NLP to great success.

Half way through the program I realised the Lawn Tennis Association was not interested. They seemed to want to bring me in to do some part-time fitness coaching and to tell me what to do and how to do it. The minute it got a bit tough for the performers, parents and coaches did not like it. The experience was quite negative. It was no surprise that I didn't hear of any of those players going on to make it on a world stage.

I think it is so important that in sports, business and life that we develop a strong resilience. There is no point in kidding ourselves by thinking we will always get an easy ride. It is important that we build mental muscle and emotional fitness.

I had been working with the Bury football club youth team since 2003 and during the football season of 2005–2006, we were producing some outstanding players. In 2003, the youth system had gone from the brink of being disbanded because of financial reasons to producing players like Colin Kazeem Richards within a couple of season. He would go on to grace the European Champions league.

Bury was winning their youth team league championship. The success of the education system we had put in place for the youth team and the players we were producing had attracted the attention of the first team. The first team had been stumbling along. While the youth team had won their division championship, 2005–2006 saw the first team lose 6 of the first 9 games under manager Graham Barrow.

The directors at the time offered Barrow my assistance. The board wanted me involved to help get the team out of a difficult situation. He refused. Then the unthinkable happened. Manager Barrow got sacked. Because Bury was routed at the bottom and tipped for relegation, and with Barrow being sacked, youth team coach Chris Casper got the first team job.

With that, Chris took me into the first team. Because the club was in a difficult financial position, we had to sell players. Still, despite all that, we managed to turn around the first team fortunes. I think the turning point came just before Christmas against Wycombe. They were unbeaten all season and at the top of the league. Even though they were leading 1-0 up until the final minute, we beat them 2-1. We scored two goals in as many minutes.

It was a fantastic achievement, a football miracle, and we survived that season. Much of the work I had done with the team to get them to that point was underpinned by NLP.

It was a huge change of fortunes in a short space of time. While it surprised a lot of people, it did not surprise me.

I would eventually leave the club not long after it beat Sunderland 2-0 in the Carling Cup first round. I had seen some excellent players like Colin Kazeem Richards, David Nugent, David Worral, Nicky Adams and several other young players come through. I helped generate revenue for the club and the first team went on to an extended record of unbeaten games.

PERSEVERANCE

> *"Boys, there ain't no free lunches in this country. And don't go spending your whole life commiserating that you got the raw deals. You've got to say, I think that if I keep working at this and want it bad enough I can have it. It's called perseverance."*
>
> —Lee Iacocca

Many people who embark on a career in business give up just when they are about to break through. Sometimes it is easy to think that people who make it to the top are privileged, more talented, have gone to a better school, are luckier, and so forth. Well, let's look at some people who have made it to the top.

Some of the world's billionaires took themselves from the streets to the top of the Forbes' list. Despite mounting evidence that it's becoming increasingly difficult to build such wealth, these 15 incredible stories are proof that it is possible to overcome life's toughest challenges and create something better for yourself. This list includes just a handful of the many "rags-to-riches" stories out there.

◢ Guy Laliberté ate fire on the streets before introducing Cirque du Soleil to the world

The Canadian-born Laliberté began his circus career busking on the streets: playing accordion, walking on stilts and eating fire. He gambled by bringing a successful troupe from Quebec to the Los Angeles Arts Festival in 1987, with no return fare. The bet paid off and the circus group was eventually brought to Las Vegas where they became the world famous Cirque du Soleil we know today.

Today, Laliberté is the CEO of Cirque, a professional poker player and space tourist, with a total worth of $2.5 billion.

Source: Celebs101

◢ John Paul DeJoria lived in his car before John Paul Mitchell Systems took off

As a first generation American, DeJoria had it rough from the beginning. His German and Italian parents divorced when he was two and he sold Christmas cards and newspapers to help support his family before he turned 10. He was eventually sent to live in a foster home in Los Angeles.

DeJoria spent some time as an L.A. gang member before joining the military. After trying his hand as an employee for Redken Laboratories, he took out a $700 dollar loan and created John Paul Mitchell Systems. He hawked the company's shampoo door-to-door, living out of his car while doing so. But the quality of the product could not be denied, and now JPM Systems is worth over $900 million annually. He also created Patron Tequila and has a hand in a variety of industries, from diamonds to music.

Source: Forbes

▲ **Ursula Burns grew up in a housing project on Manhattan's Lower East Side and now runs Xerox**

Before the Lower East Side was cool, it was a hub for gangs. Burns was raised there by her single mother in a housing project. Her mother ran a daycare centre out of her home and ironed shirts so that she could afford to send Ursula to Catholic school. Ursula went on to NYU, and from there became an intern at Xerox.

She's now Xerox's CEO and chairwoman and the first African-American woman to be the head of a Fortune 500 Company.

Source: Bloomberg

▲ **Howard Schultz grew up in the Brooklyn projects before discovering, and now leading, Starbucks**

AP Schultz grew up in the Bayview projects of Canarsie, Brooklyn. He always wanted to climb "over the fence" and go beyond the lifestyle provided by his truck-driving father. Despite destitution, he excelled at sports and earned a football scholarship to the University of Northern Michigan.

After graduating with a degree in communications, Schultz went to work for Xerox before discovering a small coffee shop called Starbucks. Enamoured with the coffee, he left Xerox to become Starbuck's chief executive in 1987. After beginning with 60 shops, Starbucks now has over 16,000 outlets worldwide, giving Schultz a net worth of $1.1 billion. He even went on hiatus and came back as CEO to lead Starbucks out of a decline.

Source: Mirror News

▲ **Li Ka-shing quit school at 15 to work in a plastics factory and is now the world's richest East Asian**

The family of Li Ka-shing fled mainland China for Hong Kong in 1940 and Li's father died of tuberculosis when Li was just 15. Quitting school to work to support his family, Li made plastics and later plastic flowers for U.S. export.

By 1950, Li was able to start his own company, Cheung Kong Industries. While at first manufacturing plastics, the company later moved into real estate. Similarly, Li expanded his ownership of different companies and today has his hand in banking, cellular phones, satellite television, cement production, retail outlets, hotels, domestic transportation, airports, electric power, steel production, ports and shipping, and investing in cool apps, among other industries.

Source: Harvard Business Publishing

◢ **Francois Pinault was a high school dropout who now leads luxury goods group PPR**

Pinault quit high school in 1947 after being teased for his poor background. He joined his family's timber trading business and in the 1970s began buying up smaller firms. His ruthless business tactics—including slashing jobs and selling his timber company only to buy it back at a fraction of the cost when the market crashed—gave him a reputation as a "predator." He had similar tactics in the real estate business, and did well buying French junk bonds and taking government money to save businesses from bankruptcy.

His self-made worth helped him to start PPR, a luxury goods group that sells brands like Gucci and Stella McCartney. At one point he was the richest man in France and Pinault is now worth a cool $8.7 billion, has historic homes around the world and is the father-in-law of actress Salma Hayek.

Source: xfinity

◢ **Leonardo Del Vecchio was an orphaned factory worker whose eyeglasses empire today makes Ray-Bans and Oakleys**

Del Vecchio was one of five children whose widowed mother could not support them. After growing up in an orphanage, he went to work in a factory making moulds for auto parts and eyeglass frames, where he lost part of his finger.

At 23, he opened his own moulding shop. That eyeglass frame shop expanded to the world's largest maker of sunglasses and prescription eye ware. Luxottica makes brands like Ray-Ban and Oakley, with 6,000 retail shops like Sunglass Hut and LensCrafters. His estimated net worth is now more than $10 billion dollars.

Source: Forbes

◢ Kirk Kerkorian went from boxer and Royal Air Force pilot to Las Vegas mega-resort owner

Kerkorian, who learned English on the streets, dropped out of 8th grade to become a boxer. His family was a casualty of the Great Depression and Kerkorian went about learning skills to help bring home income. He became a daredevil pilot for the Royal Air Force during World War II, delivering supplies over the Atlantic using routes on which one in four planes would crash.

From the money he made running supplies, Kerkorian became a high roller on the craps table and eventually a real estate magnate in Las Vegas. He bought The Flamingo and built The International and MGM Grand, stalwarts of the Vegas scene. His net worth today is $16 billion dollars.

Source: Smart Money Daily

◢ Sheldon Adelson is another Las Vegas hotels magnate who tried his hand at a few industries

Adelson grew up in tenement housing in Massachusetts, where he shared a bedroom with his parents and three siblings. His father was a Lithuanian taxi driver and his mother had a knitting store. When he was 12 years old, he started selling newspapers and a few years later ran a vending machine scheme on the same corner.

Adelson tried his hand at a few different industries, from packing hotel toiletries to mortgage brokering. His biggest break came from developing a computer trade show. He turned that wealth into a purchase of the Sands Hotel & Casino, and later the mega-resort The Venetian.

Source: Minyanville

◢ Ingvar Kamprad was born in a small village in Sweden and created a mail-order business that became IKEA

Kamprad lived the farm life growing up, but he always had a knack for business—buying matches in bulk from Stockholm to sell to his neighbours. He later expanded to fish, Christmas decorations, and pens.

Not satisfied with the small stuff, Kamprad took money from his father (a reward for good grades) and created a mail-order business that eventually became IKEA (the name comes from his initials plus those of his village and family farm). Furniture became the company's biggest seller, and Kamprad's use of local manufacturers kept his prices low. Once one of the world's richest men, his value has fallen recently to a still-amazing $6 billion.

Source: Smart Money Daily

◢ **Roman Abramovich was an orphan who turned an expensive wedding gift into an oil empire**

After his parents died when he was just four, the Russian Abramovich was raised by his uncle and grandmother. Abramovich got his first break when he was given an expensive wedding gift from his in-laws. He dropped out of college to pursue his entrepreneurial interests, which at first included selling plastic ducks out of an apartment in Moscow.

He managed a takeover of oil giant Sibneft at a bargain price in 1995. He continued to flip his investments into ever larger acquisitions, including Russian Aluminum and steelmaker Evraz Group. Over the years Abramovich has been accused of shady dealings, from paying out bribes and protection money to having a role in the gang feuds over aluminium smelters. It seems that being ruthless has paid off for the billionaire: he now owns the largest private yacht in the world, as well as a ton of other cool stuff.

Source: Hubpages

◢ **Richard Desmond went from living above a garage to creating an empire that published magazines like Penthouse**

Desmond grew up the son of a single mother after his parents divorced. The two of them lived above a garage, during which time Desmond described himself as "very fat and very lonely." He quit school at 14 to focus on being a drummer while working as a coat-checker to help pay bills. Though he never became rich from his own musical talents, he later opened his own string of record shops.

Eventually Desmond published his first magazine, *International Musician and Recording World*. The Desmond magazine empire would expand to publications like the British version of *Penthouse* and *Ok!*, a worldwide favourite. He now owns publications around the globe and is involved in philanthropic work.

Source: The Observer

J.K. Rowling lived on welfare before creating the Harry Potter franchise

In the early 1990s, Rowling had just gotten divorced and was living on welfare with a dependent child. She completed most of the first book, *Harry Potter and the Philosopher's Stone*, in cafes, because walking around with her daughter, Jessica, was the best way to get Jessica to sleep.

The Harry Potter franchise has become a worldwide success and J.K. Rowling is now worth an estimated $1 billion dollars.

Source: Biography

Before Sam Walton founded Wal-Mart, he milked cows and sold magazines in Oklahoma

Walton's family lived on a farm in Oklahoma during the Great Depression. In order to make ends meet, he helped his family out by milking the cow and driving the milk out to customers. He also delivered newspapers and sold magazine subscriptions.

By 26, after graduating from the University of Missouri with a B.A. in economics, he was managing a variety store. He used $5,000 from the army and a $20,000 loan from his father-in-law to buy a Ben Franklin variety store in Arkansas. He expanded the chain and then went on to found Wal-Mart and Sam's Club. He died in 1992, leaving the company to his wife and children.

Source: Biography

Oprah Winfrey turned a life of hardship into inspiration for a multi-billion-dollar empire

Oprah spent the first six years of her life living with her grandmother and wearing dresses made out of potato sacks. After being molested by two members of her family and a family friend, she ran away from home at age 13. At 14, her newborn child died shortly after he was born. She went back to live with her mother, but it wasn't until her mother sent her to live with her father that she turned her life around.

She got a full scholarship to college, won a beauty pageant—where she was discovered by a radio station—and the rest is history. The Oprah name became an empire and, according to Forbes, she is worth $2.7 billion dollars.

Source: Academy of Achievement

You might not have aspirations of being a billionaire or having your own empire. However, you might be looking to move up in the company you work for or are an aspiring entrepreneur. Believing that it is possible and staying focused are essential ingredients to achieving your aims.

Not everybody succeeds at the very first attempt. If you have tried to work towards a dream or a goal in the past and did not achieve it, you're in good company. You are never beaten until you give up.

FAMOUS FAILURES

- Einstein was 4 years old before he could speak.
- Isaac Newton did poorly in grade school and was considered "unpromising."
- When Thomas Edison was a youngster, his teacher told him he was too stupid to learn anything. He was counselled to go into a field where he might succeed by virtue of his pleasant personality.
- F.W. Woolworth got a job in a dry goods store when he was 21, but his boss would not permit him to wait on customers because he "didn't have enough sense to close a sale."
- Michael Jordan was cut from his high school basketball team.
- Bob Cousy suffered the same fate, but he too is a Hall of Famer.
- A newspaper editor fired Walt Disney because he "lacked imagination and had no original ideas."

⊿ Winston Churchill failed the 6th grade and had to repeat it because he did not complete the tests that were required for promotion.

⊿ Babe Ruth struck out 1,300 times, a major league record.

COMMUNICATION

Be it business, health, sports, education, or coaching, there is some form of communication. I am privileged to have worked with many clients in the world of sports and business and to help people overcome limiting beliefs. I have been really fortunate to see people excel in their field and do amazing things by using the power of these tools and techniques.

In this book we are going to look at modelling in depth because modelling is really half of NLP. If you learn to *do* something then it is just a question of how and if you have the desire to do it. In essence, it is the way of finding out why and how one does something. Normally, we have a behaviour that we would like to emulate and learn from someone to help you do what you want to do. A more detail definition of modelling is given in chapter 5.

What is the difference between the good sports person, manager, business person, teacher, therapist, and an excellent one? The question is, "What is the difference that makes the difference?" It is an important question because it can inform us about the changes we could make in what we do. If we perform well in certain situations, how do we do that? How do we replicate that in other situations to improve performance and increase consistency?

Communication is the most fundamental aspect in human interaction. Suppose you communicate with someone, thinking that you know each other, and afterward are surprised at how they interpreted your words. Perhaps you said the same thing to two people and one responded in one way and the other responded in a completely different way. The better your communicate tools, the less likely it is that there will be any misunderstandings. Using NLP can help you to remove the likelihood of someone else's misunderstanding for a better result. We will cover communication in more detail in chapter 3.

In order to communicate with others, we must also communicate with ourselves. If you think that we do not communicate with ourselves, think back to what you said to yourself when you read that last sentence. Let's say you have a meeting and it doesn't go according to plan, or you spill coffee on your shirt before setting off for work, what do you say then? To whom do you say it?

Even though we communicate with ourselves regularly, we can improve the ways we communicate with ourselves to get better results. NLP helps us to do that.

There are numerous methods in NLP to change beliefs. Is your belief system helping you achieve the results you want? We will see in the chapter 7 that our behaviours are influenced by our beliefs. Sometimes people have beliefs that are useless, such as " I cannot be a good sales person, a good teacher, a good athlete," or "I don't have all the answers while making the presentation."

There are numerous ways to help people change their beliefs and their behaviours using NLP. Start with modelling excellence: finding out how someone does something is fundamental to NLP. How does one do that? How does the excellent person know what to do? How does the teacher know that the students have learned the topic and how can we replicate that ability specifically, even possibly with the same person in the same context?

NLP provides answers to many of these questions and provides a methodology to achieve excellence. Now that the modelling process is revealed, we can focus on strategies and on putting modelling into effect so you can get results in your life.

There are numerous, specific ways in which NLP can be used that will affect every aspect of our lives, many of which will be covered in this book. For example:

- ◢ NLP can be used by business, sales, advertising, and managing people to help build relationships, improve recruitment and leadership, to resolve conflict disputes, in negotiation coaching, and to help clients achieve their goals by increasing confidence.

◢ NLP can be used in education by teachers and students to improve teaching and self learning, or to help people learn more effectively.

◢ NLP can be used in health to help with weight loss, therapies, anxiety, and phobias.

◢ NLP can be used in sports to build confidence, improve visualisation, instil motivation, and focus mental awareness.

◢ NLP can be used to help improve relationships with friends and family.

◢ NLP can be used in many aspects of your life. In this book we will focus on the business side of your life, but NLP skills are transferable to any other facet. NLP is a powerful tool that you can use to alter the way you think about and react to every situation. It helps you to think more about what you *do* want and less on what you *do not* want. It helps people to communicate more effectively and change limiting beliefs.

With NLP, you have the ability to do what you want and reach your goals. Let's start!

Understanding People and Behaviour

"Human behaviour flows from three main sources:
desire, emotion, and knowledge."

—Plato

Have you ever wondered why people perceive things differently? Have you ever watched a programme and when you went into work the next day and talked about it, you found that some people responded to it differently than you did? Have you ever watched a sporting event and agreed when the key decision was given to one team instead of the other and one of your friends disagreed with that decision?

◢ PERCEPTION

Have you ever wondered why there are such huge differences between people, even siblings in the same family? One sibling does really well in life, becoming a respected professional person, while the other ends up doing badly, committing a horrific crime or crimes. Or why is it that two competitors can react differently to the same situation? A tennis match could be delayed by rain and one player sees it as a negative situation while the other sees it as an opportunity to get his or her head together and refocus. One person might have a tragic accident and despite that bounces back and goes on to make a massive, positive impact in the world, while someone else has everything in life given to them, has every opportunity, goes to a great school, has a good family, and yet never really amounts to anything.

You know, it's not up to me to define what people should and shouldn't do with their life, but still it makes me wonder how people can turn to substances or turn to a life of crime when perceivably they've had everything they could ever wish for in life.

Why is it that a couple walking down the road notices different things? One will notice the birds singing and one will notice the plants or the street decorations. Why is it that when a couple goes to look for a new car, one person will notice the sound of the engine and the other will notice how it drives. Why is it that some people notice what other people are wearing while another person notices how they comb their hair?

What about work and business? Why do some people see a negative solution in a certain situation and why do some people see a positive solution in the same situation? Sure, you've come across people who've seen the glass as half full and some who've seen the glass as half empty, but what's the difference that makes the difference? Why do people respond differently to similar situations?

Various questions like these can be asked and answered by using the NLP model of communication. I'm sure you've heard the expression "that person lives in their own world." Well, yeah! We all live in our own world, one that is unique to us. What forms that unique experience and influences our behaviours, thoughts, and feelings? The key factors are our filters or how we process information.

We're going to explore a model of NLP that will explain how people process information and how, as a result of processing that information, it affects their behaviour. (It's important to note that it is a model that specifically works in the world of NLP.) It is very easy to follow and it's quite interesting because it gives an insight into what affects behaviour.

Let's begin with understanding that every external event is an information stimulus that we perceive through our five senses: sight, hearing, feeling, smell, and taste. In the NLP world, sight is visual, hearing is auditory, feeling is kinaesthetic, smelling is olfactory, and taste is gustatory. In NLP, the senses are referred to as representational systems or, in other words, how we represent the external world.

We'll explore representational systems further in chapter 3. For now, let's just examine these stimuli and how they are filtered to produce an internal representation or mental image of what we think we have perceived through our representational systems.

For example, if someone is asked to deliver a presentation or speak in public and they are not used to doing this, they may have a nervous response. As a result, they experience different thoughts, feelings, and images from someone who speaks in public all the time. NLP offers a series of communication techniques and approaches to help people change their negative responses to get what they want and hence achieve their goals.

The diagram in Figure 1.1 is of the NLP communication model. Starting to the right of the head, each external event is an information stimulus that will be perceived with the 5 representational senses—sight, hearing, tasting, smelling and feeling. The elements inside the head denote what happens inside someone's mind.

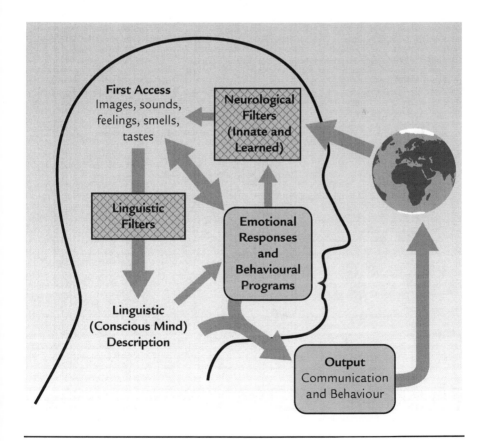

Figure 1.1   NLP Perception and Language Map

The mental image we perceive will affect how we react. If a person's mental image is pleasant, then he or she will probably feel contented, happy or another positive state. Equally, if a person's mental image is unpleasant, that person will feel upset or angry, etc. Depending on whether the person is in a good state or not will affect their physiology, such as posture and breathing. Mental images are the internal representation of the state, physiology is the external representation of the state.

We can change the physiology as a way to change the external state and the internal representations. It is common for the psychotherapists to prescribe exercise for people who are depressed. The exercise is meant to change the physiology, which then changes the state and therefore their mental images. All sports people know the highs that come after a successful exercise session. Standing up with your shoulders back will improve the way you are feeling, while looking down and having a frown on your face will adversely affect the way you are feeling.

Internal representations of a state in physiology are important because they affect our behaviours and these behaviours affect our health. Think of someone that you know relatively well. You know when he or she is in a good mood because you pick up on all the physiological signs of an upbeat mood: posture, actions, and voice. Conversely, you know when they are in a bad mood because of physiological signs that signal anger or depression. We will expand on this later in the book.

◢ PROCESSING INFORMATION

Normally, the conscious mind can handle only 7 (± 2) items of information at any given time. Of course, many people can't even handle this number—I know people who can handle only 1 item of information (± 2). How about you?

Try this: Can you name more than 7 products in a given product category, say cigarettes? Most people will be able to name 2, maybe 3 products in a category of low interest and usually no more than 9 in a category of high interest. There is a reason for this. If we didn't actively delete information all the time, we'd end up with much too much information coming in. In fact, you may have even heard that psychologists say that if we were aware of all of the sensory information that was coming in at any one time, we'd go crazy. That's why we filter the information.

So the question is, when two people have the same stimulus, why don't they have the same response? The answer is, because everyone deletes, distorts and generalises the information that comes in from our senses based on one of five filters. Those filters are: meta-programmes, belief systems, values, decisions, and memories. These filters will be covered in subsequent chapters of this book.

DELETION

It has been estimated that there are more than one million bits of outside information stimulus happening to us every second. In 1956, cognitive psychologist Professor George A. Miller of Princeton University's Department of Psychology, estimated that we can process approximately 7×18 bits (126 bits) of information per second. It is estimated that there are millions of bits of information available to you in any given second, so a lot of information is being deleted.

Even if these numbers are not entirely correct, you are still probably not aware of the feeling of your existence in a chair, the texture of the pages of the book you are holding, the sound of people around you, or the material of the cloth you are wearing. To be aware of all this information simultaneously could be overwhelming. To avoid a mental meltdown, we only focus on some of the information that comes in.

So when we go into a noisy room, we delete most of the extraneous sounds so that we can tune into the conversation that we are having. We are therefore deleting a huge amount of information from our conscious awareness. There is a difference between deleting and ignoring. Deletion is not a good or a bad thing, it is just what humans do. How can you use this knowledge usefully?

Be aware that people also communicate indirectly using body language. People pick up on these subtle clues and you can use them to reinforce what you are saying to make it more memorable. This would be important when parents give information to their children about safety, when bosses are briefing colleagues, and when talking to staff members in an office environment.

Communication involves emotional chunking. According to Professor Miller, people can take in 5 to 9 chunks of information before becoming overwhelmed. We can increase the amount of information we can take in if we organize it into grouped chunks and we will come back to that in a later chapter.

While communicating with others, remember that people can handle only a little bit of information at a time. So, keep it simple and keep to the point when giving instructions, especially when there is some pressure. For example, when a coach gives a halftime talk or when a business manager gives a pep talk on a busy day, they always need to remember that when giving instructions, some people won't take in all of the information because they've taken in all the information they can and everything else will be deleted.

DISTORTION

We all distort the information that we take in and this is not good or bad. It is just what we do. An example of distortion would be when we mentally compare how we see ourselves in our external memory to what we really are. We distort information when we buy properties or decorate rooms. We distort information when we play sports, coach a game, plan an event, think about a particular move or an attack. What if the phone rings while you are in the shower? You imagine it was your boss or a colleague and when you think about how they reacted when you didn't answer the phone, you imagine them as being annoyed and that causes you some stress. What if your boss calls you into his office later that day and your reaction when you engage in the meeting could be based on how your perceptions distorted the reality you experienced in the shower? Distortions can be limiting or useful depending on the situation. We can adjust a situation before it happens to our advantage or to our disadvantage. Now that can be a good or bad thing.

How about adjusting a situation after it happens? If you went for a job interview and didn't hear anything for a few days, you might think you're getting the cold shoulder, that you haven't got the job.

What if they lost your number? Should you phone back to find out if you got the job? Your mind goes into overdrive, flooded with questions, coming up with all sorts of scenarios. These questions are like meaning-making machines. They can take the terms and events of your life and distort the meaning, separating reality from what your mind has created.

GENERALISATIONS

When we generalise, we take one piece of information and assume that other similar things are the same and that the pattern will repeat. Generalisation can be useful when learning. For example, if you have learnt to drive a car on a course, you can generalise about what you then need to do when you are driving to work. You might have a system at work and you can generalise how to use it to accomplish a task at home.

Deletions, distortions and generalisations can be useful. For example, when you train hard in the gym it makes you feel good outside of the gym and helps you to feel confident that you will perform your best at work. Because a previous meeting went well, you believe this meeting will go well. When you have been prepared for an interview in the past, the interview went well, so, because you have prepared diligently for an upcoming interview, you feel confident that you will do well in this one.

However, generalisations also can be negative. If you deal with a person from a particular category and the situation becomes very negative, you might then believe that all people in that category will be unpleasant. Perhaps you froze in your last two presentations and so you believe that you will freeze in the next presentation. Perhaps when you were younger you had trouble talking to other people so you begin to believe that you are not very good at making conversation.

Many generalisations are expressed in beliefs
because beliefs are often generalisations.

Generalisations can be changed. If instead of saying, "I can't do public speaking," you instead say, "I can learn to do public speaking," you are starting to change a generalisation. For most people, the first sentence restricts the creativity in the internal representation system, while the second creates possibilities. Changes in way you use language will change the internal representations you have. Think of something about which you have a negative belief, about something that makes you say, "I can't." Now change the wording and replace the negative words with positive words and notice how your internal representations change.

Pay attention to the way you express your faults, especially ones that live in you. Find a way to express these in a more positive way; at all times, choose the words you use carefully. Your words create your beliefs.

Suppose for a moment that you have an interview for a new job at 9:00 am on Monday morning. On Sunday night you set your alarm for 7:00 am but when you get up on Monday, it is 8:00 am. It will take you an hour to drive to the interview, so you're in a mad rush. You put on your suit or your dress and in your haste you spill coffee down the front. By then it's 8:30 and you don't have time to change. You get in the car and the streets are clogged with traffic. It's just one thing after another going wrong! What do you think you will believe about the rest of that day?

It doesn't take a great deal to form a belief. Experiences have an effect on your beliefs. Remember that grandmother who lifted the car? The whole experience had a massive impact on her beliefs about what she could and couldn't do. That story did finish with a happy ending. She went back to college, got a degree, and did things she had always wanted to do. It's never too late, regardless of how old you are or what you want to do.

I was working with a client with chronic fatigue, a condition with which I had worked in the past. Because of the fatigue, she suffered from several acute problems, including severe anxiety and debilitation. She was only in her late teens and had had the condition since her early teens. By the time she had come to me for help, she had seen a number of consultants, doctors, and therapists but she still was not moving forward.

In my conversations with her during our sessions I discovered that she had received conflicting advice from those different consultants. Some said to train through it and some said to rest. One consultant had told her to learn to live with her condition as there was nothing that could be done.

Can you imagine being told in your early teenage years that you had to learn to live with a debilitating condition for the rest of your life?

I deployed some of the NLP techniques described in this book, such as anchoring, new behaviour generation, and logical levels to help her move her life forward. I used a heart-rate monitor to ascertain her graded physiological recovery from exertion. Graded physiological recovery is like a mobile telephone being on a charge. Whenever the charge falls near 80%, the phone is plugged back in so it can rest and recharge. It is important for everyone, but especially this young woman, to maintain her charge above 80% by resting and recharging.

She worked with me for six sessions and during that time she accomplished more than she had in the four years of working with anyone else. She managed to turn her life around—she socialised, travelled, enrolled at college, and even started training. Her improvement was so marked that one of her medical consultants wrote to me asking for my input and thoughts on her condition and how she had managed to improve.

The key to working with anyone, whether it's business, sports, or life, is to understand *that person's reality*. Meet them in *their* world and take the time to understand where they are. After all, everybody is different and having this awareness can help guide people towards a positive outcome.

I will share with you an email sent to me by this client:

> *Hi Jimmy, just wanted to drop you an email to let you know how I was doing and to see how you are. I'm currently in Abersoch with my mum and dad. We've come for a week and I drove here!! I've finished college now and the last couple of months my attendance was full! I've had some grades back and out of 5 subjects, I know I've got at least two As and one A+! I've also been exercising more every week, trying to go to the driving range once a week, playing 9 holes once a week, and I have started to salsa! Although I'm still having days when I struggle and thoughts that I sometimes find hard to deal with, my good days are*

getting much more frequent and I feel like I'm starting to find myself again. Thank you!!!!!!! Wondered if I could maybe see you sometime before September? I'm starting a degree in September and want to make sure nothing is going to stop me!! Hope you're well. I will never be able to tell you how much you have helped me!!!

◢ "THE MAP IS NOT THE TERRITORY" AND REPRESENTATIONAL SYSTEMS

The map is not the territory means that the way we represent the world is because of our own personal reality, it isn't actually reality itself. We don't respond to reality. We respond to our internalized map of reality. We all live in our own distinct reality and we all see the world completely different. We can look around and clearly see that we are all unique, but what we sometimes fail to realize is that while we are all different in the way we look, we are even more different in the way we think about the world around us. It is important to remember this when we interact with people.

Our behaviour is influenced by language, memories, attitudes, values and beliefs, decisions, meta-programmes, time and space, matter, and energy. These make up our internal map. How we represent reality is based on our interpretations of this internal map. Interpretations may or may not be accurate. All maps are inaccurate to some extent. A map of a street would need to be as large and detailed as a street to be completely accurate, but a map that large is unreasonable so the maps we use are summaries of what we deem to be the important features.

Our brain does the same thing by encoding these important features using our five senses: visual, auditory, kinaesthetic, olfactory and gustatory. These five senses are the language of our brain.

Our verbal language reveals the maps and models we use to guide our behaviour. Communication is how we explain the world to others and ourselves.

Let's take a moment to think about why do we do what we do? It is safe to say that most people who smoke are well aware of the dangers of smoking but they carry on smoking. Most people know what foods to eat and that exercise is good for them and either act or don't act on that knowledge. Let's explore and gain an understanding of why we do what we do, and by gaining that understanding we can change any negative patterns which aren't helping us live our lives to the fullest.

◢ **Exercise: Perception**

1. What does the word "relationship" mean to you?
2. Now ask five different people what the word "relationship" means to them and take note of the answers.
3. Is every person's answer different?
4. Interpret the information by looking at each person's
   - ◢ language
   - ◢ memories
   - ◢ attitudes
   - ◢ values and beliefs
   - ◢ decisions
   - ◢ meta-programmes
   - ◢ time/space, matter, and
   - ◢ energy
5. How do the above components influence their behaviour?

We all make sense of the world in our own way. The interpretations to events that are going on outside of us are perceived differently from person to person and, as a result, the behaviours that people manifest are different.

OUR CONSCIOUS AWARENESS

Take a moment to think about all the thoughts and feelings that are going through your mind this very second. What are you aware of: the objects around you, your past, your future, your life, and a multitude of other thoughts? Some of them you may have stopped to think about: what is for tea, have I put the bins out, I should make that phone call later, what's on TV tonight, I might go for a drive, and the list goes on. What we notice and don't notice, what we think about at different times, depends on what we focus on.

At a conscious level we are limited in how many things we can focus on at one time. It is estimated that your brain receives about 4 billion nerve impulses every second. Are you consciously aware of all of this information? No! For example, are you aware of how your feet feel on the floor? Unless you have sore feet I suspect that you were not aware of how your feet felt until I mentioned it. Why? Because it was not important at the time and it was filtered out.

Of the 4 billion bits of information, you were only consciously aware of approximately 2,000 bits, or about 0.00005 percent of all the potential information. To take in and process more than that would either drive you crazy or be such a distraction that you could not function. Do you consciously remember every action you perform while driving to work in the morning, the traffic lights you stop at, the gear changes you make, the people you see, the shops you drive past?

So, of all the billions of nerve impulses our mind receives every second, how does everyone interpret the information the way they do? How and why do we all see things differently and what is the impact it can have on our lives? How do we decide to interpret the information? What are the key components in breaking down this information to a manageable level in order for us to make sense out of it? Of the 4 billion nerve impulses that hit our mind every second, all of our past memories, and future plans, every event that is happening, all our interests, we filter, delete, distort, and generalise this information to the point we can make sense of it. And we all delete, distort, and generalise differently.

LANGUAGE (WORDS)

Words are a form of code to represent your interpretation of something. Try this exercise, get a group of people together and have each independently write down five words that for them means *exercise*. I bet that nobody comes up with the same five words as you do; as a group you may have a few words in common or you may not have any words in common. The word *exercise* is a code for what exercise means for you and I suspect that your friends have a completely different meaning for this word.

A perfect example of how we perceive words differently is when we talk about *relationships*. We enter into long and sometimes heated discussions with our loved ones about "our relationship", without ever really discussing what "relationship" means to any of us. No wonder even close family members can sometimes misunderstand one another.

BELIEFS

Suppose you have a belief that you are unattractive or you're not a clever person. How would you react if someone approached you and said, "You look very nice in that shirt or dress," or "that was an intelligent point"? Depending on the circumstances, you may dismiss, discount or deflect their positive feedback. Internally you may think they have not looked at the situation in detail and when they do they will find something wrong and change their opinion. Suppose all day, people tell you that you're attractive or clever—do you really hear them? Not likely! And then one person points out that your nose looked a bit big on those holiday pictures, or the point you made at work last week was bit odd. Does this resonate for you? You bet it does! It verifies your belief about yourself. From a *filter* perspective, you have deleted and distorted the positive feedback and focused on the negative. What beliefs do you have about yourself, about others, about the world, that limit who you can be or what you can accomplish?

DECISIONS

You make decisions (i.e., you generalise) so that you do not have to relearn things every day. If you want to make a cup of tea, you learnt a long time ago (made the generalisation) that you turn on the kettle, place a tea bag in the cup, and pour the hot water from the kettle into the cup—you do not have to go through the whole process of relearning how to make a cup each and every time.

Generalisations are useful but they can also get us into trouble. How many of us know how to open a door? In an experiment, researchers put the doorknob on the same side of the door as the hinge. What do you think happened when they left adults in the room? The adults would go up to the door, grasp the doorknob, twist and then try to push or pull the door open. Of course, it would not open. As a result, the adults decided that the door was locked and they were locked in the room! Young children, on the other hand, who had not yet made a generalisation about a doorknob, simply walked up to the door, pushed on it, and exited the room. The adults, because of their decisions, created a reality of being locked in the room when in fact they were not. So how many of your decisions (generalisations) about yourself, your partner, your boss, the way it is at work, leave you "locked in", when others are not stopped by it? One of our challenges is to discover those filters we have put in place and how they affect what we see, hear, feel; how we react to others and what we create in our lives. Once you become aware of filters that do not serve you, you can consciously choose to modify or remove them.

INTERNAL REPRESENTATIONS

Do you remember the first time you fell in love, do you remember driving into work the other morning, do you remember when you first passed your driving license? How do you remember it? Do you see a picture in your mind or are there smells or tastes? Were there sounds? Perhaps in your mind you can hear a radio? To remember an event, your mind uses pictures, sounds, feelings, tastes, smells and words.

These *perceptions* of the outside world are called *internal representations* and are a function of your filters (i.e., your beliefs and values). Your perceptions are what you consider to be *real*; in other words, your reality.

If you and I went out for dinner, our internal representations or perceptions about dinner will most likely be similar and different in some way depending on what is important to each of us (our filters). Dinner is not very controversial. But what about our views on a conflict such as a war or political situation. Given our different backgrounds, we may perceive a situation very differently with significantly different reactions (behaviours).

Filters

Have you ever gone to see a movie with a friend, sat next to each other, saw exactly the same movie and one of you thought it was the best movie ever and the other thought it was terrible? How could that happen? It is quite simple. You and your friend filtered the information differently (different beliefs, values, decisions, etc.). In other words, you perceived the movie differently and hence behaved differently in your reaction to it.

By the way, who put your filters in place? You did! These filters are based on what happened in your family as you grew up, the teachings of your church (or absence of church), the beliefs and values in the part of the country where you lived, decisions you made about the world (it's a safe place or a dangerous place), etc. If your filters are not creating the results that you desire, you are the only person who can change them. The first step is to become consciously aware of the filters you have and what kind of reality (results) they are creating for you.

Internal Representations and Behaviours

Would you like to see the effect internal representations have on your behaviours? Try this: think of a really happy event in your life. Close your eyes and get a picture of it in your mind. Bring in any sounds, feelings, tastes and smells you remember. Fully experience the event in your mind. Once you have done that, notice if there were any changes in your physiology. Maybe as a result of these memories (internal representations), you had a smile on the face, or sat up straighter, or maybe breathed deeper. I am sure that your physiology changed in some way. I did not ask you to change your physiology, did I? What this demonstrates is that the pictures, sounds, etc. (internal representations), that you make in your mind influence your physiology and, as a result, also influence your choice of words, the tone of voice you use, and the behaviours you manifest.

Now, sit up straight, put a big smile on your face, and breathe deeply. While you do that, feel sad. I bet that you cannot feel sad without changing your physiology (e.g., shallow breathing, rounded shoulders, etc.). This illustrates that your physiology influences your internal representations (feeling sad or happy). Next time you are feeling sad or down, what can you do? Participate in some kind of physical activity such as a brisk walk or exercise that requires you to breathe deeply and keep your body from slumping over.

Based on your previous experiences, you filter information about the world around you. The resulting internal representations are how you perceive the world (your reality) and this drives your behaviours, often reinforcing that your perception of the world is "correct". Does this work for you or make you happy? For me, one of the benefits of discovering the filters I had put in place and how they affected what I saw, heard, and felt was that I could change how I reacted to others and what I created in my life. Once you become aware of those filters that do not serve you, you can consciously choose to modify or remove them to help you take control of your life and create the life you want, helping you break negative behaviours, unproductive thoughts, and limiting beliefs.

◢ THE CONSCIOUS AND SUBCONSCIOUS MIND

The mind is made up of three parts: the Conscious Mind, the Subconscious Mind, and the Unconscious Mind (Figure 1.2).

THE CONSCIOUS MIND

The Conscious Mind governs four aspects: how we rationalize, how we analyse, our will power, and our temporary (short-term) memory. The Conscious Mind is the rational, analytical part of the mind. It's the thinking, judging part of the mind. The Conscious Mind is where we spend most of our time, but it is actually the weakest part of our mind.

Rationalise

Humans must have a reason for everything. Our ability to rationalize our actions is what keeps us sane. For example, a smoker will rationalise his or her actions by saying "smoking helps me to relax and focus." The truth is that cigarettes raise the heart rate and hand tremors by a large percent. So much for relaxing! So, our rational mind is not always correct, but, as long as our rational mind can come up with some reasoning for our actions, we will be at peace.

Analyse

Our analytical mind recognises problems, such as it ascertains that a tire is flat then figures out how to fix the tire.

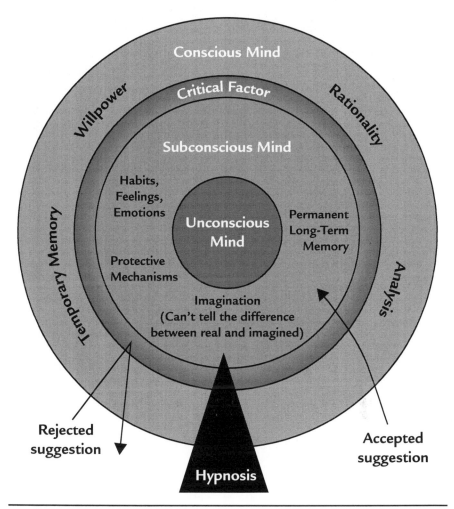

Figure 1.2   Parts of the Mind

Will Power

How many times have you tried changing an old habit by using will power? Were you successful? Probably not because will power is only temporary. It gives us short bursts of energy to help us get through a situation but then it fades away. Will power cannot affect internal change. Change has to come from within our deeper mind (our Subconscious Mind).

Temporary (Short-Term) Memory

Temporary memory is very limited. It's what we are currently aware of or thinking about. We use it to remember a phone number just long enough to dial the number. After that, it's gone. We can store information in short-term memory for approximately 20 to 30 seconds. Scientific research has proven that our Conscious Mind can only hold very small amounts of information at one time and then not for very long. Overall, the Conscious Mind is a very weak mind compared to the Subconscious Mind.

THE SUBCONSCIOUS MIND

The Subconscious Mind is part of our Autonomic Nervous System, or things over which we have little or no conscious control, such as breathing, heart rate, and blood circulation. When we cut ourselves we don't have to tell ourselves to heal, when we sleep we don't have to tell ourselves to breathe; the subconscious part of our mind takes care of that for us.

The Subconscious Mind is the most powerful part of our mind. This is the part of our mind that is actually in control and it will help you to achieve your goals. The Subconscious Mind is the part of the mind that we work with in hypnosis. This is where imagination, permanent (long-term) memory, habits, feelings, and emotions are stored.

Imagination

Imagination is more than just creativity. Imagination is also our perception of the world around us and everybody's perception is different. Everybody's unique perception is the truth to them. Remember that perception is not reality; it's just a perception.

Permanent (Long-Term) Memory

Every piece of data we ever received through any of our five senses is stored in our Subconscious Mind. Starting from when we were in our mum's tummy, everything we heard, felt, or experienced leaves an imprint on us. Using that data, we begin to build a database of information that develops into beliefs and habits, and all of this develops us into who we are today. We will think our next thought, act our next action, and feel our next feeling based on everything that has happened in our past. We are the sum total of all our past.

Our permanent memory is like a hard drive on a computer. It is a highly organized system and we know that because it works by association. For example, if you hear an old song, feelings come back of some old friend or memory associated with that song. Just like the hard drive on a computer, sometimes we need to reprogram our Subconscious Mind.

Habits, Feelings, and Emotions

The Subconscious Mind is the feeling mind. Habits, feelings, and emotions are stored there. If you are dealing with an emotional issue, being in a state of relaxation can help you become aware of the feeling or emotion that is connected to your issue. When you allow this to happen, you are on your way to making a permanent change!

THE CRITICAL FACTOR

The critical factor resides in the Conscious Mind but it takes orders from the Subconscious Mind. Think of it as being located somewhere between the conscious and the subconscious.

This is the part of the mind that we sometimes need to bypass to make changes. The Critical Factor's job is to protect the vulnerable nature of the Subconscious Mind. Think of it as a filter. It takes in every incoming suggestion from the outside world and stops it. It then compares that incoming suggestion to every perception we hold on the subject. If the new suggestion is not in harmony with our old perception, the Critical Factor's job is to stop the new suggestion and reject it. If, however, the new suggestion is found to be in harmony with our inner perception, the Critical Factor opens up and lets it in.

Remember, every piece of information we have ever received in our life is stored in our Subconscious Mind. So, any new information trying to come in is compared to the old. For instance, if you read a magazine article that convinced you that you should exercise three times a week and your Conscious Mind says yes that is a good idea, I should do that, the Critical Factor is going to compare that to what is already in the Subconscious Mind. If your Subconscious Mind believes that exercising only twice a week is what you should do, it will reject the thought of exercising three times a week. However, when you are in a relaxed state, you can bypass the Critical Factor and insert good, positive suggestions into the Subconscious Mind where they will be accepted. When you bypass the Critical Factor you can accept suggestions to change your habits, remove limiting beliefs and accept new ones, and resolve internal conflicts, all of which will help you succeed in reaching your goals. Being in a relaxed state can help you program yourself for success!

BRAIN WAVES AND FUNCTIONS

The human brain produces electrical activity that can be measured as brain waves. An electroencephalogram (EEG) measures brain waves in frequencies, also known as cycles per second or hertz. The four different wave states and how brain waves are related to the conscious and subconscious minds are explained in Table 1.1.

The Beta State

When you are awake, your brain waves are operating in the beta state of activity, that is, 14–30 hertz. In beta, you are alert and wide awake. Your conscious mind is dominant.

The Alpha State

When you close your eyes, become relaxed, and engage in creative endeavours such as imagining, visualizing, or daydreaming, your brains waves register in the alpha state. This is the brain wave state of heightened creativity and inspiration. The alpha state is where your brain waves would register if you were to go into a light

Table 1.1   Brain Waves and Functions

Brain Waves	States of Consciousness	Frequency
Beta brain waves	Waking conscious state, alert	14–30 Hz
Alpha brain waves	Daydreaming, creative, relaxed, closed-eyed	8–13 Hz
Theta brain waves	Dreaming, hypnotic, meditative, subconscious, athletic "in the zone"	4–7 Hz
Delta brain waves	Unconscious, asleep, deep sleep	0.5–6 Hz

trance (light hypnotic state). In the alpha state, your Conscious Mind is less dominant and the Subconscious Mind is coming to the forefront. The Subconscious Mind does not register the difference between imaginary reality and physical reality.

The Theta State

When you are dreaming, meditating, in a deep trance, or "in the zone" in sports, you are in a theta state. Any repetitive movement or sound will easily take you into the theta state. This state is the one in which much of your subconscious potential lies and where the Subconscious Mind is totally dominant. The theta state is where your brain waves of past experiences and emotions can be accessed.

Many people can go into an even deeper theta state where hypnoanaesthesia can be experienced. Hypnoanaesthesia occurs when a person is so deeply relaxed that surgeries can occur with sensation but without pain. More people are using hypnoanaesthesia as an alternative to anaesthesia during childbirth and dental procedures.

The Delta State

When you fall asleep and go deeper than the theta state into total unconsciousness, you are in a delta state. In this state of consciousness you will not remember what you are experiencing.

Simultaneous Brain States

Your brain can be functioning simultaneously in more than one brain wave state. For example, you can be in a beta state as you enter into an alpha state. You may be completely awake one moment and then feel more relaxed and close your eyes all in a few seconds. You could also be dreaming (the theta state), rise up into wakefulness (the beta state), and then go back into a theta state but at a higher frequency than previously.

Understanding brain wave states can help you connect your experiences with the brain wave activity in your brain. Most people attempt to change habitual behaviour consciously in the beta state in which the conscious mind is dominant. Potentially, there will be too many filters, such as beliefs, values, ethics, and past conditioning, to allow suggestions to take hold in this state.

◢ ACHIEVING YOUR GOALS

Understanding brain wave states is only part of the equation. Determination in achieving your goals is crucial. Having all the knowledge and talent in the world without determination will get you nowhere.

Caleb Patterson-Sewell is a professional footballer who, at the time of this writing, is playing as a goalkeeper for Vitória Setúbal in the Primeira Liga. He came over from Australia and had been on the road undergoing trials at numerous clubs. He contacted me to do some work while I was working at Bury FC as a performance coach.

While I was working with Caleb, I recognised he had an immense level of talent, but he didn't seem to be getting the breaks. We focused on changing his perception and thought processes using various brain wave states. Caleb went on to play a few games with Sheffield Wednesday youth team and caught the eye of a Liverpool youth team. Things seemed to be turning around.

But then he told me he was heading back to Australia because his visa was expiring. At that point, his dream of being a professional player could have fizzled out. However, one thing that had always struck me about Caleb was his sense of self-belief and determination. Where many would of given up, he persisted.

His determination took him to America where eventually he broke into the New York Red Bulls. After a time he was signed to Vitória Setúbal in the Portuguese league. I would like to think I played my part in his success by introducing him to NLP at the right time in his career.

Asking Questions

"I've always been really curious about things and slightly confused by the world, and I think someone who feels that way is in a good position to be the one asking questions."
—Terry Gross

I received a call from a high-powered businesswoman about booking a session. She told me over the phone that she was going through a hard time with a lot of stress in her personal life. She was a senior manager for an organisation and a successful entrepreneur, but she was struggling to keep it together. I sent her a questionnaire and followed it up with a call prior to the consultation. On the surface of things it appeared she was overwhelmed with her workload. She asked me if I could develop a stress-management plan for her, which I was happy to do.

When she arrived at the consultation, we discussed the contents of her questionnaire and what she wanted to achieve. As we went into depth and the conversation developed through the questioning process (which I am going to demonstrate in "Transcript From A Course" starting on page 60), it became apparent that she was struggling to hold it together and was bordering on a breakdown. Her son had been very ill for a while, her husband had walked out on her, and she was finding life and work hard to cope with.

She had, in her own words, hit rock bottom and it became apparent that in her situation a stress-management plan was only scratching the surface. By asking her some key questions she was able to connect to the problem at a deep level and take positive steps forward with her life and get things on track.

Over many years of working with several thousands of clients around the world, I have found that very often when I ask the client what they want, more often they will tell me what they don't want. For example, when I work with clients who say they are nervous delivering presentations, I ask them how they want to feel and what outcome do they want. What do they want to happen? And they will say, "I don't want to feel nervous anymore. I don't want to mess things up."

Imagine going into a presentation thinking you don't want to be nervous and you don't want to mess things up. Imagine running with that in your mind. Thinking about what you *don't* want is unlikely to help support a positive outcome. Being clear about what you *do* want gives you extreme focus. Imagine changing the words, "I don't want to feel nervous" to "I am going to be confident," and changing, "I don't want to mess things up," to "I am going to connect to the audience and deliver a powerful presentation."

In truth, most people are not clear about what they want. They don't know how to ask the right questions and find it difficult to connect what they say with what they are thinking in the depths of their mind. (This is something we will explore a bit more later in the chapter when we look at a meta-model.) The ability to ask the right question at the right time is an essential skill for business success and can be transferred to many areas of your personal and professional life.

◢ASKING QUESTIONS

Asking questions can help you better understand the perspective of your colleagues and customers. More specifically, questions should facilitate the thinking of your colleagues and customers and assist them with identifying goals, devising solutions, and crafting plans of action. You can also use questions to restate something a client, colleague, or customer has said so they know they have been heard. Let's look at various types of questions and which are most, and least, effective for interacting professionally or personally.

Asking questions, or inquiry, lies at the very heart of being successful in business and is the focus of this chapter. We will explore the question types that are the most effective for coaching, business, questioning strategies, language, focusing and challenging, the relevant meta-models, and more. We'll also look at how to identify outcomes and needs and devise an individual plan of action for each member of a staff.

QUESTION TYPES

Effective Question Types

In my experience as a coach, *open-ended questions* are highly effective as a guided method in looking for solutions. These questions cannot be answered by "yes" or "no" and often begin with the words *who, what, when, where,* and *how.* Open-ended questions may also begin with the word *why,* but be very careful asking *why questions* (see "Question Types to Avoid" on page 48 for more on this subject). The other effective question types that we will cover are *powerful questions,* using a particular meta-model, *you questions,* and *follow-up questions.* Follow-up questions are subcategories of open-ended questions.

Examples of Open-Ended Questions

1. What are the alternatives?
2. How can you reach a win–win outcome?
3. Who exhibits behaviours that you admire?

Follow-up questions can be asked to provide more information about something someone has said, possibly in response to another question. They provide an excellent way to fine-tune your interactions, tailoring your responses to the needs of the individual staff, colleague or customer. Follow-up questions require excellent listening skills and the ability to use the information gathered through listening to craft a question that will lead the client to the next step or level.

Examples of Follow-Up Questions

1. Tell me more about Marty and what you admire about his behaviour.
2. When have you displayed similar behaviour?
3. What are three different actions you can take to further your project?
4. How can you begin to take these actions immediately?

Powerful Questions

Powerful questions will set up a strong framework on which you can base your interactions with clients.

Examples of Powerful Questions

1. What would you do if you had only one year left to live?
2. Imagine the perfect scenario. How can you bring it about?
3. How would you proceed if you knew you could not fail?

"You" Questions

"You" questions seek to determine the views of colleagues and customers, shorten the problem-solving process, and pave the way for specific change recommendations.

Examples of "You" Questions

1. What is your current view of the situation?
2. How would you like to feel?
3. What existing skills and abilities do you have to help you achieve XYZ?

Question Types to Avoid

Closed-Ended Questions

Closed-ended questions can be answered with "yes" or "no." Sometimes these questions are necessary or beneficial during a meeting, but they are generally not as effective as open-ended questions. Try to limit your use of closed-ended questions.

Examples of Closed-Ended Questions

1. Did you complete your action items last week?
2. Does this plan feel good to you?

Why Questions

Why questions are a type of open-ended question, but they can elicit justifications, rationalizations, or a defensive stance, which may not be beneficial to what you and your colleagues, staff, or customers are attempting to accomplish. In my experience, if a client wants to quit smoking and they inform me that they smoked three cigarettes during the past week, asking why may cause the client to justify their entire habit of smoking. Your next question or intervention may have to "undo" this line of thinking, so it's best to avoid the why question altogether. Be careful and mindful when asking these kinds of questions.

Examples of Why Questions

1. Why did you do that?
2. Why didn't you explain your thinking?
3. Why not try it this way?

The use of the why question can be powerful in eliciting someone's motivation strategy, which we will look at in chapter 7: Beliefs and Values

Leading Questions

Leading questions carry with them an implied correct answer and do not allow a people to think fully for themselves. These types of questions should be avoided.

Examples of Leading Questions

1. You're in agreement with these terms, right?
2. I expect you're happy with how things are going?

◢ **Exercise**

Practise formulating effective questions using the question types. Think of questions you would want someone to ask of you if you were in need of support or guidance. Create a list. Then practise asking these types of questions when you're talking with friends and family members, being careful to avoid closed-ended, why, and leading questions. Notice what works and what doesn't and then modify your question list accordingly.

Questioning Strategies

Crafting excellent questions is a process that requires laser-sharp listening skills and an intuitive sense of the other person—who they are, what they want, where they are, and where they want to go. Questions provide one of the most powerful tools you have to assist people. A series of carefully crafted questions becomes a questioning strategy.

Esther Fusco, in her book *Effective Questioning Strategies in the Classroom*, makes some key points about questioning that are equally applicable to coaching. She identifies a *questioning cycle* that involves keeping the goal(s) forefront and centre. The basic steps of the cycle are: (1) establishing the goal, (2) planning the question, (3) asking the question, (4) allowing time for the answer (a "wait time" of 5–10 seconds), (5) listening to the response, (6) assessing the response, (7) asking a follow-up question, and (8) re-planning based on the response (11–12 seconds). The steps of this questioning cycle show how the questions are not pre-established; they are guided by the answers that have been given.

In short, effective questioning asks that you develop a mindful concentration. The process of listening and questioning are, in fact, two halves of a whole.

The Present and Desired States

In a person, the *state* is the total gestalt of thoughts, feelings, and physical processes (physiology is the term often used for the *physical state* in NLP). Identifying the present state of your clients, colleagues, and customers is key to helping them to understand where they are and identifying where they want to be, or the *desired state*. When achieving that desired state, they need to think about what outcome(s) they want to achieve (see Figure 2.1).

One way of thinking about any kind of change is to regard it as a movement from the *present state* (how things are now) to a *desired state* (how you want things to be). In order to get from the present state to the desired state, we may need to apply resources. These can be new beliefs, new actions, evoking positive emotions, money, a new physical environment—anything that will bring about the desired change.

It is important to be clear about what the desired state is and whether you really want it. If you are not sure of your motivation, this may be a sign that the *ecology* of the desired state (the effect it will have on the whole life of the person and the systems of which they are a part) may need attention.

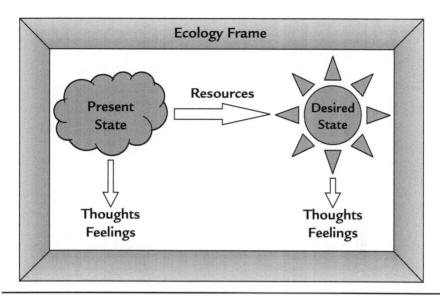

Figure 2.1   Present State and Desired State

Some people in NLP refer to the present state as the *problem state*, perhaps reflecting the earliest models of NLP that came from therapy. But remember, there will be resources available in the present state and also resource memories and strategies available from the past that may be useful.

A CLIENT INTERVIEW

The following is a real-life example of an interview with a client who had been going through a challenging time and was looking to make some changes. I have set off the unspoken desired state in parentheses. This is what I used to help the client to change her vocabulary to reflect what she wanted. It may seem strange, but the mind can't process a negative instruction. If I say, "Don't think of a blue elephant," what do you think of? For the mind to accept a declaration about a desired state, it must be in the positive.

Jim: What is your present state?

Client: I am always thinking that I will be happy once I change certain things in my life. Happiness is always somewhere off in the distance. I feel I don't deserve to be happy and successful and I destroy opportunities in my life with my negative thoughts. I also feel I am completely transparent with my flaws and others see them and I will not be liked and will be rejected because of them. I am working hard, but then something gets destroyed and I have to start again. I feel my energy is always leaking out of me. I am often in a state of "the end of the world", of something bad is going to happen. This is especially heightened when good things happen to me.

Jim: What is your desired state:

Client: I want to have an abundance of energy (I don't want to feel on edge and on guard all the time). I want to be positive and have positive people around me. I feel that being positive and happy is a fleeting feeling (because happiness is a fragile state), much more so than sadness. I want to have support from those around me (I want to believe in myself and embrace opportunities and bounce back from failures and disappointments). I want to be at peace with myself and with my imperfections. I want to feel "whole". I want to do things even if I feel afraid. I want to embrace happiness, live fully, love deeply (not get so upset when things go wrong or people disappoint me). I want to know that I am capable of supporting myself emotionally and financially.

I then asked the client to focus on the outcome she was looking for. She told me she wanted:

1. Inner peace and acceptance of the way I am.

2. Belief that I deserve happiness and success in all its forms.

3. I want to embrace opportunities and relationships and not be so scared or disappointed when things don't turn out as I'd hoped.

As you can see, the desired state the client wanted was not defined with a clear outcome. If you don't have a clear outcome how are you going to hit the target? The desired states the client said she wanted were just states of mind. For example, asking for happiness as an outcome is vague. Asking for opportunities presupposes you don't have opportunities, asking to be confident means nothing on its own, as I am sure nearly everyone is confident about something, whether it is driving or just making a cup of tea.

Instead, the outcome should be stated in clear terms, such as, "I want to have the confidence to deliver a presentation to 30 people on a specific topic."

Remember: It is important that we specify what we want as a positive instruction because the mind can't process a negative instruction. We also need to be specific about our outcomes. As you can see from the example, many people state what they want in the negative and by doing that the mind processes exactly what they don't want.

A RADIO CHALLENGE

I was invited to do the phobia-release technique on City Talk Radio. I was told it was the biggest talk show outside London. I decided to take up the challenge. As far I was aware, I was going to have time to conduct some sessions. I thought I would initiate a session then the show would carry on with its schedule and they would come back to me towards the end of the session and discuss the outcome.

Little did I realise I would have, at most, two to three minutes per person; it was obvious I didn't have much time for a pretalk. So, I thought if I could get some clarity about what was going through the person's mind related to the phobia, I could work with that to help them overcome it even in that short amount of time.

Ironically, the first person that arrived was waiting downstairs in the foyer of the radio station. I asked the producer why this man wouldn't come up. The City Talk building is one of the tallest in Liverpool and the producer replied that the man was afraid of heights.

I asked if I could chat to him, and the producer said I could, but prior to that I needed to work with the first person scheduled for the show, who was already waiting in the studio. I had the designated two to three minutes to work with him but after that the radio station would break to get an update on a football game.

So I talked to the first man on the schedule who told me he worked in theatre and had a fear of broken toes. I asked him if someone had to live with his phobias, what would they experience in a sequential manner and what would they see, hear, and feel.

He told me that an injury to his feet would mean he would not be able to work and that was his biggest fear. I asked him what he wanted to experience and what outcome did he want. He said he wanted to feel calm, relaxed, and focused. He also wanted to be focused during audition performances.

From there I had something to work with! I worked on his fear and achieved a positive outcome. That set the tone for the rest of the evening, including helping the man with the height phobia. It was a massive learning experience for me. It taught me how important and powerful it was for someone to be aware of their strategy when pursuing an outcome in any given context.

◢ COMMUNICATING USING THE DEEP STRUCTURE/ SURFACE STRUCTURE META-MODEL

This meta-model was developed by linguistics guru Noam Chomsky. It describes how what we *think* is translated into what we *say*. We never say the whole of what we are thinking—it would take too long and much of it would be irrelevant to what we want to say.

> *"At first, I see pictures of a story in my mind. Then creating the story comes from asking questions of myself. I guess you might call it the 'what if—what then' approach to writing and illustration."*
>
> —Chris Van Allsburg

THE DEEP STRUCTURE LEVEL

The deep structure is actually made up of images and feelings that cannot be expressed precisely in words. We have an idea of what we want to say—the *deep structure*—but the words we actually use—the *surface structure*—cannot fully represent everything we mean. Every time we speak, we unconsciously do three things:

1. We select only some of the information available in the deep structure and leave out or delete the rest.
2. We simplify what we want to say, which results in some distortion to the meaning.
3. We generalise, leaving out exceptions and qualifiers that are irrelevant.

Then when we hear the surface structure of someone else's conversation, we apply our own deletions, distortions and generalisations to fill in the gaps to make our own deep structure.

THE SURFACE STRUCTURE LEVEL

The surface structure—the words that someone uses—contain clues both to the deep structure of what they really mean and to the model of the world in which that deep structure is set and from which it is generated.

This level of the meta-model is a way of recovering the deleted, distorted and generalised information in both the deep structure of what a person is saying and in the person's surface structure model of the world. It reminds us to be aware of our own distortions, deletions and generalisations and not to apply them automatically.

For example, a client or a colleague might say, "I am fed up at work." What does that mean exactly? You could make an assumption based on your map of the world, though that is not likely to be an accurate reflection of what the problem might be. It is almost like someone telling you they are going to the shop and you making an assumption of which shop they are going to, what they are going to buy, how long they will be, who they are going with, and so forth.

CONSIDERATIONS FOR USING THE DEEP STRUCTURE/ SURFACE STRUCTURE META-MODEL IN COACHING

The deep structure/surface structure meta-model is often presented as a set of *violations* and the *challenges* to use on them. You can use the meta-model as an inner guide for following what a person is saying to you and recognise the thought patterns that show up in their language, with the option to ask a question when that would be useful. However, aggressive questioning will come across as very confrontational.

Always remember you have two purposes in using any meta-model:

1. to recover lost information, and
2. to help the client loosen up their model of the world.

When you are talking to someone, remember to ask the questions that are most relevant to these ends. Decide what level of information you are after. Go for the biggest chunk size you can while maintaining rapport.

You can use this particular meta-model to:

1. clarify your own thought processes and communication,
2. check your understanding of what another person is saying,
3. help other people to become aware of their own mental maps, unconscious beliefs and thought processes, and
4. help them to solve problems by reconnecting their thoughts with sensory experience and identifying gaps in their thinking.

Table 2.1 lists some examples of deep structure/surface structure meta-model patterns. You don't need to memorise all the patterns, just get an understanding of people's patterns of distorting, generalisation, and deleting information. Then look for the sort of the response you can use to help loosen the clients map of the world and fill in the missing gaps.

EXAMPLE OF USING THE DEEP STRUCTURE/ SURFACE STRUCTURE META-MODEL

It was 28 April 2007 during a game between Accrington Stanley and Macclesfield Town. I had been helping Accrington Stanley FC literally do a Houdini act to get out of what many called an impossible position in order to stay in the league.

The Macclesfield team was managed by Paul Ince. He got a lot of publicity for working towards helping Macclesfield maintain their position in the league. The irony of that was that Paul Ince had been given money by the then-owners to bring in better players. Accrington had no money to bring in anyone at the time.

Prior to the game, one of the players to look out for was young Nick Blackman, who now plays for Reading FC. I had taught Nick before when I was working part time for an organisation teaching footballers a scholars education. Then he had been in a group of footballer scholars that had seen teachers come and go. I was brought in and instituted a strong disciplinary regime, which players like Nick objected to. He was not a model student and there were times when he and the other students tested my patience. On a positive note, I got the students through the course.

Table 2.1 Examples of the Deep Structure/Surface Struction Meta-Model Patterns

Patterns	Examples	Responses
Distortions		
1. Mind Reading	"You must think I'm stupid." "He wants to humiliate me."	How do you know…?
2. Lost Performative (a value judgement presented as a fact)	"She's beautiful." "It's selfish to go for what you want."	Who says? By what standard do you judge…?
3. Cause and effect (A / B)	"He makes me angry." "Work bores me."	How does this cause that?
4. Complex Equivalence (A = B or A means B)	"She never smiles at me, she doesn't like me."	How does that mean…?
5. Presuppositions	"Would you rather wash up or tidy your room first?"	Who says/how do you know…?
Generalisations		
6. Universal Quantifiers (all, always, never, everyone, no-one…)	"Everyone says so." "Things never go right for me." "Dogs are vicious."	Everyone? Has there ever been a time when…? What, all dogs?

Table continued on next page

Table 2.1   Examples of the Deep Structure/Surface Struction Meta-Model Patterns (continued)

Patterns	Examples	Responses
Generalisations (continued)		
7. Modal Operators		
a) Necessity (must, should, have to, need to...)	"I mustn't say that to him." "It is necessary to do this."	What would happen if you did...? or (for possibility only) "What stops you?"
b) Possibility (can't, it's impossible...)	"I can't stay now."	
Deletions		
8. Nominalisations (processes that have been turned into things)	"I'm in a bad relationship."	Who are you relating to? How are you relating badly?
9. Unspecified Verbs	"Peter made things OK again."	How (specifically)...?
10. Simple Deletions	"I am unhappy."	About what?
11. Unspecified Referential Index (when it's not clear what's being referred to)	"They don't listen to me." "It's a matter of opinion." "Some people will never get this."	Who or what (specifically)...?
12. Comparative Deletions	"It's better this way." "I handled that badly."	Compared with what?

I had mentioned to Nick that in the small world of football there would be a time when we would cross paths again in the game and he would not get the same treatment he did as a student.

Well, during the warm up before the game against Macclesfield, I caught Nick's eye. His face dropped when he saw me. I went over to have a short conversation with him. I noticed Paul Ince watching us during our talk, but it was all above board, though I did use the deep structure/surface structure meta-model to get into Nick's head.

We scored first and the game was 1-0. Then Macclesfield hit back and scored 2 goals before half time. They were up 2-1. Just before half time, we scored again to make it 2-2. During half time I told our players to focus and keep with the task in hand.

As we were walking out to recommence the game, I made a deep structure/surface structure meta-model comment to Nick and he seemed to lose it. He charged towards our dugout and it did not take much to transmit his emotion to the players on our bench. I thought that this was our chance because the other team's leader was riled up even if he wasn't in the game. Soon after all the hoo-ha, we scored again and it was 3-2. Nick got into the game again too late to really affect the outcome, but because of his earlier emotion we stayed up at 3-2 and that's all that mattered.

I wished Ince, Nick and all the players the best, but Macclesfield had to go to the final game to ensure their survival.

Deep Structure/Surface Structure Meta-Model Examples

Look at the two statements on the next page. Try to keep from looking at the answers and decide for yourself which deep structure/ surface structure meta-model pattern level they correspond to. Then generate a response to challenge the statement.

Statement:

"John makes me feel sad."

Meta-Model:

This is a cause and effect pattern because the word "makes" appears in the sentence.

Response:

How does that cause you to choose to feel sad?

Statement:

"I should read more books."

Meta-Model:

This is an necessity operator model pattern because the word "should" appears in the sentence.

Response:

"What would happen if you did?"

TRANSCRIPT FROM A COURSE

The following is a transcript from a course I conducted in which a delegate stated she was a commitment-phobe and had a problem with committing herself in relationships. For confidentially purposes the person is named Client. At points in the session I make references to the class as to the deep structure/surface structure meta-model pattern I was using, which assisted them in understanding the questioning process.

Speakers: Jim and Client

Client: All right, the issue is, I don't know if I'm a bit of a commitment-phobe in regards to relationships.

Jim: A commitment-phobe. So you're not aware of whether you are a commitment-phobe?

Client: Well, I was seeing a guy and when he said he was getting feelings for me, that's when he completely backed off. At that point, instead of sticking with it, I just said, "Right, well, I don't need to be with somebody like you." Now, I don't know if that's a bad thing or a good thing, do you know what I mean?

Jim: *Okay just to give you an idea at this point, I have my interpretation of what Client is saying. She has her own interpretation, so we want to get to the bottom of what's going on and we're going to use the deep structure/surface structure meta-model to get there.* So at the moment, you're unsure whether or not you're a commitment phobe?

Client: Yeah. Everybody says you shouldn't be single, you shouldn't be this or that, and I'm like, "Well, but I'm happy as I am." Do you know what I mean?

Jim: Everybody says? Who is everybody?

Client: Pretty much everybody in my family, my friends, and my work colleagues.

Jim: Everyone in your family, your work colleagues, and your friends?

Client: Uh-huh.

Jim: So that's who you class as everybody?

Client: Yeah.

Jim: Let's go back to what we said before: everybody?

Client: Well not everybody, just a close friend of mine at work. I guess not everybody, though it feels like everybody.

Jim: Exactly. So there's a big world out there with seven billion people the last time I counted. Is one person everybody?

Client: Ok, just one close friend at work.

Jim: What do you want to happen, Client? What do you want?

Client: What do I want to happen? When I actually think about it, the whole thing of commitment and all the rest of it doesn't bother me at all. The fact is, spending the rest of my life with somebody I love dearly actually excites me. It doesn't scare me, so I don't understand what's the issue really.

Jim: So what is the issue?

Client: Because I think people are putting pressure on me, you know what I mean?

Jim: Who is putting pressure on you?

Client: Myself.

Jim: How are you putting pressure on yourself?

Client: Well, I see my friends all happy and settled with kids and I am on my own. And I am unsure as to whether this is because I am a commitment-phobe.

Jim: So you're unsure as to whether you're a commitment-phobe?

Client: Well, I have quite high ideals and I base relationships on my personal ideals. I have a good, strong relationship with my family and I suppose I have expectations about relationships because of that. When I feel as though I'm not getting what I want from a relationship, then that's it. Rather than sticking together and working towards it, I just say, "Right, well, it's not working out, see you later."

Jim: How is that a problem?

Client: Well, no two people are the same, are they? There's always going to be some sort of compromise and negotiation and all the rest of it. And coming to that compromise and actually having the guts to stick with it rather than just running away from it, I guess.

Jim: So just to answer my question, how is it a problem for you?

Client: Well, because I'm not a serial dater or anything like that. I don't want to be continually just going out with people, do you know what I mean? I'd rather just have a nice relationship and mainly the problem is getting to that point.

Jim: At this point, it's becoming a little bit more clear as to what's going on in your mind and what's happening.

Client: Yeah, it's weird. I went on holiday this weekend with one of my best friends and we were talking about it. She said, "I just don't understand it. You have really nice guys who try to take you out and all the rest of it, and then for some reason, you just pull back even if it's something really insignificant." I can understand where she's actually coming from, but it...

Jim: Yeah, so, I'm going to be a pain, and this is where the model is a pain. No, this is where the model can come across as being violating. I want you to tell me how is that a problem?

Client: How is it a problem? Well, I think because I worry about the end result. Obviously I want a nice, happy, fulfilling relationship, right? The issue I've got is that I just get scared about the smallest little thing I can. It's stopping me from getting to where I want to be.

Jim: Where do you want to be?

Client: Well, you know, in a happy, secure, healthy relationship.

Jim: So where we are at the moment, you're unsure if you're a commitment-phobe, you think it might be a problem because you know what you want out of a relationship, so you want a happy relationship and ...

Client: Yeah.

Jim: You said that being the way you are at the moment could potentially be preventing you from having that. How can it prevent you from having that?

Client: I think it's just because of my insecurities, really. It's almost like I let somebody get close and then that's it. Do you know what I mean? There's a line. On the very, very, very rare occasions I've let people get across that line, it's as if my protection mechanism kicks in. I don't know if that's really weak to actually say, but, yeah, it's just this thing of...I recently met a guy and he was absolutely brilliant, do you know what I mean? He's been a perfect gentleman and he'd do anything for me, but at the same time I'm struggling to break down my barriers.

Jim: What are your barriers?

Client: I don't know what my barriers are.

Jim: Then how do you know you've got barriers, if you don't know what the barriers are?

Client: Well, that's the label that I put on them. There's something there, some sort of fear, I think.

Jim: So it's fear?

Client: I think so.

Jim: Because you've said that you've got barriers, when I ask you what the barriers are, you don't know what the barriers are? So what is it?

Client: Well, I think there's something that's stopping me and I don't understand what it is.

Jim: There's something stopping you from doing what?

Client: To achieving where I want to be, to getting really close to somebody, something is ...

Jim: Something is stopping you?

Client: Yeah.

Jim: What's that something?

Client: I think it's fear of rejection. Being hurt. Because I place a lot of faith and trust and everything I value in my relationships with people, my family, and my friends, and it's the same with a boyfriend.

Jim: So, you've got a fear of being hurt and rejected?

Client: I would say, yeah.

Jim: What makes you think you're going to be rejected?

Client: Well, you see, this is it. I don't know. That's my perception, isn't it? And I guess that's my…what's the word…survival mechanism, and I think, "Well, if I'm never in that situation then I can't feel hurt."

Jim: What's a survival mechanism?

Client: So if I did have that unfortunate experience of being hurt and rejected, it's not having to deal with that.

Jim: Yet, what did you say you wanted?

Client: I want a healthy, happy, nice relationship.

Jim: So you want a healthy, happy, nice relationship?

Client: Yep.

Jim: And what are you doing to …

Client: Stop having a healthy, happy relationship. My own issues.

Jim: What are you doing to achieve a happy, healthy, nice relationship?

Client: Well, I'm trying. I am, you know. I am making an effort. I want to get to know people, but when it comes to people getting to know me, it's this barrier thing. You know, this …

Jim: You mentioned this barrier before.

Client: Yeah.

Jim: What was the barrier?

Client: Well, it's my fears, my insecurities. Everybody has insecurities.

Jim: Now we're relating it back to you. So your fears and insecurities are about what?

Client: About being hurt, rejected, and all that kind of stuff.

Jim: Okay. So you've got a fear of being hurt, being rejected?

Client: Yep.

Jim: And is there anything else?

Client: No, no, it's just the feeling of hurt and rejected.

Jim: So you've got a fear of being hurt and rejected?

Client: Yep.

Jim: How is that fear of being hurt and rejected preventing you from having a happy relationship like you've described?

Client: I think it's probably because I don't want to go through it again.

Jim: You don't want to go through it again?

Client: You know what I mean? It's just one of those things that once you've experienced it, you don't really want to go through it again.

Jim: You don't want to go through what again?

Client: Being hurt and rejected. And to know that you can't put that fear on somebody else, but it's very difficult, isn't it? I suppose, when you've experienced it, it's hard not to have it in the back of your mind every now and again.

Jim: So you identified fear and rejection.

Client: Yep, I am afraid of being hurt.

Jim: You've identified what you want from a relationship.

Client: Yep, I want a happy relationship I can share my life in.

Jim: Okay. What can you do to move forward and achieve that relationship?

Client: I think it's believing that no two people are the same. You have different relationships with people. I've got no reason, really, to feel like that, but it's just a case of, I think I need to ...

Jim: You got no reason to feel like what?

Client: Well, the feeling of fear and rejection. My mom and dad, they've been together 40 years. I've got a very good relationship with my brothers, very good relationships with my friends. Since I was at school I've had long-standing friendships and relationships. So really, when you look at it, my family background and everything is absolutely rock solid. It's just this whole, I don't know, I think I need to just place more faith in people.

Jim: You think you need to put faith in people?

Client: Yeah, I need to believe a bit more.

Jim: And if you believe, then you put faith in people, what would happen then?

Client: I think it will be good and give my relationships a chance to flourish.

Jim: How could it be good? What would be good?

Client: Well, the relationships. Healthy, happy relationships.

Jim: So if you believe that healthy, happy relationships couldn't go wrong, what would happen then?

Client: It wouldn't go wrong.

Jim: It wouldn't go wrong?

Client: The relationship would be allowed to grow.

Jim: So do you think if you believe it couldn't go wrong, it wouldn't go wrong?

Client: Well, I don't know. I don't necessarily believe that, because there's lots of other things that can come into play. But I think, yeah, it would help if I had that belief.

Jim: Would it help if you had that belief?

Client: Yeah, it would help if I had that belief.

Jim (to the group): *Can anyone see a pattern emerging or anything emerging based on what the initial problem was? Where are we now? Does anyone remember what the initial problem was?*

Speaker: Yeah, she was a commitment-phobe.

Jim: *So in the client's words, she was a commitment-phobe. Okay. So where are we now in the context of the problem?*

Speaker: We're identifying what the problem is and it's that she's not actually a commitment-phobe.

Jim: *Yeah. So if a client came to me as a coach to solve an initial problem, and she said, "I'm a commitment-phobe, can you help me?" If I deployed techniques and strategies to solve her being a commitment-phobe, what are the chances of me being successful without establishing an understanding as to what's going on?*

Speaker: Not as effective as they would be now.

Jim: *Precisely. So through this process we've unravelled a series of various thoughts and information that had been deleted, distorted, and generalized to the point to where we are now. So where we are now? Client has established some key areas in her own mind that are preventing her from being where she wants to be in a relationship and we're making progress. Where we carry on and where we go with the model is anybody's guess. But the main thing is, we want to aim for the outcome.*

So, if at any point during the model you feel that you've gone around the house and around the world in 80 days, what you want to do is backtrack and think, "What outcome does the client want? What does client want? What's going to work for her? Okay. And what information do I need to loosen her map of the world? And give her a level of empowerment so she can recognize that she can start moving forward to solve whatever's going on at a deeper level."

Okay. If we've got any questions, we can go from there. As I said, this can go on for as long as it needs to go on. During my consultation, the client will feel challenged to a certain extent in certain situations because I am questioning them, not just about levels of behaviour, but also about beliefs and, potentially, values to get them to an outcome they want. Obviously if I question someone's belief or a value and it isn't something they want to talk about, they can feel severely violated. But if I can get to the bottom of it and to solve the problem, that's the key and that's the most important thing.

So, let's continue on with this issue for five minutes or so. Where we are now, Client? You talked about, in your own mind, in your own words, being a commitment-phobe.

Client: Yes.

Jim: Where we are now? You've now talked about what you want in a relationship, you want a happy, healthy, nice relationship.

Client: Yep, yep.

Jim: You mention that fear and rejection potentially are in the way of achieving that. You mentioned that you thought if you could believe that the relationship you're going into is healthy and happy, that would go a long way towards achieving it.

Client: Yep.

Jim: I'm going to ask you a few questions. What is a healthy, happy, nice relationship?

Client: Well, a relationship in which you feel secure, in which you feel respected, and you can laugh together. You know you can go through problems together. It's a whole range of things.

Jim: So a relationship that's healthy, happy, and nice, in your world, is one where there's respect and going through problems together.

Client: Also honesty and trust.

Jim: Respect, honesty, and trust.

Client: Yeah, like that kind of stuff.

Jim: So these are values that you're looking for in a relationship?

Client: Yep.

Jim: Where you don't feel insecure, you said?

Client: Yeah, yeah. Yeah.

Jim: Can anybody make you feel anything?

Client: What do you mean anything?

Jim: Well, can somebody else affect how you feel? Is it possible for somebody else to make you feel insecure? Who makes you feel insecure?

Client: Nobody makes me feel insecure.

Jim: Whose choice is it to feel insecure?

Client: My choice.

Jim: Okay. So if it's your choice to feel insecure, can you choose otherwise?

Client: Yeah.

Jim: Okay. Going back to the criteria of the relationship you're looking for: respect, honesty, loyalty, and trust. Have you got a choice as to who you have a relationship with?

Client: Yeah.

Jim: Okay. And if they have that set of values, how would you feel?

Client: Great.

Jim: So you'd feel great.

Client: Yeah.

Jim: If you met someone who was loyal, honest?

Client: Yeah, yeah, yeah.

Jim: Now, you mentioned fear and rejection. How is keeping that fear and rejection going to help you to achieve what you're looking for? A healthy, happy, nice relationship with all your values?

Client: It's not.

Jim: It's not.

Client: Yeah. It's prevents me from letting a relationship develop.

Jim: It's preventing you?

Client: Yeah, yeah.

Jim: So how come you're keeping it?

Client: I think I get comfortable and because I see fear from friends who are in relationships. They're not happy.

Jim: This isn't about your friends, it's about you. How come you're keeping this fear of rejection?

Client: Well, you see, I'm happy where I am. It's like I look at one of my friends and she's in a relationship. She's been with him a long time and they are not happy. The only reason they're together is because it's...

Jim: So whatever's going on in your friend's world...

Client: Yeah?

Jim: Does that have anything to do with what's going on in your world?

Client: No, it has nothing to do with it.

Jim: So how come you're comparing yourself to your friend?

Client: Because I am happy.

Jim: And how come you're comparing yourself to your friend?

Client: Well, I just think that it begs the question, you know, of what is the point of being in a relationship because I see a lot of people who are in them, in relationships, and they are not happy.

Jim: So you see a lot of people who are not happy. Do you ever see people who are happy in relationships?

Client: Oh, yes. Yeah, totally.

Jim: So it's six of one and a half dozen of another, isn't it?

Client: Yep.

Jim: So what happens when you compare yourself to other people?

Client: It's not good.

Jim: What happens when we compare ourselves to others?

Client: You start to believe, don't you?

Jim: Can you put your friends to one side for now and focus on where you are? So you mentioned you're happy.

Client: Yep.

Jim: Okay. If you're happy, what's the problem?

Client: But I could be happier.

Jim: So you could be happier?

Client: Yeah.

Jim: Okay. What's preventing you from being happier?

Client: I think just, again, this feeling of rejection and...

Jim: Okay. This feeling of rejection.

Client: Yeah, fear and rejection

Jim: This feeling of rejection and fear. Okay, and how is this feeling of fear of rejection preventing you from being happier?

Client: Because they're stuck in me really. They are keeping me from getting to where I would like to be, I think.

Jim: And where you'd like to be is...?

Client: Is in a nice relationship.

Jim: Who controls these fears of rejection?

Client: Me, really.

Jim: So how come you keep these fears? If they're, in your own words, preventing you from being happier?

Client: I think it's just one of those things, you know, like you have natural reactions. Yeah, I don't know.

Jim: How come you keep these fears?

Client: I don't know. It's protection, I think.

Jim: Protection from what?

Client: Being hurt and rejected. I feel as though if I haven't got a boyfriend, then it doesn't really matter, does it? It's never going to happen.

Jim: Okay. So you have two choices.

Client: Yes?

Jim: You carry on doing what you are doing or you find a partner.

Client: Lose the fear. And replace it with faith and trust.

Jim: Yeah. And what happens when you place faith and trust in certain situations?

Client: You believe, don't you? You believe.

Jim: Yeah?

Client: For whatever reason, you believe that things are going to be fine; everything will be fine.

Jim: So how can you let go of this fear and rejection?

Client: By believing in something else, by believing that I have no reason to feel like that.

Jim: Yeah. And by doing that, do you think you can achieve this happiness you're looking for?

Client: I think so.

Jim: Yeah?

Client: Yeah, I think so. It's just changing my thought patterns really and believing what I want to believe.

Jim: So, moving forward toward the outcome you're looking for, which is achieving this additional happiness and building a healthy, nice relationship based on honesty and loyalty, in letting go of the fear of rejection, what will happen if you let go of this fear?

Client: It will allow me to have faith and trust in other people.

Jim: Are you happy to let go?

Client: It's not getting me anywhere, so I am happy to let go.

Jim: So you're happy to let go?

Client: Yeah, yeah. Yeah.

Jim: Okay. Fantastic.

The above transcript demonstrates how powerful the questioning process can be.

EFFECTIVE QUESTIONS

Effective questions are worded so that the person answering only needs to work on forming their response, rather than understanding the question. Effective questions also have a clear sense of purpose; for example, to gather more information, to see something from another perspective, or to create a sense of the future. Some useful examples of effective questions are found in Table 2.2 and Table 2.3. Note that they are open in intention and not restricted by an anticipated answer.

The powerful questions in Table 2.4

⬦ acknowledge the issue or challenge;

⬦ assume that a positive outcome is possible;

◢ are open-ended (what, how, when, who, why), and

◢ provokes a creative response.

◢ Exercise

1. Discuss/Write/Reflect

   Write one of your own examples for each type of question in Table 2.4, "Powerful Questions", that would satisfy a coaching approach and work towards a positive outcome.

Table 2.2 Questions With a Clear Sense of Purpose

Purpose	Coaching examples
Gather general information.	Can you say more about that?
Gather specific information.	Specifically, what is it that you're unhappy about?
	Can you tell me what actually happened?
Help someone remember something more clearly.	What else can you remember?
To refocus someone on what's important; e.g., to keep them on track, or calm them down, etc.	Ok, so what's really important about all this?
	What seems to be the most important thing for us to focus on now?
Understand someone else's values.	What is important to you about that?
	Why is that important to you?
Help someone to appreciate another person's perspective.	What might be Jody's reasons behind asking for this?
	What's important to Jody?
	If we had Jody here how would she describe this situation?
Get someone to link two thoughts, or situations, together.	How do your work pressures relate to what you said about developing the team more?
Help someone come to a conclusion.	What are your thoughts about this now?
	What is the conclusion you are drawing from this now?
Produce ideas without a sense of pressure.	What options are there?
	What options are available to you?
	What things might you do?
	What ideas are you having?
Influence someone to decide.	Which option do you prefer?
	What have you decided to do?
Influence someone to action.	What could you do about that right now?
Prepare someone to overcome barriers to taking action.	What might stop you from doing that? [Follow-up] So how will you overcome that?

Table 2.3   Questions With Open Intention

Strategised question	Question with a more open intention
Couldn't you speak to your boss about this?	What support do you need with this?
Have you considered putting a plan together to make everyone agree to the dates?	How can you get everyone to agree to the dates?
How angry are you about all this?	How are you feeling about this?
What could your HR representative do to help you?	Who else might help?
	[Or even more open] What are you thinking of doing?
Didn't you say that Dave doesn't actually want to be involved anyway?	How would Peter feel about that?

Table 2.4   Powerful Questions

Statement of issue/complaint	Powerful question
It's hopeless—we're never going to get it done by Friday because we've already got so much other work in the queue.	How can we get it done by Friday and still deal with the other work in the queue?
We'd love to have a staff summer party again, but the money needs to go on training this year.	How can we find the money for a summer party and still afford the training?
We really need to do some team collaboration, but people's roles are going to change and we don't yet know what that's going to mean.	How can we do some team building and still support the new roles in the future?

3 Communicating and Rapport

"Everything that irritates us about others can lead us to an understanding of ourselves."

—Carl Gustav Jung

Rapport is an important aspect of relationships. Rapport allows you to see the world through a client's, colleague's, or customer's point of view. In turn, it helps you to understand where they are coming from. For the other person—be it colleague, staff, client, or customer—rapport, or its absence, may register subconsciously.

◢ CREATING RAPPORT CONSCIOUSLY

In this chapter we will explore ways to create rapport consciously. To do so, closely observe and then subtly match some aspect of your client's manner, being careful not to imitate or mock. More specifically, as Jacquie Turnbull explains in her book *Coaching for Learning*, you can match body language, voice and language to create rapport. Let's look at each of these three areas in turn.

BODY LANGUAGE

Body language speaks volumes about a person's mood, outlook, comfort level and self image. Notice everything. Does the person have their legs and arms crossed or uncrossed? Are they slouching or sitting up straight? Is their torso open or hunched over? Are they holding their head or mouth in a particular fashion? Match whichever element allows you to feel most "in sync" with the person.

VOICE

One of the most subtle ways of creating rapport is to match breathing. Watch for the rise and fall of the chest and listen for the rate and quality of breathing in the voice. Then listen to voice itself.

Is it tight, breathless, low, high, slow, fast, singsong, monotonous? Again, match the aspect that feels most important to you.

LANGUAGE

Matching language is a very easy and important way to create rapport. For example, if your client says, "My head is throbbing," you might respond by asking, "Why is your head throbbing?" rather than "Why do you have a headache?" Creating rapport in these ways is an important first step in establishing effective relationships.

◢ RAPPORT IN BUSINESS

Think of a time when you went to an interview, had a meeting, delivered a presentation, or interacted with a work colleague and you were completely in sync. Go back to that time and try think what is was about that person that made you feel comfortable and attuned to him or her.

It is likely that you had some common ground. Maybe you both had kids of similar ages that attended the same school. Maybe you had both travelled or lived in a certain place and shared similar experiences. Maybe you both grew up in the same area or both your parents originated from same town, city, or country. You might have similar beliefs and values. Maybe you both had recently watched a sporting event or film that interested you in the same way; e.g., the football team you both support had just won a cup final and you discover your favourite player scored the winning goal.

Whatever drew you to that person and vice versa, will be an element of rapport. You had an understanding of each other's worlds, a bond on some level, which made you feel you knew where you were both coming from. You felt you had a mutual understanding and respect of each other's perceptions of the world.

Congruent rapport (or establishing rapport) is one of the most important skills and resources you can tap into. In business, to be successful you need to be able to get along with people. With rapport you will be able to create win–win situations in which both parties feel they will receive a benefit from the interaction you share.

Whatever your role in business, whether you're just starting out, looking to win a contract, in a sales environment, attending a meeting or interview, or working with people, the ability to establish a bond—to understand and enjoy each other's company, to work harmoniously and create win–win outcomes—is essential.

The word rapport derives from the French verb *rapporter*, translated as "to return or bring back". The English dictionary definition is "a sympathetic relationship or understanding". It's about making a two-way connection. You know you've made such a connection when you experience a genuine sense of trust and respect with another person, when you engage comfortably with someone no matter however different they are to you and when you know that you are listening and being listened to.

Rapport, used in English, implies harmony, a feeling of shared understanding and of being at one with someone else. It is the most important process in any interaction. Without rapport in business, two people will not trust each other and probably will not even *hear* each other correctly.

It takes very little time for people to form an impression of someone they have just met and that impression tends to be the same for you. A study by Harvard University psychologists found that the opinion students formed toward new teachers in the initial two seconds of a course was essentially the same as the one they held after sitting through the whole course. Of course, you cannot expect to become everyone's best friend in a few seconds, but if you make the right first impression, demonstrating that you are honest, reliable and trustworthy, you can initiate the building of a lasting rapport within 90 seconds.

Transfer that to the business world and think of the implications when you attend an interview, meet a potential customer or client, deliver a presentation and go for that promotion.

People make snap judgments about you, your skills and even your intelligence all based on a quick glance of your body language. I know, most people don't like to admit it, but we all judge others from the first moment we see them, even before the person says hello. In interactions, our communication *on every level* is key.

When people find common ground they tend to feel comfortable with each other. Think about it: people prefer to become part of clubs and associations that share similar interests and represent similar values and beliefs. Have you ever gone to a party where there was an instant bond amongst people who had never seen each other before?

Who are the people you feel more comfortable associating with? For example, who do most English people tend to feel better about, the Americans or Iranians? Easy answer. Who do the English have most in common with? Same answer.

Think about why some of the world's problems exist. Could it be because of different religions, economies, beliefs and values? Is it the emphasis of each other's differences? Deep divisions happen even in the same country based on ethnic origins and economic status. When people focus on each other's differences, problems arise.

One of the things I have learnt in life is that even though we all have unique experiences and backgrounds, we also have a great deal in common. Regardless of what ethnic origin you are or what country you were born in or brought up in, we all have the same or similar human needs, instincts and aspirations.

We are all in life together. Regardless of what nation, colour, religion, beliefs and values people have, at the very core there is a human spirit that wants to do the best we can. The person getting up to go to work to support his family on one part of the world has many similarities with a person in another part: loving his or her family, similar challenges, fears and aspirations.

So with this in mind, we can establish rapport with anyone! As the French say, "vive la difference." Respect and celebrate each other's differences.

◢ CREATING RAPPORT

We have all created rapport many times whether we're with an old friend or when we meet someone new and it feels like we've known them all our lives. People tend to think it just happens, but we can establish rapport deliberately.

To be successful in business, you need to be able to interact effectively with your work colleagues, your management, your staff, people who you see daily, people you only see from time to time, or people you see in passing. The results of the interactions you have with the people you meet will be determined by your ability to get on with them. Whether it's delivering a presentation to a group, being interviewed or interviewing, in a meeting, selling, leading, coaching, or mentoring, the degree of success you have will be based on your ability to influence with integrity, and this involves the skill of building rapport quickly and efficiently.

You may be the most talented person in your field, have the best product to sell, have a great attitude and have a lot to offer, but how you initially come across to people during your interactions in business is important.

Have you ever been in a situation when someone has tried to influence you, possibly over the phone to renegotiate a mobile phone contract, or when you have walked into a store or a car yard and a pushy sales person has been overbearing or overwhelming? How did it make you feel?

Now, think of the opposite scenario when you decided to make a purchase based on the way the sales person came across. What was the difference between the first experience, when you were put off and the second experience, when you were enticed? Did the person in the second scenario take the time to understand what you wanted, your needs?

Developing your ability to build rapport in business can help you become more successful and enhance your interactions with your colleagues. Rapport often develops naturally. Often you probably don't even notice it happening.

Take the time to reflect on your present work environment, reflecting on the situations and people with which you have good rapport. On your journey to achieving excellence in business there will be occasions when a person or people important to your business success may not be on your wave length. In that case, during the process of building a relationship with any individual or group of people it is important to establish rapport at a level necessary to support both party's outcomes.

So how do we create rapport and give ourselves the best possible chance to succeed in business? By finding or discovering common interests (i.e., you enjoy similar activities, favourite travel destinations, support the same football team, enjoy a particularly restaurant) and by associations (i.e., you grew up in the same area, went to the same college, or you hold similar beliefs).

However, all of those experiences are communicated through words, which on the face of it, is how most people consciously open up a dialogue of communication. For example a sales person going to deliver a pitch might focus consciously on what he or she is going to say to the perspective client or customer. And yet, studies have shown that we communicate only about 7% by words and 38% through the tone of voice. (Think of a situation or a time when a teacher, a parent, a boss, or a manager called your name using a certain harsh tone. It represented more than just your name.)

The largest part of communication—up to 55%—is as a result of physiology or body language. Think about the various conversations you have had with people or have heard during television interviews. What do you notice about someone who is scared? Someone who is happy? Someone who is nervous? Or confident? Chances are they did not have to open their mouth and say a word for you to have an idea of what they were communicating. The fact is, you cannot *not* communicate. We are always communicating at some level whether its conscious or unconscious. Our body language—the facial expressions, gestures, breathing, fast or slow physiological movements, timing of movements—are always sending messages.

Have you ever been to a comedy show in which the comedian got up and said things at which you would take offence if you had heard someone say them on the street? Yet, the way the comedian says it made you laugh. Have you ever watched the programmes "Dragon's Den" or "The Apprentice?" It's the physiology and tonality of the people making the decisions on the panel, or of Sir Alan Sugar pointing his finger at a candidate with a firm direct tone of voice saying, "You're fired," which draws you into the suspense of the moment. Merely trying to create rapport by the content of our conversation ignores the higher percentages of how we communicate.

The easiest and quickest way to build rapport with someone is to meet the person at a level at which *they* are comfortable. Respect and gain an understanding of the other person's perspective. Respect their map of the world. Find some common ground. Use your physiology. These are great places to start. Use this process to build rapport and a foundation of a relationship with anyone you choose. No matter how well the odds are stacked in your favor, if you don't establish rapport you limit your chances of success.

In NLP, the process of creating rapport is called *matching and mirroring*. Mirroring, or adopting a similar physiological position as someone else, is an excellent foundation on which to built rapport

---

◢ Exercises

1. Take a moment to adopt the same or similar physiological position as someone else for an extended period of time, say about 5 minutes and notice how you begin to feel.

2. Take 5 minutes to write a list of the people you get on with best in your professional or personal life or both?

3. Now take 5 minutes to write a list of people you don't have rapport with?

Do you notice any differences between the two groups of people in #2 and #3 and your role in both situations. Do you feel confident? Are you supporting each other's outcomes? Are there conflicts at beliefs and values level?

◢ USING RAPPORT

Think of a situation where you saw through someone. What did you notice about the person? If someone tries to fake rapport, it will come across as being false. People can fake it for only so long. Eventually, if the rapport is incongruent, the relationship will fall apart. The insincerity will show through in the tone of voice, language patterns and body language.

If you are in rapport with a person, the communication between you can take place on a deeper level of understanding where you are not judging them from a distance but joining them in their reality and their experiences, both consciously and unconsciously. This does not mean that you agree with them, simply that you can join them in their reality for the purpose of developing open communication.

To gain rapport with people, you don't have to be best friends. It's about seeking win–win situations and respecting each other's map of the world. You may not necessarily agree with them on their identity, beliefs or values, but by respecting their positions and taking the time to understand them, you can reach a level of respect to support each other's outcomes. From there, a more natural level of behaviour takes place.

If we attempted to gain rapport without using body language and voice tonality we would be missing an opportunity to affect the greater proportion of how we communicate. One of the people who used NLP modelling was the great Dr Milton Erickson, called by some "The Father of Hypnotherapy". Erickson was one of the most successful therapists of his generation. He learned to mirror physiology—breathing patterns, rate of breathing (fast, shallow, deep) and posture (legs crossed, arms folded and various movements). It has been said Erickson would use matching and mirroring as a means to build rapport and develop the trust necessary to help his patients as effectively as possible. He would even match and mirror some of his patients to help them out of a catatonic state. Just think of how powerful this process would be if you adapted it to certain situations in your business or work environment.

Has anyone ever said something to you and your interpretation of what they said was completely different from what they meant? Let's say your boss calls you into his/her office for a meeting and gives you some praise in a dull tone of voice while not looking at you. It is hardly going to mean anything. In contrast, if you have you ever gone to watch a band or a theatre that you enjoyed, you probably gave a loud round of applause to show your appreciation and if you wanted an encore, you cheered the performance enthusiastically, trying to get the performer to come out to perform more.

Have you ever noticed two people deep in conversation? They unconsciously adopt each other's body postures, voice tones, pace of breathing; they are matching and mirroring. How we express ourselves through our physiology is key. By matching someone's physiology, their response will probably be, "Hey this person is similar to myself. He or she must be ok."

RAPPORT THE EASY WAY

Matching and mirroring is a highly effective method of creating rapport, of helping people feel more comfortable and relaxed. At first it may seem a little unnatural, but as you practise, it becomes more natural. By now you might be wondering, "How do I match and mirror someone's physiology?"

If you watch two people in rapport, you will see them sharing movements, speaking in a similar tonality, using similar gestures, language patterns, physical and emotional responses, breathing patterns and sharing many other aspects of their behaviour. That's where you begin.

You're probably thinking that this sounds crazy. It's not! We do it automatically anyway, so why not do it consciously to help gain rapport more rapidly? Matching and mirroring is *not* mimicking. You don't have to match and mirror everything on every level. You could start with voice tone or adopting similar body language (e.g., if the person has their arms folded, you could gradually bring your arms into a folded position).

Imagine the impact that gaining rapport easily and efficiently would have on your business if done on a daily basis in situations where you wanted a positive outcome. It is so easy, anyone can do it. Matching and mirroring is a skill, like any other and the more you practise, the better you become. So, go out and practise. Practise with work colleagues and give it a go in situations where you a looking to gain rapport. Practise at home with your family, friends, or your children. I am sure they will have fun in the process.

You can match and mirror even in discussions over the phone. For example, if you are English and are talking to an American on the phone, you wouldn't start speaking with an American accent, though you could still match voice projection and speed, tonality and breathing.

Another area you could match is the person's preferred representational system (rep system) or learning style. People use all their senses to process and deliver information, though most people have a strong preference for one or two. Once you have identified some-one's preferred rep system in a certain context, you can use that to foster an even better understanding and rapport.

If someone is very visual, they will tend to use visual references, (e.g., how do you see it going?). If you explain the process in any way other than visual, the person may struggle to connect. Explain the process in a way that meets their preferred learning style and you will have a massive positive impact. See the "Preferred Representational System Predicates" on page 148 and the Preferred Representational System Predicate Phrases on page 149 for ways to gain an insight into someone's preferred learning style.

You will also find there is a certain physiology attached to peo-ple's preferred learning style. Visual people may point a lot and use exaggerated gestures. Auditory people at times may turn their ear to face you or tilt their head, possibly with less eye contact. Kinaesthetic people tend to speak at a slower pace and clutch on to something like a pen, or move their body frequently. The physical tells people use that reveal their representational systems are covered in greater detail starting on page 146.

Obviously the physical tells vary from person to person and in context to context, so you need to pay attention in your observations. However, when you can identify someone's preferred learning style and you can match it, you have taken a big stride forward in develop-ing rapport and entering into their world.

Imagine a man is looking to purchase a car and he is very audi-tory. He enters the car yard and the sales person is very visual and proceeds to show him the cars on the yard. At no point does the sales person start the car engines so the auditory person can connect to the experience. It could be an opportunity lost. Taking a moment to identify a person's preferred system could potentially have a massive implication.

I remember being in a situation when a colleague of mine had brought a football team over from Australia to tour the UK. During part of the tour my colleague's team was going to play against the same under-15s age group at an academy in Manchester City.

The game had been booked in and was set to go. However, when I arrived at the grounds, the academy coach informed me there was a double booking and another team had been booked in on the same day. Because of commercial reasons, the other team was going to take priority. The lads, coaching staff and parents of my colleague's team all looked let down.

The coach of the other touring party was also from Australia and he would not budge. He was adamant it wasn't his problem. His team wanted to play Manchester City and regardless of what anyone said or did, he just wasn't going to reach a compromise. The Manchester City coaches told us that if we could come to a resolution with the coach of the other touring team, they would be happy to come to an arrangement.

I approached the coach of the other touring team as he was walking across the field with a two bags of footballs, I asked him if he wanted me to assist him with the bags and took one off him. I carried it the same way, I walked at the same cadence, breathed at the same pace and talked with a similar volume.

When he put his bag down, so did I. We continued to discuss options in order that my colleague's team could get a game. He finally backed down from his original position and agreed that my colleagues team could play both his team and the Manchester team, using a reduced timeframe of 30 minutes for each game. This is just an example of how powerful matching and mirroring can be.

◢ BUILDING RAPPORT AND LEADING

There was a popular book written in the 1930s, still popular today, called *How to Win Friends and Influence People* by Dale Carnegie (Simon and Schuster, 1936). In this book the author told how building rapport with another person was about finding common ground and connecting with that other person on some level. Carnegie explained that pretending to like another person does not build rapport. Rather, you have to find something you can honestly like, or at least appreciate, about the other person if you are to work towards a good relationship.

The idea in the book is clear: if you dislike everything about a person it will be almost impossible to build a good working relationship or personal rapport with that person because your body language and subtle attitudes will betray your true feelings. Thus, the best way to build rapport with another person is actually to find something about them that you can identify with and like, or at least appreciate.

As an example, consider that you have a co-worker that really drives you nuts. Despite your negative feelings about this person, you have to work with him. Try as you might, you don't seem to be able to develop a good working relationship, partly because you have trouble hiding your contempt. What can you do?

You can try to reframe the situation. Try to find something about this person that you can grab on to. When you talk to him or ask around, you learn that he is a hunter (you are a vegetarian), that he has no kids (you have three) and that he lives on ten acres (you live in an apartment). The list of opposites just seems to go on. That is, until you learn he is a huge science fiction movie fan and you love science fiction too. Now, you have found something in common.

Talk to him about this topic, form a connection on this one topic, find movies you both liked (sweeping any disagreements on the movies under the carpet). Now, when you interact with him instead of thinking about the things you don't have in common, think about your shared enjoyment of science fiction and use that as a basis for an honest reaction of agreement with this person.

This idea of finding something to like about a person helps you develop a foundation for a relationship, so you are not beginning from a place of contempt. But what is rapport really and do you have to like another person to have it? Rapport is what happens when two or more people are communicating effectively. These people are understanding each other, they are actively listening to what the other is saying and they are actually accomplishing something with their communications.

Though a mutual affection can make rapport easier, you do not have to like a person to be in rapport with them, you simply have to be listening and communicating well. One way that an outsider can tell that two people are in rapport is to watch their body language. People who have a good rapport will mirror each other. These people will use similar body language (perhaps both leaning towards each other, both alternately touching each other lightly in agreement, both tilting their head, etc.). They will mirror their body language,

Figure 3.1   An Example of Subtle Matching and Mirroring

their vocal tone, volume and tempo, their posture, eye contact and more. When people have good rapport, they have built trust.

The great news is that you can actually use your own body language to create this rapport. You do this through mirroring, as related in the section on the Australian coach. Mirroring is a way of matching the body language of another person. It is *not* about mimicking or mocking, but rather aligning your body languages (Figure 3.1). For example, if the person you are speaking with is very formal, you should remain very formal. Imagine for a minute that you are meeting a high-level president of your company. You can build good rapport by matching his body language, being formal when he is formal and becoming more causal and familiar as he does. Remember, to suddenly act very informal could alienate the person to whom you are talking.

When you create rapport you show the other person that although you might not necessarily agree with them, you do respect and appreciate what they are saying. You do this by mirroring their stance, their use of vocal tones, their arm movements and so forth.

However, you should stop mirroring and start leading if the person you are talking to starts to show body language that is upset, angry or aggressive. You may want to bring that person back to a calm state, to find a way to diffuse their anger. This comes in handy because most people unconsciously mirror people that they are in rapport with. Here's how to take the lead and turn a situation around.

You are talking to an acquaintance and things started out fine; you felt as though you were establishing rapport and communicating well. Then the conversation turns towards politics, which you can see is a hot topic with this person. You do not hold the same opinions and this person is growing increasingly agitated. You notice that their jaw is clenching, their pupils have constricted, they have crossed their arms tightly over their chest and are talking more quickly...it looks bad.

You want this person to be your friend and not to be upset at such a conversation, so you try to turn around their feelings with your own body language. First, you begin by mirroring that person by adopting a similar stance, tone of voice and other body language actions, but you do so just one step down from them, not quite so angry. By doing this your bodies are in rapport; they are on the same level of emotional display.

Now, you can start to lead this person, pulling their anger down. You do this by slowly, subtly reducing your anger displays and giving the other person time to unconsciously follow. First, you lower your voice a bit and slow down your words. After a moment, you uncross your arms and a little later you open your arms up wider in a, "Hey, it's ok," gesture (similar to the "I'm open to you" gesture that you often see in Jesus and Madonna statues).

As you calm down and show more open body language, the other person is likely to follow and calm down themselves. You can use this same process in other situations. You can use mirroring and leading to help reduce the stress that you sense in a person who is nervous to meet you or to be in a particular situation. You can use it to help someone who is embarrassed, sad or experiencing a variety of other emotions.

There is a school of thought that matching and mirroring is manipulative, but actually it is a natural process. When you are in rapport with someone, or people are in rapport with each other, they naturally begin to mirror tonality, physiology, etc. Even when you mirror someone else, you will always be you. It is just a process you're adopting that requires some thought as you are entering the other person's world.

Notice the next time you deliver a presentation, or are in a presentation, how people in rapport will gradually sit the same way as they begin to get comfortable with each over (e.g., crossed legs, adopting similar breathing patterns, etc.) It is entirely subconscious. Matching and mirroring, as well as using representational systems such as visual, auditory and kinaesthetic language references, is a powerful process you can use to connect, engage and communicate on the level of the other person and improve understanding.

Think of some powerful speakers you have heard. They have an ability to create rapport and engage an audience while making their point clear and understood. Successful businesspeople also tend to have this ability to create rapport. When you enter into another person's world and then work towards an outcome, the resolution is nearly always a win–win

Being able to gain rapport is not a natural ability, but it is something we can all achieve more consistently with practise. Remember, you are looking for things you can mirror as comfortably and unobtrusively as possible. Don't put on a foreign accent or adopt a physiological position that isn't natural (such as limping if the other person is limping) because that is more often perceived as mimicking or mocking.

By practising as often as you can, you will reach a point when it becomes an unconscious competence. Then implementing matching and mirroring in situations will help you gain rapport to achieve a positive outcome. You will become more consistent at understanding the other person's map of the world. Once the other person feels you understand their map of the world, they feel a connection and rapport and then you can them get them to follow you. Regardless of what differences you have, or whether it's a formal business meeting, interview or presentation, client or friend, whatever the situation and however you meet, once you have a high level of rapport by using similar tonality and gestures and the person becomes comfortable and feels a strong enough connection to follow you unconsciously, you can then gradually lead the other person's behaviour to be consistent with achieving a desired win–win outcome.

One of the questions I am often asked when I am teaching rapport on my NLP courses is what someone can do if they are dealing with a person who is extremely angry or aggressive. It depends on the situation and how confident and comfortable you feel. If it's a situation where you might be in danger, then it's probably best to keep yourself safe. That said if you find yourself in a situation that is not dangerous but in which there is still conflict or aggression, you could either match and mirror the anger and use that to escalate the negative tension, or you could break the person's state by using matching and mirroring at a slightly lower level to interrupt the person's thought process. Once you do that, you can then lead them into a state in which they are more relaxed.

Have you ever gone into a meeting feeling angry, frustrated and disappointed and by the end of the meeting the presenter had made you feel great? Your mood had been enhanced and you were in a more productive mindset. It's possible that the presenter used matching and mirroring to lead you back into a more relaxed and receptive state.

Remember, rapport isn't about trying to be someone's best friend. It is about gaining enough of a connection to work towards a positive outcome that supports both parties. In those cases, it may be acceptable to enter the world of someone's anger.

I remember being in a meeting for a company I once worked for in which the team was underperforming. The manager stood up and expressed his anger as disappointment as to what was going on. I listened carefully and realised he did it because he cared. However, getting angry with the staff was not going to solve the problem. So I stood up and matched his mild aggression and led him into a more relaxed, focused state. It was a case of powerful interaction and communication that had a positive effect for the rest of the team.

The key to achieving rapport is having mental flexibility. Many people make the assumption that everyone has the same mental map as their own. With that kind of inflexible thinking, rapport cannot be achieved.

◢ **Exercise**

1. Write a list of the best and most effective communicators you know?

2. What do they do well?

THINGS YOU CAN MATCH

Use the following list to match and mirror in order to create rapport in various situations iwith your work colleagues, clients, customers and staff. Taking time to create rapport in business requires some effort and time, but it will pay off.

Body posture: You'll notice people doing this unconsciously. However, if you do it consciously, use with care! People don't like to be mimicked. Matching the angle of the spine works well and is not obvious.

Breathing: Breathing has a rhythm that you can match. It can be deep or shallow. People also breathe from the chest or the abdomen.

Voice tone: This includes volume, speed, tonality and speech rhythms. An accent not your own is probably best left alone!

Movement rhythms (crossover matching): This is a slightly more complicated form of matching. You can match someone's gestures with a different part of your body. People do things they are almost unaware of—scratching their chin, flicking their hair, crossing their legs—and you can match this subtly by some equally natural-looking movement, like tapping a pencil or jiggling your foot.

Representational systems: (see previous section "Rapport the Easy Way" on page 83).

Metaphors: Listen to the metaphors that people use and match them.

Language: The key words a person uses.

Values: What people hold as being true and important.

Experiences: Common interests.

Matching and mirroring: This can take place at the behavioural level. Direct matching of gestures by doing the same thing can be counterproductive as people can spot it very easily.

POWERFUL COMMUNICATORS

In my extensive studies of powerful communicators, I have found that the great ones can adapt to a given situation. They come across as being charismatic but they also adapt their language, gestures, breathing, tonality and expressions to support the outcome they are looking for. Essentially, they are able to engage in their listener's map of the world.

As a communicator, it's about *you* taking responsibility for getting through to the person you are communicating with. You can know all there is to know about your profession, whether you're a physiotherapist or a sales rep, a doctor, a lawyer, or a manager, but if you can't connect to the other person's map of the world, your knowledge accounts for nothing. That's why the best business people are the ones that can establish rapport.

The best sales people, managers and leaders, have the ability to gain rapport and then lead. You can give any two people the same script to work with and one person will stand out while the other never fulfils their potential, both because of how either expresses the information and how well they establish rapport.

One of the most fantastic things about rapport is it is something anyone can learn. Your journey to becoming a master communicator begins now.

A great place to begin is by getting curious about the people around you—those you work with, colleagues, customers, clients. There may be some key individuals that you'd like to get to know better. It could be the manager of a project or someone who is interviewing a potential client. Perhaps the bank manager is somebody with whom you'd like to establish rapport!

Use the following exercise to create a checklist you can fill out about anyone with whom you'd like to have better rapport. Writing down your responses will make you stop and think about the other person's map of the world. You don't have to get it perfect right away; you can always come back to revisit the list at a future date. Good relationships take serious investment and time to build and nurture.

◢ **Exercise:**

Identify a situation in which you want to gain rapport. It could be a meeting or a presentation. The questions below require you to think about your needs and also the other person's needs. Rapport is a two-way street.

◢ Name: _____

◢ Company/group: _____

◢ What is your relationship to this person?

◢ Specifically, how would you like your relationship with this person to change?

◢ What impact would this have on you?

◢ What impact would it have on the other person?

◢ Is it worth investing the time and energy?

◢ What pressures does this person face?

◢ What is most important to them right now?

◢ Who do you know that you could talk to who has successfully built rapport with this person? What can you learn from them?

◢ What other help can you get to build rapport?

◢ What ideas do you have now in moving this relationship forward?

◢ What is the first step?

You can build rapport in business with:

1. prospects so that you have more chance of making the sale,

2. interviewers so that you are more likely to land a job,

3. customer service agents in order to obtain lower prices or better service, and

4. audiences so that your presentation will achieve the outcome you want.

While you may prefer to spend your time with other people who are just like you, the business world is full of a wonderful variety of people with special skills, opinions and backgrounds. Rapport is the key to success and influence in both your personal and professional life. It's about appreciating and working with differences. Rapport makes it easier to get things done. It means you can provide good customer service, understand people better, be understood and give yourself the best possible chance to succeed.

If you show no particular interest in another person's efforts or don't try to gain rapport, you are unlikely to succeed. Lasting rapport requires sincerity and receptivity. Take the time to understand the other person's reality and unique perspective.

◢ **Exercises:**

1. Think of a time you couldn't gain rapport no matter what you tried. What was happening?

2. Think of a situation where you have gone for an interview, delivered a presentation, had a business meeting, interacted with a work colleague, client or customer, when a better relationship would have been good for both of you. Imagine meeting that person. Notice his or her posture and body language. Are they sitting or standing, legs crossed, arms folded? Are they breathing fast or slow? Do they use gestures when they are speaking. How does their voice sound? Raise or lower your voice and pace to match. Listen carefully to what the person has to say to explain and describe their point. When you speak, use similar words, metaphors and language patterns. If they are explaining a process or are a customer or client explaining what they are looking for, instead of using your own preferred words, substitute them with ones that are similar to the ones used by the person to whom you are speaking. You don't need total precision when matching, just something that is similar. It may seem unnatural at first, but it works. It is helping you to understand the other person's mind-set and sends a strong messages that you have a connection with them.

KEY POINTS

Rapport is a process, not a thing. Rapport is something we do with another person. Rapport is responsiveness—you don't have to "like" the other person.

There are things we can do to establish rapport. The nonverbal aspects of communication known as paralanguage (voice tone, body language) convey information about our relationship with the listener. This forms the context in which the content of the words is understood; e.g., "That was really good!" conveys the opposite meaning if the voice tone is sarcastic and the body language dismissive.

Psychologists have discovered three elements to rapport: mutual attention, when each person is tuning in to the other; shared positive feeling, mostly conveyed by non-verbal messages; and synchrony when people unconsciously respond to each other's movements and gestures

If you don't have rapport, you won't achieve your outcome. In any conversation, neither of you will get anywhere until you have established rapport.

How do you know when you have rapport? You'll feel it. Or get a sense of being at one with the other person. Conversely, if you lose rapport, or put a foot wrong, you'll feel uncomfortable. We've all had that experience. But you can just do some more matching and get back into rapport again.

You'll experience pacing and leading. *Pacing* is a word from NLP jargon meaning matching someone, falling into step with them, entering into their model of the world. You can pace someone's ideas, beliefs and experiences as well as their words and behaviour (you don't have to *share* those ideas, you just have to fall into step with them for a while). Human beings have a natural tendency to fall into step with each other. So after you have matched someone for a while, you can do something slightly different—slow down your breathing, uncross your legs, or scratch your nose—and if you have rapport, the other person will follow you. If they don't, do some more matching.

You'll notice skin colour changes. When people feel relaxed, capillaries in the skin dilate so the skin appears darker (in dark-skinned people) or pinker (in light-skinned people).

The other person may tell you. They may say something like "I feel like I have known you for ages" or "I've never told anyone this before, but..."

PRACTISING RAPPORT SKILLS FOR BUSINESS

There are a number of ways you can practise and sharpen your rapport skills.

1. Notice examples of people in rapport around you—on the train, in a bar, at work, anywhere that people gather.

2. Practise non-verbal rapport with strangers. You can unobtrusively match someone's posture or breathing (just as you may have done unconsciously many times in the past). Don't be surprised if they strike up a conversation with you.

3. Choose a different aspect of rapport to practise every day or even for a week. One week you could do voice tone; when you've mastered that you could move on to breathing, then representational systems and so on.

4. Watch TV. Notice the type of words that people on the TV are using. Listen to the representational systems rather than the content. Does the character or presenter use mainly visual words, mainly emotional words, or what? Practise until you can spot the dominant representational system and get the content of what they are saying at the same time.

5. When that gets too easy, rephrase what they are saying in a different representational system. Never again will there be "nothing on the telly tonight."

◢ USING BODY LANGUAGE TO BUILD RAPPORT

In this section you will learn to detect the difference between aggressive and assertive body language and how to read what the other person is feeling about you and what you are saying. You will learn how to use personal space as a communication tool and how to develop positive relationships through your body language. You will also learn in more detail how to calm down another person and even lead people where you want them to go with your body language. Finally, you will learn how to read the non-verbals of a person as relates to their torso, hips, chest and shoulders.

Through your reading, reflection and exercises you will come to understand the following:

1. The difference between aggressive and assertive body language.
2. How to develop relationships and build rapport using body language.
3. Recognise various non-verbals of the head/neck, torso, hips, chest and shoulders.

As I have continually noted, *how* you say something is as important, perhaps more important, than *what* you say. While you may be busy choosing your words, perhaps altering your tone and controlling your facial expressions, there is a good chance that you are ignoring your body, the core of you, which is everything right down the centre.

You need to be aware of the body core and how it affects what you project to others. You need to be aware of the importance of making first impressions, specifically when it involves building rapport with others. And you need to recognise aggression and stress in the body language of others. These all can be gleaned by being proficient in reading the non-verbals of the body.

NON-VERBALS OF THE TORSO

Your main body core, often collectively referred to as your torso, houses your body's organs and keeps your vital centre protected. This area of the body includes your hips, chest, belly and shoulders, but we will also discuss the neck and head that sit upon your torso. You may wonder how this centre area of your body can truly have much to say, thinking it capable of little independent movement. But there are actually many physical tells that you exhibit with this part of your body.

Leaning

One big way that your body core sends a signal is through the way it leans. People tend to lean towards things they like and away from things they do not like or they fear. For example, if a couple are on a date and they are leaning towards each other, they are probably both having a good time and feeling comfortable. However, if something changes, or if one of them is not having a good time, they will pull back, leaning their entire body away from the other person.

Extreme examples of this leaning action can be observed in very unpleasant situations. Imagine a person who runs over something in the road and gets out to investigate. As they approach they see that it is a dead animal. Most people will pull away in disgust at the sight, leaning back. Picture an elevator full of people standing quietly; the door opens and a strange looking man with wild hair and crazy eyes steps in. Everyone in the elevator immediately moves their body away so as not to be associated with this person and they do it subtly, trying not to draw attention to themselves.

Facing

Another way that we use our entire torso to communicate is by the way that we face. In anatomy, we call our front side "ventral" and our back side "dorsal". When it comes to body language, putting our front side towards a person is called ventral facing. It is a way of showing comfort with or like of the person we are facing. When we turn so that our backs are facing someone, then we are dorsal facing and we are showing a discomfort with or dislike for the person or for what is being said. This latter position, that of dorsal facing, is actually where the term "turn your back on someone" comes from; when we are not interested or do not like something, we "turn our back" on it.

Of course, we usually turn our backs towards people subtly. Sometimes, we do not give them our entire back, but rather we slightly shift our body in our chair so that we are not ventrally facing the person, or we adjust our bodies slightly as though we are trying to inch towards an escape.

An example of this would be if you were at a party, talking in a circle with some friends, laughing and having fun. A man walks up and joins the group. At first everyone allows him into the circle, facing him and saying greetings. Then, the man starts to talk about work, complaining about this and that, bringing the group down.

One by one, people start to turn their backs on him, engaging in conversations with other people. After a few moments a single person has been trapped into conversation with the man; this person looks annoyed, with their arms crossed, a fake smile on their face, toes pointing away as though they want to run any minute.

Everyone else in the previous circle has now broken into smaller conversation groups, their backs to the annoying, negative man.

On the other hand, when we are excited to see someone, we present them with our full front, body language that is open and inviting. You can imagine this when a parent greets their child after a long day at work, or when someone welcomes a long overdue visit from a loved relative, facing fully forward, arms spread wide for an embrace.

When we continue to keep our full fronts facing another person we show that we are comfortable with them and pleased with the situation. If we begin a conversation ventral facing, then we shift so that we are more dorsal facing, we are likely revealing that something has just caused us to change how we feel about this situation— perhaps we don't like what this person is saying.

Head and Neck

Of course, which way we lean or orient our torso is not the only way in which we use our body to communicate. There are three main ways that we communicate non-verbally using our head and neck:

The head tilt: People most often tilt their head to the side when they are genuinely curious about and interested in something. The head tilt is a positive sign that things are well, that a person is comfortable and interested. We rarely tilt our head when we are unhappy or in the presence of a person we dislike; our bodies do not go off centre like that when we are nervous. Rather, the head tilt is reserved for people with whom we are comfortable.

Muscle tightening: Our muscles also give away our subconscious feelings simply by constricting under stress. That is why some people will clench their teeth during stress or tighten their forehead and jaw muscles. In some people, you can see the strain of the muscles as they fix the jaw into place, a sure sign that they are uncomfortable or experiencing anxiety.

Covering the neck: Other than unconscious muscle tightening, covering the neck is the most common way people send non-verbals using the neck. When people are uncomfortable, they often put their hand to their neck or throat, leaving their arm to cover their chest. This is a type of protective manoeuvre. We see women do it by playing with their necklace or simply messaging the base of the neck where their collar bones meet. You might see a woman do this when she is watching something that makes her uncomfortable, perhaps an overly zealous public display of affection between young lovers or while being told that her credit card was denied at her favourite high-end fashion store. Men do the same thing, often by adjusting their collar or neck tie. You see this in businessmen a lot when a deal is not going the way the man wants it to.

Shoulders

We use our shoulders to communicate consciously all the time, particularly when we shrug. You might think that a shoulder shrug is simple, that a person lifts their shoulders up towards their ears when they are saying, "I don't know." But there is a bit more to this area of the body. Sometimes people make a half shrug, just a non-committal moving up of one shoulder. This usually symbolizes that the person is unsure about what they are saying. It is possible that such a person knows more than they are saying. Usually when people are answering with the full truth they will give a full shoulder shrug, with both shoulders rising. In fact, the more defined the shoulder rise, the more likely the person is certain about their response.

Other than shrugging, we also use our shoulders, in combination with our neck, to indicate discomfort. This is most often done to indicate a negative reaction such as insecurity. In this way we sometimes raise our shoulders towards our ears and somehow seem to make our necks disappear, almost as though we are trying to retract our head like a turtle, hiding from some unhappy circumstance. You see children do this a lot when accused by their parent, you see criminals do it when they are arrested or on trial and you see average people do it when they are uncomfortable, lacking confidence, or simply trying to disappear.

Chest

One way that we use our chest to communicate is the ventral and dorsal facing that we discussed earlier. Another is something called "shielding." People will use their arms to shield themselves, shielding their faces and bodies, but there are other ways that we shield ourselves without using our arms.

We see this often with women who will shield their body with their purse, perhaps by setting it on the table in front of them or on their lap when on a bad date. Men often use their clothing to do this, for example, buttoning up their business suit when they are displeased by something or someone, or unbuttoning their suit and loosening their tie when they are relaxed and comfortable. Of course, we often do this by crossing our arms, but people will often use other things, including a coat held in their arm, a pillow from the couch next to them, a stuffed animal, a shopping bag and so on.

Whichever way we do it, our chest and stomachs are the areas we shield most, as if by protecting these areas we are protecting our entire selves from real or emotional threat.

Hips and Belly

We use our hips and belly in two main ways when we communicate, some aspects of which we have already discussed. We tend  to hide the belly or abdominal area behind our arms or a bag, as though to protect that area of our body. With our hips we usually face our hips towards things we like and away from things we do not like, just like the ventral and dorsal facing.

Now that you know how people use these different body parts to communicate, let's look at their impact on building rapport to get what you desire and how you can use them to detect aggression.

AGGRESSION AND STRESS IN BODY LANGUAGE

One of the biggest reasons for any person to learn to better read body language is to help them detect when other people are unhappy, specifically when that unhappiness might translate into aggression or violence. Fortunately, those trained to read body language can learn to identify stress, anxiety and even aggression in another person and react accordingly.

Body language can reveal comfort, confidence, anxiety and aggression, among other emotions. When a person is comfortable, 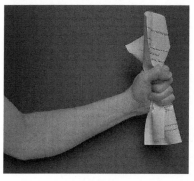 they tend to be physically open, their muscles appear relaxed, their head may tilt and they may face towards or even lean towards the people they are talking to. The trick is to learn to look for *changes* in the behaviour of an individual; look at their baseline, their normal behaviour and watch for deviations. One individual might be really comfortable with their arms crossed over their chest; this position may simply be a physically comfortable spot for them and it does not mean they are closed off or protecting anything like it might mean in someone else. However, if they suddenly move their crossed arms to arms akimbo and step forward into someone else's personal space, this could indicate that they feel the need to assert their power. Something has happened to change their mood.

A person exhibits confidence in themselves and in what they are saying when they are physically open (not protecting body parts) and ventral facing. They show comfort with another person if they are not tense, are not using pacifying behaviours, like biting their nails or wringing their hands, and they maintain eye contact. However, people can hear, see, or think something that changes the way they feel in an instant and their body language will change right along with it. For example, when a person stands up and makes themselves taller, perhaps using arms akimbo, they are showing power and authority. If a person steps into your personal space they are showing aggression. Some of the differences between confidence and aggression may be subtle, but you probably will recognise them subconsciously.

Confident body language includes the following:

◢ Eyes forward with good eye contact indicates comfort and confidence.

- Shoulders back and spine comfortably straight, standing tall, looks confident.
- Smiling that reaches the eyes makes others feel you are honest and confident.
- A handshake that is firm, but not too firm, shows confidence.
- Relaxed arms that swing freely show comfort.
- Arms akimbo shows confidence and power, but when paired with other signs of aggression it can mean more.

Aggressive body language includes the following:

- A person who seems to be staring "through" you, not looking at you, may be dangerous because they are not connecting with you. Similarly, if a person seems to be staring hard at you, like you are a target, this could be a sign of impending aggression.
- A person who maintains lengthy eye contact that becomes "staring" could be plotting an act of aggression.
- A person whose arms are unnaturally still or tight may become aggressive.
- Clenching the fists and jaw is a sign that muscles are tightening, perhaps in preparation for attack.
- Stepping into another person's personal space is a clear sign of aggression. Angry people who do not plan to attack will usually step away from what is making them angry, but aggressive, potentially dangerous people will step towards it.
- Mock, suggestive attacks can portend a real attack; such behaviour includes shaking an accusing finger or a fist.
- Sudden movements, such as a mock attack, may be done by an aggressive person to gauge the other person's response and reaction time.

I hope your personal interactions go well. Now that you understand the value of body language you may not need to watch for these aggressive signals. However, you should know them, just in case.

◢ **Exercises**

Enhance your learning by performing one (or all) of the following exercises based on your interests.

1. **Watch the Arms**

   Go to a public place and watch the people around you. To begin, choose a person who is likely to stay in your view for some time, perhaps a person waiting for their flight or a patron at a restaurant. Look at their arm movements and interpret what you think they are feeling. Watch their faces and, if you can hear them, their words, trying to confirm what you observed in their arms.

2. **Observe Body Language**

   Look at the photo of the couple to the right. List at least three things that show they are comfortable with each other.

3. **Check the Nuances**

   The same body language can mean different things; you have to look at other clues to the meaning. Look at the three pictures above, each of a person with their arms crossed. Match each picture (left, middle, right) with the proper description of the emotion this person is expressing:

a. casual comfort

b. anger or concern

c. confidence

◢ BODY LANGUAGE SKILLS FOR BUSINESS AND COACHING SUCCESS

So far in this chapter we have talked about how powerful matching and mirroring can be and the power of understanding someone's non-verbal messages. Now we dive deeper into how you can really use body language as your secret weapon. You will learn about various applications for reading body language in others—areas in your life where you can use your knowledge of non-verbals as a tool or as a weapon.

HOW TO USE BODY LANGUAGE AS YOUR SECRET WEAPON

In this section I will demonstrate various ways that you can read non-verbals to detect lies and read emotions. You will read scenarios of how law enforcement agents, business people and others have used their body language skills to better understand the truth behind what others are saying. You will also learn to detect various non-verbals of the face, seeing how the smallest wrinkle or change in a person's expression can speak volumes about what they really mean and what they are not telling you.

Through your readings, reflection and exercises in you should understand the following:

1. The value of reading the body language of other people.
2. Recognise that you can intentionally communicate with your own body language.
3. Recognise the various non-verbals of the face.

We all use body language every day to some extent. When a co-worker comes to work with puffy eyes and slumped shoulders you might assume either that she slept poorly or is upset. We look at faces and detect anger, happiness, frustration, weariness, surprise and more. But most of us can recognise only the most obvious signs and signals.

When you learn to read people better you set yourself apart from everyone else. If you can read the fine distinctions of body language, you can be better prepared to react to what they say, to help them with issues they are keeping private, or simply better understand their behaviour. Unfortunately (or perhaps fortunately for those who do) few people know how to really read body language. Thus, when you develop this skill you join a small group of people with the ability to more accurately communicate with and influence others.

You can use your body language tools to read others, detect potential deception, make better business deals, help people in trouble and communicate from a position of power. The reading (and using) of body language can become like your super power, a weapon that you can use for the good of yourself and others.

Recognising Non-Verbals of the Body

Your teenage son has been hanging out with the "wrong crowd". You are concerned with one friend in particular, who you know does drugs and has been arrested for auto theft. You have told your son that he is not to spend time with this boy, but you suspect that he is hanging out with him behind your back. You want to know for certain.

Your son comes home for dinner and your family is sitting around the table. Your son seems comfortable, his shoulders are back, his hands are splayed very open on the table and his face is relaxed.

As you talk, you casually bring the conversation around to this friend. You mention that you are glad your son is not hanging out with him anymore. Your son maintains his comfortable stance, still eating. He agrees, telling you that he is not hanging out with the boy.

Your son's apparent calm leads you to believe that he is adhering to your wishes and not spending time with this boy. Then, you ask your son who he is spending time with. Suddenly, your son's body language changes. He stops eating and his shoulders droop. He puts his hands on his lap and replies, without looking at your face and with some non-committal language about "just friends."

Now, you are suspicious. Your son may be telling the truth about not hanging out with the previous friend, but he seems uncomfortable about who he is spending time with. This body language does not give you details, but it certainly indicates that you should pursue this line of questioning and get some more details about your son's new friends.

Recognising Non-Verbals of the Face

We've mentioned before that most people concentrate only on the face when they are looking for meaning behind the words a person does or does not say. It is unfortunate to limit one's reading of body language to the face; however, that does not mean that there is no significant value in properly reading a face.

Non-verbals of the face can manifest themselves in the eyes, eyebrows, forehead, lips, nose, jaw and skin. Head tilt is also important, along with the shoulders and torso. So, let's look at each of these areas on their own, to make it clear what can be learned from the face.

The Skin

The skin can tell a lot about a person in general. Smooth skin usually denotes youth, while wrinkled skin usually shows age. Historically, tanned skin was a symbol of poverty, as only the poor toiled outside, whereas pristine white skin was a sign of wealth and elite status. Of course, today a tan is often associated with youthful vigour and good looks, as tan skin has been in vogue for the past couple of generations. Still, overly tanned skin often reveals a person's vocation, such as the reddened, leathery skin of a construction worker or others who toil in hot, sunny locations. But the skin tells more than just our vocation or level of outdoor activity.

The skin receives much of its colouring from the blood vessels that lie beneath and nourish it. Sure, melatonin in the skin is responsible for skin colour variations, but blood flow plays a role. When a person become frightened, severely stressed or upset, blood is diverted away from the skin causing the person to go pale. We sometimes call this a "ghostly pallor" in deference to its frequent origin in fear.

Similarly, when people are extremely angry or embarrassed, blood often rushes to the surface, perhaps in an attempt to cool down the organs of the body. This results in a flush of red across the face which we commonly associate with these negative emotions. Of course, the colour of one's skin (whether the blood moves to the surface or away) is completely unconscious. No matter how attuned you are to your body you simply cannot control your blood flow. Thus, the colour of the skin becomes a great tell for how a person is feeling.

The Forehead and Eyebrows

The forehead can be extremely expressive, particularly when it comes to showing stress, anger or concern. People often squint and furrow their forehead, creating that telltale pair of wrinkles between the eyes. People probably won't even realise that they are doing this.

Have you ever had a particularly gruelling day at work when you were running around dealing with problems and being annoyed? Then, at the end of the day you went home and relaxed and suddenly realised that your forehead muscles were actually sore from furrowing all day. This is partly how some tension headaches begin, from excessive, lengthy tightening of the facial muscles.

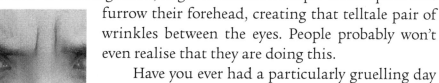

By contrast, when a person is surprised, their eyebrows often go up as their eyes widen (left). This creates the series of two or three horizontal lines that seem to etch themselves more and more deeply into our foreheads as we move into our thirties, forties and fifties.

In the image below, notice how the eyebrow and the squint of the eye work together to show a subtly different emotion. The eye is rel-

atively relaxed, with a normal pupil and a slightly furrowed brow. Even from this extreme close-up, you can tell the man is exuding either confidence or calculating concern. He seems to be relatively relaxed, with perhaps just a hint of confidence or suspicion. This man could be staring confidently at a girl across the room or holding his ground when being questioned by police.

Conversely, this man is exhibiting a widened eye and dilated pupil. On top of this, his eyebrow is drawn down towards the inside of eye and up on the outside of the eye. He looks like a man who has been startled or has just heard shocking news which has truly outraged him. This is the eye of a man experiencing a high amount of raw emotion.

We use our eyebrows and foreheads in a seemingly endless number of ways. We squint our eyes and furrow our brow to examine something closely or to demonstrate distrust or disdain. We sometimes squint to show curiosity, but a sort of distrustful or disbelieving curiosity. We arch our brows up and open our faces to show happiness, surprise and other positive emotions or genuine curiosity.

The Eyes

The eyes are very close to the eyebrows and thus these often work together to showcase our various emotions. They say that the eyes are the windows to the soul. Certainly we often feel as though we can sense love or hate in the eyes.

In addition, the eyes seem to add to any smile, making it seem more honest, more sincere. When a person is truly happy their eyes seem to glow. We can often see tears in the eyes to further demonstrate emotion. For the student of human body language, there are a variety of ways that the eyes provide details to how a person is truly feeling.

Pupil Size

Our pupil size also tells much about how we are feeling. Our pupils have the ability to dilate (become large and black) to let in more light and see something better. They can also constrict, becoming smaller, when they want to focus narrowly on a perceived threat.

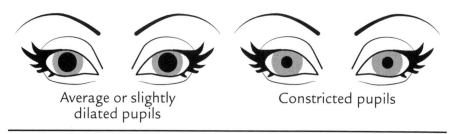

Average or slightly   Constricted pupils
dilated pupils

Figure 3.2   The Pupils Will Tell You More Than Words

Thus, when you see a person's pupils suddenly get larger it is likely that they just heard or saw something that interests them, something that they want to know more about. Imagine a child's eyes widening when presented with an unexpected gift (Figure 3.2).

When you see a person's pupils suddenly constrict, it often suggests that they heard or saw something disagreeable, either something they are subconsciously trying to block or something they are questioning. For example, in business if you are negotiating the terms of some contract and the other party suddenly constricts their pupils, you can be sure that this subconscious change in the eyes indicates that they are unhappy with some of the terms. If their pupils suddenly dilate, then the contract is likely more than they had hoped for and is very pleasing.

Eye Movements

Despite our propensity to say that we sometimes misspeak because we speak without thinking, humans actually do have to think in order to speak. We often see thoughts manifested in body language before they actually form into words. One way that we see this is with eye movements.

As we think we often move our visual focus to a neutral location—we look away to think. Neurologists call this the *lateral eye movement* (LEM). Some who study body language call it *eye accessing cues*. You can look at the focus of the eyes to determine how the person is thinking.

Specifically, research has shown that when we visualise something that actually happened in our past—when we try to recall a memory—we move our eyes up and to our left. However, when we try to imagine something that we have never seen—when we are making something up—we tend to move our eyes down and to our right. We can use this knowledge to detect potential deception.

So, if you ask a student why they did not turn in their homework and they look down and to the right, you know that they are likely imagining something and may be making up a fictional scenario. Law enforcement officers often use these eye accessing clues when questioning witnesses to help determine what they actually remember and what they are fabricating.

Even closed eyes tell us something. Obviously we close our eyes when we blink and when we sleep. But we also close our eyes to reveal our emotions. For example, one's blinking rate can change based on our state of emotion. Some people will simply stare ahead and blink rapidly when they are confused or confronted with some information that they do not understand and are having trouble accepting. People slow down their blink rate when they are captivated by something, like when a person is working hard and staring at a computer screen or a stalker is carefully watching a potential victim.

People often close their eyes briefly in response to some negative information. Think about the last time you saw someone hear bad news about the health of a relative or some other important information. It is likely that they closed their eyes in an extended blink as if shutting out the information. People will often close their eyes tightly in severe situations, as if refusing to let in the information.

Many of the facial cues you will observe in others, particularly in response to stress or bad news, is a type of blocking behaviour (Navarro & Karlins, 2008). Just as a person will raise their arm to protect their face from an anticipated blow, so do we close our eyes or shield our eyes in various ways against negative information and emotions.

The Lips

Our lips can also speak volumes and not just through the formation of words. When a person is genuinely pleased or happy, their smile is wide and their lips are full. Many people, when relaxed and comfortable, part their lips slightly in a state of casual rest.

Full, relaxed lips usually show basic comfort. Thin, disappearing lips indicate some level of displeasure. Watch a person who is comfortable as they hear news that is disagreeable to them. You will notice their lips become smaller and smaller, eventually disappearing almost entirely as they compress them. We also compress our

lips to express disbelieve or annoyance, often in the form of a "smirk" like the little girl in the picture to the left.

We also show concern by concealing our lips. People will tighten their lips to the point that they almost disappear when they are anxious, stressed, or trying to conceal information. These "tight lips" are how the body tries to shut down and keep quiet. "Loose lips sink ships," as the saying goes. While this compression of the lips does not necessarily mean the person is lying—or lying by omission— it is indicative of stress and is often seen in those who are not telling the whole truth.

There are even many different types of smiles. Researchers have actually determined that a genuine smile born of pure, positive emotion uses totally different muscles than an artificial smile. This is partly why some actors use a type of acting called *method acting*, in which they generate emotional displays by tapping into their own past memories of experiencing a similar emotion.

Only by actually feeling happiness can one truly show an honest, happy smile. A true smile will also raise up the corners of the mouth. When the smile is really big it will actually *lift the ears* and cause "laugh lines" to appear on either side of the mouth and just outside the corners of the eyes. A "polite" or "forced" smile will never leave the lips.

Another interesting phenomenon is the frown. This act of turning one's smile into an upside down "U" is one of the most truthful tells. That is because, for most people, it is not possible to fake a full frown. Look in the mirror and try; without the emotion behind it most people find it impossible to turn the corners of their mouth down on purpose.

Thus, if you see this expression on someone, you know that it is likely genuine. Police can use this when assessing how upset a spouse is at the death of their partner. Many facial cues are difficult to fake properly. The police often also look at subjects who purse their lips (pucker them), as this often indicates disagreement (Navarro & Karlins, 2008).

The Nose and Jaw

As expressive as the eyes, eyebrows and lips are, other areas of the face can reveal almost as much. You may wonder what a nose can do, but believe it or not, it can show emotion.

Specifically, when people are aroused, they flare their nostrils. That is, their nostrils will actually open wider. The top photo shows normal nostrils while the bottom photo shows flared nostrils. This can happen when a person is angry or full of adrenaline and ready to fight. It also happens during sexual arousal.

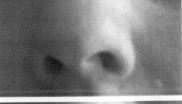
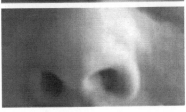

Most often people will flair their nose when they intend to engage in some type of physical action (Navarro & Karlins, 2008). It is rather like the typical image of a raging bull flaring his nostrils before he charges. People will flair their nostrils when they are about to lift a heavy weight, engage in a fight, or become involved in sexual activity. If you see flaring nostrils you know it is likely that something is about to happen. Nasal flaring can be subtle, but if you look closely you can see a widening of the nostrils.

By contrast, tightening of the jaw tends to denote a more passive anxiety. People often tighten their jaws, even when alone. Many people find that they tighten their jaws or clench their teeth in response to stress, even stress that does not represent an immediate threat. For example, many people will clench their teeth while working on their homework. These people often find that their teeth or jaws hurt when they finally finish their work and withdraw their focus from their task and relax. Similarly, people in a conversation that is becoming upsetting will often tighten their jaw or clench their teeth in response to something that they do not agree with or that makes them angry.

WIELDING YOUR OWN BODY LANGUAGE WEAPON

When you understand the various body language signals of other people, you give yourself an advantage over lesser mortals. You can use your ability to read the body language of others to better understand people. This puts you in an enviable position.

Imagine that you are at work, negotiating a contract. If you understand body language you can better tell what areas of a negotiation are important to the other party and which are less important. For example, if you notice that the other party does not seem interested in a portion of the contract about copyrights and patents, yet this is important to you, you now know that you can likely ask for more in this area without hitting any real opposition. Yet, if your company is asking for more time and the other party shows anxiety when discussing timing, you know that getting the job done quickly is of the utmost importance to them.

This knowledge gives you great bargaining leverage. You know you can probably ask for more money and more intellectual property rights if your company is willing to speed things up.

You can also use your understanding of people's body language to make people feel more comfortable. This can help you to excel in dating and other personal matters. For example, imagine you are on a first date. Your dating partner seems uncomfortable and is showing this by averting their eyes, smiling a fake and nervous smile and pursing their lips. You notice this and feel bad; you want your date to feel more comfortable and open up.

One way you can encourage them is by demonstrating your own comfort and by showing that you like this person. Give them a genuine smile that reaches your eyes. Keep your own body language open, arms wide, torso revealed, lips full. When they sense your comfort, openness and cheer, they will start to feel more comfortable unless they are truly hiding something. We will discuss this more in the section on building rapport in chapter 6.

The point is that understanding body language allows you to read people better. When that happens, you are working from a place of more knowledge than they have and you can use this knowledge to serve your own purposes. Does this mean you should take advantage of your skills? Of course not. But it means that you can give yourself a leg up in business or make yourself a better friend or parent with your body language reading skills.

In addition to reading body language you can also use your own body language more effectively. This means that you can learn how manifesting certain behaviours can make others think a certain way. Let's look at an example.

Say that you work at a company where you don't get along well with your boss. However, you are close friends with your boss's boss. Sometimes, that big boss friend gives you some insider information about the company that you probably should not have. One day this big boss friend tells you, in confidence, that you are going to be assigned as team lead of a large, high profile account. You are thrilled and you show it. Your big boss friend tells you that you are not supposed to know this until your immediate supervisor tells you. The big boss friend asks you to seem surprised when your supervisor approaches you with the news later that week. Now, you know that to show surprise you should open your eyes wide and raise your eyebrows. Then, let your expression change to one of happiness.

While most body language is unintentional and subconscious, we all use our body language consciously every day. When you reach out to shake a person's hand this is a somewhat conscious choice; to not shake a person's hand is a similarly conscious choice which certainly sends a signal.

If you truly understand body language you can learn to be more aware of yours and to ensure that you are sending signals that you wish to send. This can be about hiding your nervousness or hiding the fact that you have a stronger position than you really do. Think about this in terms of gambling.

Gamblers, particularly poker players, try to control their body language so as not to show when they have a particularly strong or weak hand. Unfortunately for them, most poker players think only of the tells their faces may be giving off. They work hard to keep their smile from emerging when dealt a good hand but fail to realise that their foot just reached for the sky in a clear show of jubilation.

Later in this chapter you will learn other physical movements that are easier to feign and will subtly ensure your boss that you had no idea this assignment was coming. The point is, when you know how the body subconsciously behaves in certain situations you can often learn to send out these signals intentionally to subtly let people think you are feeling the way you want them to think you feel. You will know to raise your hands in the air to appear happy, even when you are not and so much more.

We will learn more about how to use hand and feet movements effectively. We'll discuss this concept of wielding your own body language effectively and how you can change your own emotions through body language in more detail later in the chapter.

Remember, when you know how to read body language, you can also learn how to wield that body language as a weapon.

Recognising body language can serve you well in work, school, parenting, relationships and much more; it is not just for police and gamblers.

While the face is the most truthful area of a person's body, you can still learn much by watching people's eyes, eyebrows, nose, mouth and more.

◢ **Exercises**

1. Look at the photo of the man to the right. Consider the various features in the man's face. Be sure to look at the forehead, eyes, eyebrows, nose, mouth and jaw. Looking only facial tells, write a separate paragraph about what each tell reveals about his feelings at this moment. Be

specific. If you want to know more about various expressions, do additional research.

2. The boy in the photo to the right is smiling. Answer the following questions:

> Is this a real smile or a fake smile? How can you tell? List at least two reasons.

> Do you think this boy is truly happy? Why or why not?

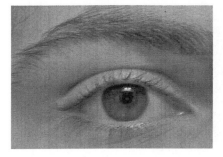 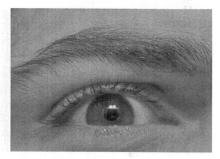

3. Look at the eyes in the photos above. Considering the left photo as the baseline, describe the changes that appear in the right photo. List at least two changes and describe what they could possibly mean.

◢ ENHANCING YOUR BODY LANGUAGE VOCABULARY

As you learn to glean clues to a person's true feelings, you will also learn to use your own body language more effectively. In this section you will learn to communicate how you feel to others, how to appear confident using only non-verbals and how to make better use of hand gestures, facial expressions and eye contact to imbue your words with more meaning.

WE START LEARNING WHEN WE ARE YOUNG

When you were a child you had a lot of ideas in your head but a limited ability to express them. As you matured, you learned more and more words, enhancing your verbal vocabulary and greatly improving your ability to communicate what you truly meant to others. You learned to discriminate between subtle meanings. You knew to say you were scared when something truly frightened you, but to say that you were startled when something suddenly surprised you. You learned the difference between lending and borrowing, to, too and two, and so much more. But it was a long path to learn all of this.

The language of the body is similar. From birth you had the ability to recognise basic non-verbals. You were able to recognise a happy, smiling face when you were just days old. This is a basic skill because even our doggy companions have the ability to "read" certain non-verbals. A dog will come to us, tail wagging if we look happy, but back away and be submissive if we furrow our brow and look angry. Or course, our canine pals are limited in what they can learn, but we humans have the capacity to expand our body language vocabulary immensely. You can even learn how to change your own attitude by understanding and using body language.

For example, your boss assigns you to design and present a training conference on a new software system in your office. Your boss gave you this assignment because you know the software well, having used it before and having been part of the initial team to choose this software.

However, despite your technical knowledge you simply are not comfortable speaking in front of audiences. Thus, you are extremely nervous as you prepare to enter the conference room. You respond by slouching a bit with your head sunken into your shoulders. Despite the fact that your arms are wrapped around your body as though you are cold, your hands are sweaty. A co-worker asks if you feel alright because you are very pale.

Your fight or flight response is telling you to flee, which is exactly what you want to do. Then, you remember your body language course. You know that the brain manifests subconscious emotions into physical actions. You also know that this process works in reverse. If you can force your body into a position of confidence and authority, you can help yourself feel more calm and in control.

So, you stand up straight, your shoulders back and open, head held high. You tilt your chin up and force your forehead and eyebrows to relax. You stand like this for a moment, breathing deeply. After a minute you feel noticeably better and you head into the conference room. Throughout your meeting you are aware of your body language. You also read the body language of your audience and respond appropriately. You are brilliant and the training goes well.

NON-VERBALS OF THE HANDS AND FINGERS

Human hands are not only very useful, with our opposable thumbs and all, but they are also quite expressive. Our human hands are capable of the most amazing acts of intricacy and detail. Human hands can transplant organs, paint masterpieces and build space stations. Unfortunately, human hands are also capable of terrible actions, having the ability to molest, torture and kill. But for the most part, human hands are marvels that make our lives easier and more expressive. In fact, we use our hands and fingers to express a great many emotions, every day.

We use our hands when we meet other people to their shake hands or clap them on the back. We also use our hands when we are pensive (imagine the famous sculpture, "The Thinker," with his chin on his fist) or to rub the bridge of our nose in stress or exasperation. Truly, our hands tell how we feel often much better than our words. Let's look at some specifics.

Hand signals are used effectively in a variety of contexts by many groups. Think for a moment about sign language, when those who cannot hear use their hands (along with their facial expressions and other body language) to actually speak. Sign language can be beautiful and artful to watch; it is an amazing example of how much can be said without ever uttering a word.

Other, sometimes more unsettling, examples of effective hand gestures can be seen in the military and militant groups. Every military in the modern world uses some type of salute. This is usually done with a flat hand brought to the forehead and then pushed away sharply. This salute is a sign of respect and deference to authority.

The malevolent dictator, Adolf Hitler, used a modified military salute to create a powerful feeling of deference to his authority. This "Heil Hitler" motion was a way of giving people a physical manifestation of his power and their dedication. Once a person associated their admiration (or fear) of the infamous man with the salute, doing the salute would no doubt cause emotions to manifest in the brain. This is a great example of how behaviour can change or elicit an emotion.

Other hand motions are less deliberate and thus are more indicative of a person's true emotional state. We can read the hands and fingers to determine what a person is thinking.

Touching Others

One way that humans demonstrate emotion is through touching. We hug people we are close to or stand back to avoid a touch from people we do not like or are uncomfortable around. The quicker

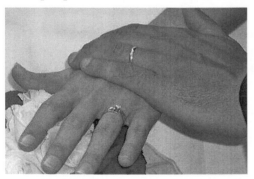

the hug the less comfort and affection it denotes. Similarly, a one-armed hug shows less dedication and can indicate either discomfort or a low level of liking for a person.

Even how we casually touch with just our hands says a lot. Often people will touch others when they talk, perhaps to make a point. One way we see this is when a person says something and punctuates it by leaning over and touching the other person's arm. A light touch of only fingertips reveals a moderate level of comfort; a full touch with the palm shows a more significant level of comfort (Navarro, 2010).

Hiding of the Hands

When people hide their hands this is often a subconscious way of hiding something else. Pay attention the next time you are talking to someone and notice if you have an emotional response when the person withdraws their hands from the table; most people do. When we can't see another person's hands, we distrust them or become suspicious. So, if you are meeting the family of a new boyfriend or girlfriend for the first time, be sure to keep your hands on the table or in plain view and you will better elicit their trust.

Quivering Hands

The muscles of the hands can sometimes show uncontrollable shaking or quivering when a person is aroused, nervous, threatened, angry, or under stress. Sometimes, hand quivering is not very noticeable until a person picks up an object, such as a pen and you can observe the pen shaking. Often a person whose hands are quivering will attempt to hide it by removing their hands from the table, which again demonstrates stress and discomfort.

Observing quivering hands is a sure way to know that a person is aroused in some way. While this often denotes stress, it can also occur when we are happy. For example, a man may shake out of nervousness when he proposes marriage to his girlfriend. Then, the new fiancée may begin to shake out of sheer elation.

Again we see that much body language is about context as well as how a person's movements deviate from their baseline behaviour. Some people have various physical and neurological disorders that cause their hands to shake, resulting in quivers, shaky writing and so forth. Obviously in this person, hand shaking cannot be read for emotion. In other situations it is up to you to observe other tells to determine if the hands are shaking out of joy or negative emotions.

Comforting Behaviours

FBI agent Joe Navarro often writes about how people use certain behaviours to comfort or pacify themselves. This is much like a child who sucks their thumb or holds a stuffed animal when nervous. Adults do it in more subtle ways. When it comes to the hands, adults will often engage in subconscious pacifying behaviour when they are nervous or anxious. This behaviour can include wringing the hands or rubbing the palms together. A person might rub the palms on the thighs, as though to dry them off.

The Worst Thing Ever

Even a quick perusal of almost any body language book or of body language research will reveal one significant "do not" that every person should know. Thou shalt not point. It's true. Pointing is commonly considered the most rude display of body language in all cultures.

Certainly this means that you should never point a finger at a person as you chastise, or point to someone to imply guilt. You should even avoiding pointing with a single finger in more innocent situations, such as suggesting which direction a person should go. People respond more favourably if you point with your entire flat hand.

American President Bill Clinton was well known for using this flat hand gesture frequently and with good reason. Whether you are giving your children a lecture or engaged in a heated business debate, single finger pointing is rude and demeaning and should simply not be done.

Temperature

Even the temperature and "feel" of a person's hands is a type of body language. A firm handshake denotes confidence, while an overly harsh shake can demonstrate dislike or an intense need to make a strong impression. But it is not just about the firmness of the grip.

A warm hand shows that the hand is receiving blood; this occurs when we are comfortable (Navarro, 2010). By contrast, blood flows away from the hand when we are uncomfortable, making them cold. Of course, sometimes hands are cold because it is cold outside, so it is important that you take the context of the situation into account before you read too much into any bit of body language.

Finger Territory

Many parts of our body take up additional space when we feel confident. That is, when we feel like we know what we are doing, that we are masters of our universe, we make ourselves larger. We spread our arms and stand up straight—we simply take up more space. This is true of our fingers as well. Usually fingers that are taking up space are confident. For example, when a person folds their fingers together, interlocking them with palms touching (like a child might pray) they are taking up less space; this position indicates some level of discomfort or concern. However, when a person steeples their fingers, spreading them out and touching them tip to tip (like the hands to the right), with space between the fingers, this is a show of confidence and security.

Remember to look for changes in behaviour. For example, if you are a police officer you might see a suspect sitting with open, steeple hands. Then, when you start a certain line of questioning their fingers come together and then interlock. This demonstrates that the person has become less comfortable.

Grooming

One thing we will touch on sporadically throughout this course is the affect of dress and grooming on body language. Certainly the jewellery you wear, the tattoos you sport and how you groom yourself say something about who you are and how you feel.

Long nails are viewed as feminine, thus most men will want to keep their fingernails clipped short. Also, avoid tattoos on the hand if you are in business or plan to be taken seriously. Despite their seemingly increasing social acceptance, tattoos still tend to give off a certain signal that a person is tough or of low socio-economic status. Many people feel they are not acceptable for those in business, law, or medicine (Navarro, 2010).

If you are fond of tattoos (photo to the left), have them done in areas that you can easily cover up when appropriate. A wrist tattoo, for example, can be covered by a thick bracelet, or a finger tattoo by a ring. Ensure that arm tattoos do not extend past the cuff and can be covered by full sleeves.

Grooming yourself while talking to someone is also impolite body language. Nail biting is negative grooming behaviour. When a person, male or female, bites their nails it usually denotes nervousness or insecurity. Another example is picking lint off your shirt or getting the dirt out from beneath your fingernails. Both show a lack of interest in and a lack of respect for the other person. This is dismissive behaviour. Of course, picking off one piece quickly may not be noticeable, but excessive preening of any type is disrespectful.

Then again, it must be pointed out that some mutual grooming can be seen as a body language display of comfort and closeness. Just as monkeys pick bugs off those they are close to, so will some humans pick a piece of fuzz off a friend's vest, a girlfriend may wipe some stray mustard from her boyfriend's lip, or a mother will fuss over a child's hair or face. Again, as with all body language, context is important.

The Cover Up

Another way that we use our hands to denote stress, anxiety and potential hiding of information is through the cover up, or shielding. People often will use their hands to shield their eyes when they hear disturbing, unwelcome news. People shield their nose by rubbing the bridge often when distressed or pulling away in thought. They also use hands to cover the chest and neck, an unconscious way of protecting vulnerable areas during stress.

Imagine a nervous housewife being asked by her spouse if she is cheating. Often her hand will go to the base of her neck or she will fidget with her necklace, covering this sensitive area.

It is very common for people under stress to cover up their torso by crossing their arms. This is similar to how you would reflexively raise your arm to shield your face against a blow. But covering the neck is one of the most common indications that something is wrong. Men often do this by straightening their tie, women by either just putting a hand to the base of the neck or by playing with their blouse collar or necklace.

Police sometimes use this knowledge to look for truth. For example, most women engage in the neck cover up when they are under stress. So, a woman reporting that her husband abuses her will usually cover the neck as she recounts the painful details of her story. In this situation, the lack of a neck cover up could indicate untruthfulness; if a woman does not cover this area when providing supposed details police may suspect that she is not emotionally engaged in the story and perhaps it is not entirely true. As always, we must look for clusters of tells and read them in context.

SAY WHAT YOU WANT TO SAY

Most body language is universal, though a few specific gestures might have culture-specific meanings. For example, crossing one's arms is a sign of being closed off or anxious in pretty much every country around the world. However, the thumbs up symbol, which is positive in much of the western world, is actually an insult in Iraq, Iran, Greece, West Africa, Russia and more (Axtell, 1997). Similarly, the "OK" symbol that many westerners make with their index finger and thumb as a sign that everything is just fine, is a highly offensive gesture in Brazil.

Despite these and a few other exceptions, it is important to remember that most of the body language we discuss is largely universal. You can use these tells to better understand people of any culture. Of course, when it comes to travelling, you may want to brush up on your understanding of culturally-specific body language.

Body language is relatively consistent at any age. Children exhibit much of the same body language that adults exhibit and they can understand a lot of body language as well. Children, in fact, are often even more honest in their body language than adults because they have not yet learned to limit their expressions or mannerisms in any way. This is why some of the examples and images in this book show children. As a parent or teacher, when you better understand body language you also better understand and communicate with children.

One way teachers can do this is through mirroring the body language of their students. If a student is talking to a teacher with their legs crossed, the teacher can cross his or her legs to create a subtle rapport. We can also use our awareness of body language to ensure we are sending the right signals.

When you understand body language you can ensure that your actions say what you want them to say. In his book, *What Every Body Is Saying*, FBI agent Joe Navarro (HarperCollins, 2008) tells how he has seen confident businesswomen steeple their hands but they do so on their lap, beneath the table. This is unfortunate because the hand steeple demonstrates confidence. However, by hiding it under the table the person they are speaking with is not able to read their confidence and may in fact assume they are lacking confidence.

It is important to recognise that when we understand body language we can work to give off the signals that we want others to read. We can give a thumbs up when things are good, we can be sure our steepled hands are in view. However, we can also use this knowledge in an effort to avoid sending off signals that we do not want others to read.

Imagine you are at work. The economic times are hard, so your company is combining annual performance reviews with a round of workforce reductions. This means that everyone is having a review meeting with the boss. Some people are being fired after this meeting. The boss has announced publicly that no one will be receiving raises this year due to tough times.

You arrive for your meeting and are nervous when you walk into the room. The meeting goes surprisingly well. The boss tells you how pleased he is with your work and that you are not part of the reduction. In fact, your boss relays the surprising news that you are actually receiving a raise. The boss cautions that few people are getting raises and asks you not to share this news with your co-workers.

As you exit your boss's office you try not to smile, knowing that a smile would reveal that you are pleased with the outcome and could possibly hint to more than simply keeping your job. This would offend those whose situation is not so good; thus, you manage to control yourself and not smile.

However, as you exit the office you quickly realise, because of your awareness of body language, that there is a bounce in your step and your hands are splayed wide apart in a display of confidence. You immediately recognise your mistake, slow your gait and fold your hands in front of you, interlocking your fingers to appear more sombre and concerned. You are now putting off signals that you are closed, that you don't want to talk about what happened in there, which would imply to others that it was not a cheerful occasion. No one asks you about anything and you do not even have to lie about your evaluation.

If we can learn to avoid giving off certain signals we can ensure that we do not broadcast emotions that we prefer to keep in check. Spies have to learn this; they must learn to avoid showing nervousness or indicating they are watching someone, either of which would arouse suspicion.

Think about newspaper articles you have read in recent years since terrorism has struck the western world. You may remember examples in which acts of terrorism were averted because the terrorists could not adequately control their body language. In fact, the U.S. Department of Homeland Security has been testing electronic monitoring devices that look for specific body language in people to spot would-be terrorists (Johnson, 2009). The devices monitor pupil dilation, body heat, gaze direction, respiratory rate and blink rate to detect anxiety. Fortunately for our security, many of these body language tells are nearly impossible to hide or change.

There are signals that, if you have an understanding of body language, you can learn to control to avoid sending them out into the world. You can also learn to make better use of gestures to generate comfort and confidence in others, to increase your use of facial expressions and to use eye contact positively—all ideas that we will discuss further in chapters 5 and 6.

◢ CHANGE HOW YOU FEEL

It may surprise you to know that learning to use body language effectively is not all about communicating with others. Sometimes, you can use body language to actually communicate with your own brain and to change the way you feel.

We've all heard it said that if you smile the world smiles with you. In many ways this is true, people are affected by the emotions and body language of those around them. We often subconsciously mirror others, taking on their attributes. This is why police hostage negotiators stay so calm when dealing with kidnappers, they hope that their calm behaviour will bring the kidnapper to a similarly calm state.

What you may not know is that your brain works in a similar way. Let's look at the process.

Usually, your brain will receive some outside information through the senses, news that it must process. The primitive limbic system often turns this information into an appropriate emotion even before the thinking brain can form a response. Thus, our body language reveals how we are feeling before we can verbalise it. We hear good news and we feel a rush of "butterflies" in our stomach, we feel good and then the smile emergences, all of this nanoseconds before we can tell someone how happy we are. The emotions generated tell the body how to react by quivering or smiling.

The interesting thing is that this process can also work in reverse. This is why people will tell us to "put on a happy face." This is good advice because science has demonstrated that when we exhibit body language that is associated with a certain emotion we can actually generate that emotion.

That means if you are having a bad day and you feel unhappy, you can actually improve your mood by smiling. Really! Try it. Right now you are probably in a relatively neutral state as you read, neither really happy nor sad. So, pause a moment, look away from your computer or book and smile. Just sit there for a full five to ten seconds and smile.

Now, access your mood. Do you feel at least a bit more joyful? You probably do. This is because your body knows that smiling equates with happiness. Just like your body will feel happiness and then prompt the muscles in your face to smile, so too will your body sense the smile muscles flexing and in turn send out signals of happiness.

We often experience this in the reverse, becoming sad when a loved one is sad. You may be having a great day that started with a healthy breakfast, continued on to a good day at work and light traffic on the way home. You are feeling happy and satisfied, only to arrive home and learn that your partner had a rotten day at work and is depressed. Your fantastic mood immediately dissipates in the face of your partner's bad day.

The great news is, by using mirroring, matching and leading, there are ways that you can use body language not only to bring your own mood back to your happy place, but also to raise your partner's mood along with it.

When you study body language, you learn not only how to read others, but you also learn how to better control your own language:

- You can use your body language to make others think that you feel a certain way; for example, exuding confidence even when you are nervous.

- You can read a person's hands and fingers to detect comfort, confidence, stress, anxiety and more.

- You can use your own body language to actually change your emotions.

USING BODY LANGUAGE TO INCREASE YOUR PERSONAL IMPACT

You can use your body language to increase your personal impact; that is, to make an immediate impression upon others, the impression that you intend to convey. You can use your body language to hide any fear or other negative feelings that you have, portraying to others only what you want them to see. You can use your body language to engage an audience, large or small and to communicate in a confident, professional way. You can learn how to use non-verbals of the arms to communicate clearly and how to read these non-verbals in others.

START WITH A GREAT FIRST IMPRESSION

You never get a second chance to make a first impression. This popular saying is a reflection on the fact that in the first seven to ten seconds of meeting a person we form an opinion of them and decide whether we like them or not. This opinion can be extremely difficult to change once it is formed. Making the right first impression to someone is of the utmost importance. This is especially important if you work in an area that requires you to address audiences or give speeches. The first impression you give can determine how people remember your speech.

To ensure that you make the best first impression possible, you need to master not just how you look and what you say, but also what your non-verbal communication is saying about you. It may surprise you to know that your arms actually have a lot to say.

THE ARMS TELL ALL

It's your first date. The movie was enjoyable and dinner is even better. The food is great, the wine is tasty and the conversation is interesting. You and your date are getting along great, both leaning in to talk intimately. Suddenly, your date leans in even closer and, indicating something over their shoulder, makes a derogatory comment about the race of someone who just sat at a table nearby.

You are immediately turned off by the racist comment. You lean back in your seat, pulling your arms onto your lap. You may even subconsciously start to play with your napkin or pick at your fingernails. The rapport is broken, the mood is gone and if your date has any knowledge of body language they will immediately know that the racist comment offended you.

However, because most people do not understand any more than the most extreme body language, your date will likely patter on with no idea that you have just emotionally withdrawn.

We use body language a thousand times every day to communicate how we feel. We smile or frown, shake or nod our heads, but we also do much more subtle things, including making movements with our arms that say a lot about how we are feeling at the moment.

Non-Verbals of the Arms

We all use our eyes, lips and faces to communicate every day with words and expressions, both conscious and unconscious. But what many of us do not realise is that the arms also have a lot to say. Sure, we all know some people or ethnicities who gesture wildly when upset or enthusiastic; often we think of such highly articulate arm gestures as isolated to certain expressive cultures, but the truth is that we all use arm language every day.

Our arms are amazing appendages, strong and agile. We use our arms to help carry weight, to push ourselves up from a lying or sitting position, to protect our body from an impending blow and more. In fact, we often think of our arms as our strength, our protectors. This is in many ways related to how we use our arms to communicate.

One way that your arms can communicate to show fear or anticipation is by coming up in protection of your body. We see this done consciously in boxers or martial artists who keep their arms and hands up in front of the sensitive neck and face. But we also see it in women who unconsciously hold their hands and arms in front of their belly when pregnant, as if cuddling and protecting their unborn child. We see it in ourselves when we are walking in the dark, our arms slightly up, in front of our bodies, shielding us from unseen spirits or, worse yet, solid walls.

So instinctive is the habit of pulling our arms up towards our heads in protection that even when we were to hear bullets sound or a bomb go off, our hands spring up in what is likely a futile attempt to protect our heads; we simply cannot help using our arms to protect ourselves. This tendency to shield ourselves with our arms is exactly why we hear the officers on police murder shows or forensic television programmes always talking about "defensive wounds." Any person who is conscious while being attacked in some way almost always has wounds on their arms that they incur while holding up their arms in protection of their body, neck or face.

Likely, this is one of the uses of our arms that nature intended. Yes, our ribs serve to protect our vital core organs, but the femurs and ulnas of our arms are much stronger than the ribs and they can be repositioned to protect weak areas, like the sternum or belly. Imagine if you are a parent and your four-year-old son decides to practise his football class head butt on your stomach. Instinctively your arms go to your stomach to block the blow. In many situations this instinctive movement can save you a painful gut blow or even a cracked rib.

These instinctive movements of the arms to fly to our defence, without our need to consciously direct them, is what makes them so helpful to us. It is also what makes them very truthful. The ability of our arms is not limited to protection or showcasing our anticipation of a blow; the arms have other tales to tell.

Our arms can also indicate our moods, particularly in naturally expressive people. For example, imagine a person who is sad or subdued. Picture such a person in your head, like someone at a funeral.  What are their arms doing? Likely, the person's arms are very still, either they are hanging straight at their sides or are in front of them, secured by clasped hands.

Now, imagine a contrasting scene, such as a child who has just kicked the winning goal in a football match. This child (and likely the entire team) will hoist their arms into the air in triumph and wave them in myriad other ways, showing clear enthusiasm and joy. American FBI agent Joe Navarro calls happy behaviours like these "gravity defying behaviours." He notes that when people are happy they are more likely to raise parts of their body into the air, defying the pull of gravity. He makes a good point. When we are happy we kick our feet into the air, we widen our eyes, raise our eyebrows, raise our lips up in a smile...and, we raise our arms above our heads triumphantly or cheerfully.

It doesn't necessarily mean we are celebrating victory every time we move our arms, but it usually indicates positive emotions. Think about the simple act of walking. In most situations, a person who is sombre, concerned, anxious, or lacking confidence will walk with their arms very still. A person who is happy, confident, or feeling otherwise positive feelings is more likely to swing their arms as they walk. If you are a child of the 1970s or 1980s, think of the strutting walk of TV character George Jefferson or John Travolta's movie alter ego Tony Manero, with their flamboyant arms (among other expressive body parts).

How much we move our arms and where we put them says a lot about our emotions. While we often use our arms to protect ourselves from physical harm, we also use our arms in an attempt to protect ourselves from emotional harm. Most people—women in particular—will cross their arms over their chest or body, or even combine an arm cross with knees pulled up to the chest, in an effort to protect themselves. This is often seen in women who have been the victim of assault or abuse, but can also be the result of strong heartbreak or other negative emotions when the person feels the need to protect themselves.

While arm crossing can indicate a need to protect one's self, crossing the arms actually can mean many things. People often cross their arms when they are trying to look comfortable and casual; for example, when leaning against a wall waiting for someone. People cross their arms when they are cold to pull in body heat or when they are bored. Arm crossing is very common when a person is angry or does not agree with what is being said. This is another example of why it is so important to read body language cues in concert with other hints and observations. Let's consider an example.

A young boy called Sam is practising football in a field. Another boy called Tom walks towards him. Tom is a boy that Sam knows and against whom he has a high need to compete. As Tom approaches, Sam puts his foot on his football and crosses his arms over his stomach. This could be either a show of concern, that Sam fears Tom will start trouble, or it could be a defiant behaviour, like Sam is saying to Tom, "I'm a better player than you so don't try to mess with me." To know what the body language means you would need to also look at Sam's facial expressions and other behaviours. No one piece of behaviour tells an entire story on its own.

Remember, it is *changes* in behaviour—a change from the person's baseline—that tells you something important. Think of a couple sitting in a restaurant. Both partners are leaning in, talking, smiling, arms on the table, hands not touching, but close together. Suddenly, the woman sits up, pulling her hands off the table and leaning back. There is a very good chance that the man just said something that upset her because withdrawing one's arms is a very common way of demonstrating that a person is withdrawing emotionally. We pull back our arms when we do not feel close to this person anymore because they have said or done something that changed our attitude.

It is also important to note that an absence of movement can mean a lot. Think for a moment of the cliché "deer caught in headlights." This is a deer who is crossing the street when a car comes around the corner; the deer sees the headlights of the vehicle and instead of running, it freezes. People do the same thing, usually when scared or shocked. We particularly see it a lot in children. In fact, here is an example of one upsetting manifestation of this freeze response in children:

A girl called Sara is on the baseball field having a great time with friends, running bases and playing. After play, she comes over to her mum who says, "Look Sara, Mr. Michaels from next door came by to see your game." Sara looks at Mr. Michaels and freezes, saying nothing, not moving. This should be an immediate sign to Sara's mum that something is wrong, something about this situation is scaring Sara into a freeze response. Police and teachers—those trained to protect children from abuse—should always be on the lookout for such freeze behaviour which indicates that something is wrong and that this situation requires some investigation.

In short, remember that a person who is not moving their arms much is potentially under some type of stress. Thieves casing a store, for example, will keep their arms tense and move them less than average people, as do drug users looking around for a score.

There are a few other things to touch upon as relates to arm movements. Arm movements tell us how welcome we are in a situation. If a person puts out their hand to shake, they are welcoming you. If they keep their hands hidden, they are not welcoming you. Notice how many high level people such as doctors or lawyers will stand with their hand or hands behind their back. This is a way of keeping their distance and telling you to keep yours. In fact, you can see this stance if you watch footage of the British Royal Family, who, by keeping their hands behind their backs, subtly indicate that they are not to be touched.

MAKING A POSITIVE IMPRESSION

Your body language is an important part of how you make an impression on someone when you meet them. This applies to your arms, as well as your entire body. When we make eye contact and extend a warm (but not sweaty) hand, we show that we are confident and comfortable. In fact, the best way to make a positive impression on another person when you first meet is to smile, lean forward (which indicates that you feel positive towards this person), make and maintain eye contact and, if appropriate, extend your hand in greeting.

We can use our arms to make an impression of strength, guardianship, friendliness and more. Police officers and military personnel use their arms to show dominance and control. One way they do this is through a stance called "arms akimbo." This is a way of standing with their hands on their hips, elbows out so that the arms form a triangle. When you stand with arms akimbo you show dominance and authority. This is not just a position reserved for law enforcement or the military; anyone who feels a need to assert their power uses this stance. For example, a younger manager who wants to assert himself over a group of older employees or a female manager looking for an extra display of power over predominantly male employees might use this stance.

We also use our arms to claim territory. You can see this in prisons, where many prisoners will eat with one arm on the table, wrapped around their food dish in protection of it, claiming that space as their own; that is how much table space their arms (and even their belongings) take up. You also see it in how people sit. A person who feels powerful, or who is trying to appear powerful, will take up more space than those around her or him. In a business situation this might mean putting a briefcase on the table or spreading papers over a wide area. A women might claim territory by putting her purse on the table.

We also claim territory in how we stand. For example, the way that you use personal space tells how you feel about the person you are meeting. If you step in close to another person you indicate that you like them, or at least that you are amiable to meeting them. When you keep your distance you show that you distrust or dislike this person, hence the saying, "keeping them at arm's length."

To continue to show positive feelings about the person you are meeting you should maintain open body language. That means keeping your arms at your side so that they are not covering your torso and keeping your body facing this person. When your arms are open, you appear open. If you do not wish to be approached, then you should close off your body language. The best way to close off while still retaining a look of confidence, is to stand up straight with your arms behind your back.

If you are a public speaker, your body language can also help you to connect to your audience, to elicit their trust. Much of this is done through your face. Obviously you want your face to be open and smiling, eyes wandering the group making as much eye contact as you are able. But in a large group setting, your body can do much more than your face, particularly your arms.

In speaking engagements you want to appear confident and professional. The best way to do this is to maintain open body language. Avoid hiding any part of your body by standing behind a podium. You should stand or sit in the open, where everyone can see your entire body, especially your face, arms and hands. Then, learn to use your arms and hands for maximum effect. When you are speaking in public you should gesture frequently, arms wide and inviting, torso open. If you keep your body language open and move sufficiently to show enthusiasm but not so much that you look fidgety, then you will be an effective speaker, at least visually.

HIDING NON-VERBALS YOU DON'T WANT OTHERS TO SEE

One reason to learn all of these body language principles is so that you know what body language you should avoid in certain situations. The good news is, you can learn what body language means and thus know what you want to avoid. The bad news is that controlling your unconscious body language is difficult. You may start a conversation controlling your movements well, but once you become embroiled in the conversation—when you are lost in the moment— you will likely forget yourself and let your subconscious take over.

Does that mean that you should not try to control the non-verbals that you don't want others to see? Of course not. But it means that you also need to have a back-up plan. Let's consider, for a moment, meeting another person.

Say that you are about to meet your daughter's boyfriend. You do not like what you have heard about him and you are quite sure that you won't like him. However, you fear that showing your dislike will just make your daughter want to see him more so you want to hide your negative feelings. Before you meet the boy, imagine how you will feel and what expressions, arm movements and so forth you are likely to have. In fact, stand in front of a mirror, close your eyes and imagine meeting the boy. Then open your eyes and look at what you are doing. Did your arms cross? Or did they flatten unyielding to your sides? Did your expression become grim? Identify any negative body language.

Now, practise the body language that you know will be more positive. Practise keeping your arms to your sides, but casually, not on your hips or glued to your body. Practise facial expressions and cocking your head just slightly to the side, in a positive gesture of comfort.

The only way that you can hide negative body language is to identify it and prepare for it. When you are going into a situation where you anticipate having a response that you'd rather not reveal, practise for it. You must practise replacement behaviours that send off the signals you want to send. The more you practise, the better you will become at controlling your behaviour.

To review, we all use our eyes, lips and faces to communicate every day with words and expressions, both conscious and unconscious, but the arms also have a lot to say.

- We show fear or anticipation by bringing up our arms in protection of our body.

- We pull our arms up to our heads in protection. If we hear the sound of bullets or hear a bomb go off, our hands spring up in what is likely a futile attempt to protect our heads; we simply cannot help using our arms to protect ourselves.

- They indicate our moods, particularly in naturally expressive people.

- We use our arms in an attempt to protect ourselves from emotional harm.

- Arm movements tell us how welcome we are in a situation. If a person puts out their hand to shake, they are welcoming you. If they keep their hands hidden, they are not welcoming you.

◢ We use our arms to claim territory.

◢ HOW TO READ OTHER PEOPLE'S BODY LANGUAGE

We've discussed how you can recognise aggression and other emotions in people's body language. We will now delve into reading the non-verbal cues that other people unknowingly send us. We will look at how you can use these non-verbals, including eye movements and more, to detect deception in others. We will also look at the micro-expressions people do not even know they exhibit and how you can become attuned to these non-verbal cues. Finally, you will learn to recognise and interpret various movements of the feet and legs, using them as clues to the real emotions that a person is trying to contain.

FINE-TUNE YOUR READING

Of course, throughout this entire chapter we have been talking about how to read other people's body language. But in this section we will go into more detail, particularly looking at how to notice and read things that a person may not want you to see, such as micro expressions and micro gestures and more.

Communication is a two-way street. It requires that each person send out words or signals and also receive words and signals from another person. This means that one part of effectively communicating with another person is in trying to understand the other person's emotional state, to figure out the real meaning behind what they are saying or doing. When you study body language you learn to better interpret the truth behind a person's words and actions.

Some people can identify only the most obvious clues to another person's emotional state; they only notice yelling, crying, hitting, tantrums, laughter and other such exaggerated displays. But with practise, you can learn to tell how a person really feels long before any emotions are displayed. Once you can read body language accurately, you can practise mirroring and leading.

Part of detecting another person's true feelings involves looking at their arms, hands, torso, head and other things we have discussed already. But it also involves their feet and legs (yes, really), as well as what we call micro expressions and micro gestures, things that a person does fleetingly before they realise it and cover it up. In this section we will concentrate on these tell-tale signs of the truth within a person and will also touch on a topic that is of interest to most people as we explore whether you can really use body language to detect deception.

NON-VERBALS OF THE FEET AND LEGS

You are walking down the street and you bump into a friend that you have not seen in a while. You both stop to say hello. You notice that the friend's expressions change a lot in the first second you catch their eye, moving from surprise, to what looked like dismay, but then to friendliness; you brush it off thinking you must have imagined the expression of dismay.

Your friend is being friendly, asking how you are, but you notice that they keep glancing away from you in the direction they had been heading. Then you look down and notice that their body is turned, their legs twisted as their feet face towards the direction they had been walking but their body is facing towards you.

Your friend is politely listening to you tell them about some event in your life as you notice this, so you pause and ask, "Do you have somewhere you need to be?" The friend apologises, looking down at their watch in distress and says that actually they are late for an important meeting with their child's teacher.

You suggest that the friend give you a phone call later so you can catch up and prompt them to be on their way. Visibly relieved, the friend thanks you and heads off.

According to body language specialist, Joe Navarro, the feet are the most honest part of the body. That is mostly because people rarely pay attention to what their feet are doing, other than getting them from here to there. However, the feet most certainly have stories to tell, if you know what to look for.

The main reason that our feet give such honest descriptions of our feelings is rooted in our DNA and our limbic system. Our limbic system is our primitive brain, the part of our brain that is responsible for emotional responses and also for fight or flight. Of course, humans don't have wings, so by flight we actually mean running away, which we do courtesy of our legs and feet.

This means that our legs and feet have a special relationship with our limbic system. They are wired to respond quickly to emotions and run towards something (such as a child falling into a pool of water) or run away from something (like a bear, venomous snake, or your boss). Whatever the situation, our feet stand ready to serve.

If you really stop to think about it, our feet certainly show our emotions frequently. If you are walking down a dark road alone and you hear a noise from a nearby alley you will likely freeze, your feet stopping your movement so that you can be quiet and assess the situation. Of course, if you identify some threat, your feet will suddenly leap into motion, carrying you away from the danger as fast as they are able. But more than fight or flight, our feet demonstrate other emotions.

Children stomp their feet when they are angry, as do some less mature or highly emotive adults. People sometimes stomp their feet in unison to make noise in support of their team at a sporting event. Imagine that you are sitting in a sports arena watching a game and the home team scores. If you look, you will see many people in their audience who remain sitting but raise their knees and feet up into the air, along with their arms, as they scream in joy.

We use our feet in celebration when we dance, particularly with the wild and exciting foot movements common to Irish dancing and other celebratory cultural dances.

When we are truly excited, we sometimes jump into the air. Most of us have seen the corny television soap opera or commercial where the woman in love lifts her foot while her Prince Charming kisses her.

Children often swing their legs when they are sitting in a chair and are excited. Adults will sometimes jiggle or shake their leg to show anxiety, nervousness, or boredom. Truly, our legs are a window to our emotions, if not quite our soul.

Unfortunately, most people watch only for body language of the upper body and they neglect the legs and feet. Thus, if you learn to watch for, recognise and decipher these leg and feet cues you will definitely have a leg up (pun intended) on everyone else around you.

Remember, the main reason that leg and foot body language is so honest is because of the link between the legs and our primitive limbic system. But there is one other reason why the legs are the place to watch if you want honest clues as to a person's feelings. While most people have trained themselves (or been trained) to control the emotion that they show in their face and maybe even in their hands, few people give any thought to what their feet are saying.

Like all body language, foot and leg movements are about observing changes from baseline posture. Many people jiggle their legs or feet as a nervous habit or even some disorder. But if a person is sitting still and they suddenly bounce their legs, you know they likely heard something agreeable. On the other hand, if a person is bouncing their legs and they suddenly freeze, it is likely that they just heard or saw something that they did not like.

Another way that we use our feet and legs is in how we point them. Just like the ventral and dorsal facing of the body that we talked about earlier, we also face our feet towards things we like or want to go towards. Thus, if you are talking to a person and notice that their feet are facing away from you or inching in another direction, this may be a sign that they need to be somewhere else or want to leave. Sometimes a person will face one foot away, perpendicular to the other. This is a clear sign that the person wants to make their exit.

People will also do this when they are seated and talking to someone. If we are having a cheerful, comfortable conversation we usually face the other person with our body, legs and feet. However, if we want to leave we will shift our feet and legs in the direction in which we want to flee. Or, if we know that they cannot leave, we may cross our legs so that our knee is blocking the person we are speaking with, as if shielding our body from what is being said.

People tend to cross their legs towards people they like and conversation they are enjoying and away from things they do not like. Then again, people who have back, hip, or knee problems may need to shift positions often, so their movement may mean nothing. You must look at the context of the movement and look for signal clusters, as we will discuss in chapter 8.

We sometimes cross our legs (particularly when standing) as a blocking behaviour to indicate physical or emotional discomfort. Conversely, when a person is talking to someone with whom they are very comfortable, they may also cross their legs at the ankle, a sign that they are not in a hurry to go anywhere and are pleased with the conversation. Usually, when a person is uncomfortable to the point that they wish to flee they will open up their legs into a stance that allows for a quick exit.

We also show that we are in a hurry to leave when we lean forward in our seat and put our open palm on our knees—"clasping" the knee—almost as though to give ourselves momentum to stand and leave. This is one of the body language signs that many people do recognise and that we consciously use to indicate that we want to wrap up a conversation.

People use their legs in a hundred different ways to communicate. By knowing these basics and looking for other more subtle foot movements in your own interactions, you can learn to better understand people's emotions and motivations in your personal and work interactions.

MICRO EXPRESSIONS AND MICRO GESTURES

Previously we talked about the expressiveness of the face and hands. Now we will take these ideas a bit further and talk about micro expressions and micro gestures. Micro expressions and micro gestures are those fleeting, subconscious looks and movements that a person makes when they first hear some news or first have some type of emotional reaction.

We can illustrate these reactions best by imagining a criminal for a moment, such as a woman who has killed her adulterous husband and tried to make it look like an accident. As the police question her she has her poker face on. In her attempt not to smile at her jubilation, she is being unnaturally calm and still. For now the police are assuming that she might be in shock and thus are not overly suspicious yet.

The investigating detective is asking the woman various questions about where she was and how she found the body. Then, he switches gears and asks something the woman had not expected.

Had her husband been cheating on her? For just a moment the woman's face shows shock or anger, not having anticipated this question and feeling "caught" in her motive. She quickly regains herself and puts her sad face back on, shaking her head that no, her beloved spouse would have never cheated.

A less seasoned detective, one not experienced in body language, might miss this micro expression, this flash of shock or perhaps even anger that appeared just briefly before she could cover it up. A slightly better detective might notice the look but may shrug it off, figuring the woman was just shocked by such a personal and suggestive question.

But a detective experienced in body language knows that this micro facial expression is a hint that something may not be as it seems. Likely, this detective will change the subject, asking more innocent questions and then later suddenly return to the topic of the cheating husband and look for a similar reaction or some other body language to confirm his suspicions.

There are many times when we might exhibit such micro expressions. You might hear news that someone has died, someone who you were not very fond of. Your initial blank expression, or even a quick note of sarcastic frown, might give away your true feelings before you can affix your mask of expected empathy or sadness. There are many times when our initial, honest reaction sneaks past our conscious censors for just a brief moment before we can put on the face that we know is better appropriate for the situation. It is these flashes that are much more honest than the face we replace them with.

Micro gestures are the same as micro expressions, except that we do them with our bodies. The difference is that micro gestures can sometimes be done intentionally. Many of us have seen a person or movie character surreptitiously give a rude finger gesture. We sometimes see passive aggressive anger when a person expresses dislike of another person by pushing their glasses up using their middle finger, or wringing their hands together but letting a sole middle finger poke up for just a second. These conscious micro gestures are rarely noticed, but when they are, a new aspect of the person's attitude and behaviour is revealed.

A micro gesture can also be a quick subconscious flash of movement before a person controls themselves. For example, when your spouse introduces you to a person from work, someone that you know your spouse cannot stand to be around, you unconsciously start to move forward to shake hands. Suddenly, you realise how upset this will make your spouse, so you pull your hand back and do something else with it, perhaps putting it in your pocket or smoothing your hair. This micro gesture, to anyone who noticed, would show that you initially felt positive about this person and were about to reach out to him, but that some other thought pulled you back.

We also see this with parents who are watching their child do something that makes the parent nervous, like participating in a sporting or gymnastics event. The parent might lean towards the child, almost lunging when they sense danger, but then restraining themselves.

We make and correct these micro movements frequently, often in situations that surprise us. These are among the most difficult body language signals to read, but they are also the most difficult to hide. Thus, if you learn to detect and read these signals you will obtain valuable information about the true feelings of people around you.

DETECTING DECEPTION

If you are like many people, your initial interest in body language was probably cued when you saw something on TV about how law enforcement agents use body language to detect deception. Let me be very straightforward—in our current world there is no foolproof way to tell when a person is telling the truth or when they are lying. No machine can detect lies with 100% accuracy and neither can any human. Now, that being said, many people can and do use their knowledge of body language to detect potential untruthfulness or partial truths.

I have said repeatedly in this book that reading body language is about looking for deviations from baseline behaviour. That is, you look at how a person holds themselves when they are relaxed, then, during your interactions with them, you look for changes from this baseline, changes that may indicate stress, anxiety, lack of comfort, an urge to flee and so forth.

If you are talking to a person and they seem comfortable, but then you ask them a certain question and they suddenly appear uncomfortable, what might this tell you? Well, you know that this question or topic makes them uncomfortable. So, you might wonder whether they are uncomfortable because they don't like the topic, because they don't want to tell you the truth, or because they are telling you a lie.

By looking at body language signals and signal clusters, you can make some very educated decisions about whether or not a person is telling you the whole truth. Let's look at an example.

You own a small business and you just sent an employee on an errand that you figured would last an hour. Three hours later the employee returns from the errand. You really needed the employee in the office sooner to get some things done, so you ask him what took so long. The employee looks you straight in the eye and says that traffic was a nightmare, that there was a huge accident and he was stuck at a standstill for 60 minutes. As he tells you this he gestures with his arms to emphasise his points. His feet are set shoulder length apart. He is demonstrative and somewhat animated, maintaining an open body language. His pupils are wide and he looks up and to the left as if remembering something as he relates his tale. There are no signs that he is hiding anything. At the end of the story he plops into a chair, apparently exhausted, legs spread wide and arms at his side. All of these behaviours are signs that he is telling the truth.

However, if he answers you while refusing to meet your eyes, looking down and to the right (as if imaging something), crossing his legs or crossing his arms over his chest, or otherwise blocking his body, these are all signs of discomfort, signs that perhaps he is not telling you the whole truth or is not comfortable with what he is telling you. These signs would indicate that you might want to probe a bit deeper to see what really went on in those extra two hours.

Body language can suggest discomfort and place suspicion on a person's truthfulness, though it cannot detect deception on its own. However, when you become adept at reading body language, you will find that what their body says gives you a very good idea of whether their words speak the truth or if you should be asking more probing questions. Of course, looking for multiple tells, or signal clusters, is the best way to be more sure of what you are seeing.

◢ REPRESENTATIONAL SYSTEMS

Have you ever had a conversation with someone and thought to yourself that you may as well have been speaking in two different languages? Or, at the other end of the spectrum, have you ever just clicked with someone from the off and had an immediate connection?

Within our vocal vocabulary we process information using our senses, predominately visual, auditory and kinaesthetic, but also olfactory (smell) and gustatory (taste). We may also use nonsensory auditory–digital. Each of us will have a preference for communicating through one or two senses and it can be contextual.

Developing an understanding of how people process information and their preferred processing style helps us to connect with people better. We can transmit information more effectively, gain better rapport, help people develop a skill set and teach and present information to ensure people's learning styles are met. If you were explaining a process at an interview and the interviewee was very visual, you might draw a diagram or use visual sensory-based words. If you were selling a product and the perspective buyer was kinaesthetic, you might let them test drive a car or use a TV remote control. If someone was very auditory, you might let them listen to a sound system by turning up the volume.

Take a moment to think about a time you went to view a new house. What did you notice most? The sounds outside, the way the garden looked, the feeling you got from walking in?

What did you notice most the last time you bought a car? That new car smell, how it drove, how the seats felt?

A colleague of mine, familiar with NLP, was doing some work with the Accrington Stanley football club. It was the season of 2006–07 and there were roughly 10 games to go. With the threat of being deducted points for fielding ineligible players, the morale in the team was low. Accrington Stanley was stuck in the relegation zone and as it was its first season back after many years in league football, the prospect of being relegated was financially catastrophic.

My friend told me she didn't seem to be getting through to the team. She had put together these amazing power point presentations, was articulate in her presentations and had some of the most powerful tools and techniques at her disposal. She asked me to assist her.

I was in the room about to deliver my presentation when I could see the players were getting restless. I looked at my colleague and thought, "That's it!" I had recognised that the team was made up of predominantly kinaesthetic learners.

I took them out of the class room and did a variety of physical activities underpinned by NLP techniques. The players did not realise the psychological process, but at the end of the session they gave me a big round of applause.

And that set the tone for the rest of our involvement throughout the season. We managed to go on a winning run and stay up. This illustrates the importance of understanding the learning styles of the people with whom we work to get the best out of them.

THE SIX REPRESENTATIONAL SYSTEMS

Representational systems (rep systems) are how we gather and process external events through our senses. The main information processing styles are called:

- visual (sight),
- auditory (hearing),
- kinaesthetic (feeling),
- auditory–digital (nonsensory),
- smell (olfactory) and
- taste (gustatory).

They are also referred to as *modalities*. When information reaches our brains, it is given meaning and form and our representational systems are the ways we *represent* our subjective experience of the world.

PREFERRED REPRESENTATIONAL SYSTEMS

Although everyone uses all of the rep systems, we all tend to have a preference, just like there are people who prefer certain types of food. Statistics suggest that in a developed country, approximately 60% of the people are predominantly visual with another 20% auditory and 20% kinaesthetic. It is worth bearing this statistic in mind when creating marketing or advertising material.

The representational system that we prefer is our own special language of our experiences and it embraces the mental processes of thinking, remembering, imagination, perception and consciousness. By understanding these more clearly, it allows us to communicate better with ourselves and others and controls the way we interpret things.

We can think of our rep system preference(s) as a combination of numbers comprising a pin code to open a safe. Being aware of someone else's preferred rep system, or pin code, is the key to unlocking how to present information to them in a way that is relevant.

This is important in professions such as delivering training, presentations, teaching, management and sales. For example, you want to purchase a new wide-screen television and you have an auditory preference. You go into the local electronics store to purchase a television and the sales representative, who has a very visual preference, proceeds to show you all the televisions in the show room but doesn't take the time to let you listen to the television's sound. As a result, you might decide to go to another store because you didn't feel engaged in the experience.

This explains why it is not only important to be aware of other people's preferred rep system, but also to be aware of our own. Being aware of our own rep system can help you be more aware, flexible and adaptable; to think beyond the box in the way you communicate with people.

Representational Predicates

You can recognise a person's preferred representational system by how they use predicates. The predicate words in Table 3.1 and the predicate phrases in Table 3.2 will help you to spot people's preferred representational systems.

Using Tells to Spot the Primary Preferred Representational System

There are key indicators you can use to spot someone's primary preferred rep system.

Table 3.1 Preferred Representational System Predicates

Visual	Auditory	Kinesthetic	Auditory Digital
Appear	Be all ears	Catch on	Change
Clear	Be heard	Concrete	Conceive
Crystal	Deaf	Feel	Consider
Dawn	Dissonance	Grasp	Decide
Envision	Harmonise	Hard	Distinct
Focused	Hear	Scrape	Experience
Foggy	Listen	Slip	Insensitive
Hazy	Make Music	Tap into	Know
Illuminate	Question	Throw out	Learn
Imagine	Resonate	Touch	Motivate
Look	Rings a bell	Turn around	Perceive
Picture	Silence	Unfeeling	Process
Reveal	Sound(s)		Sense
See	Tune in		Think
Show	Unheard of		Understand
View			

Visual

Visual people tend to do things more quickly whether that be moving or speaking. *A picture says a thousand words* and these people are describing in words the images that are flying through their mind. They may speak in a higher pitch and tend to sit more erect on the edge of their seats, with their eyes up. They generally breathe more shallowly from the top of their lungs. They use gestures a lot that tend to be nearer head height and have no problem throwing their hands in the air.

They generally have a neat, organised and well groomed appearance and like things to "look right." They find it difficult to remember verbal instructions because their minds tend to wander when receiving them. They are less distracted by noise and they use visual

Table 3.2   Preferred Representational System Predicate Phrases

Visual	Auditory	Kinesthetic	Auditory Digital
Appears to me	Afterthought	All washed up	A particular way
Bird's eye view	Call on	Boils down to	Can you comprehend
Catch a glimpse	Clearly expressed	Come to grips with	Change your mind
Clear as day	Describe in detail	Control yourself	Consider both sides
Clearly defined	Earful	Cool, calm, collected	Consider your options
Dim view	Give an account of	Firm foundation	Decide what works
Get an eyeful	Give me your ear	Get a handle of	Deem it correct
Get a perspective of	Grant an audience	Get a load of this	Discern the answer
Hazy idea	Heard voices	Get hold of	Distinctly differently
In light of	Hidden message	Get in touch with	Experience the best
In person	Hold your tongue	Get the drift of	Gain knowledge of
In view of	Idle talk	Hand in hand	Get them motivated
Looks like	Inquire into	Hang in there	Get to know them
Make a scene	Keynote speaker	Heated argument	Give me your opinion
Make it out	Loud and clear	Hold it!	I sense I know

Table continued next page

Table 3.2 Preferred Representational System Predicate Phrases (continued)

Visual	Auditory	Kinesthetic	Auditory Digital
Mental image	Manner of speaking	Hold on!	I suppose I can
Mental picture	Pay attention	Hot head	I think you're right
Mind's eye	Power of speech	Keep your shirt on	I understand
Naked eye	Purrs like a kitten	Know-how	Know the details
Paint a picture	Rings a bell	Lay your cards out	Know what it's about
Scope it out	State your purpose	Pain in the neck	Know what's wrong
See to it	To tell the truth	Pull some strings	Learn about yourself
Showing off	Tongue-tied	Sharp as a tack	Learn what to do
Sight for sore eyes	Unheard of	Slipped my mind	Make your mind up
Staring off into space	Utterly	Smooth operator	Perceive the truth
Take a peek	Voiced an opinion	Start from scratch	Practice till perfect
Tunnel vision	Well informed	Stiff upper lip	Process this
Under your nose	Within hearing	Too much of a hassle	Sensitive subject
Up front	Word for word	Underhanded	

predicates like, *I see what you mean* or *I get the picture*. Physically, they are often thin and wiry and their hands will reflect this too with long slender fingers. Their handwriting will also likely have more sharp points to it and be written quickly.

Auditory

People who are predominantly auditory do things more rhythmically. Their voice tends to be mid-range and they talk to themselves, either internally or externally. They may even move their lips when they're reading. They breathe from the middle of their chest and use some hand gestures, but not extensively. They can repeat instructions back to you easily but are distracted by noise.

Auditory thinkers often tilt their head to one side in conversation, as if lending an ear or as if they holding a the telephone between their shoulder and head. They memorise things in steps or sequences and like to be told things and hear feedback in conversations. They tend to use auditory predicates such as, *that rings a bell* or *that clicks* and are interested in what you have to say. They can be excellent listeners and enjoy music and the spoken voice. Their handwriting is between the visual and kinaesthetic styles.

Kinaesthetic

Kinaesthetic people typically breathe from the bottom of their lungs so you'll see their stomachs going in and out. They do things much more slowly than a visual person and have a deep voice. When they speak, there are long pauses between statements and they process things that are said to them to determine how they feel about something.

They respond well to touch and physical rewards. They use few hand gestures and generally stand close to the person they're talking with. They use predicates such as, *I want to get a handle on it* or *a firm foundation* and will be able to access their emotions more readily. Physically, they tend to be more solid looking and generally their hands are larger or chunky (so that they can get to grips with things). They are interested in how you feel and memorise instructions by walking through the process or doing it. Their handwriting is more rounded and it is likely that they'll push more firmly on the page.

Auditory–Digital

The auditory–digital person will likely manifest characteristics of the visual, auditory and kinaesthetic rep systems. In addition, they will talk to themselves a lot and like to *make sense* of things and *understand them*. They place a high value on logic and also like detail.

They use words which are abstract with no direct sensory link. They use predicates like, *I understand your motivation* or *that computes with me*. As a result of their emotions being attached to the words that they're using to describe something, they often are less emotionally attached to outcomes (double dissociation).

Olfactory and Gustatory

You may sometimes hear phrases or words with an olfactory (smell) or gustatory (taste) connection such as, *that puts a bad taste in my mouth* or *that smells fishy*. When creating rapport, simply match these expressions when they occur and consider them as the kinaesthetic rep system.

LEARNING STYLES

An effective coach can best support a client's learning by gaining an understanding of how people learn and think. An awareness of the different ways people process information can increase a coach's ability to ask appropriate questions and provide accessible "homework" options. Visual learners associate ideas and concepts with images and techniques. They prefer to see or read the material they are learning. Auditory learners depend on hearing, listening and speaking in order to learn. Kinaesthetic or tactile learners prefer to learn through doing.

To further understand each of these learning styles, it's important to understand how each might approach the task of learning how to change a flat tyre. A visual learner will want to read written instructions or watch a video demonstration of the process. An auditory learner may also benefit from an instructional video, though more from the verbal explanation than the visual cues. A kinaesthetic learner will just want to roll up their sleeves and change the tyre, learning as they go.

Understanding learning styles can be helpful and informative for both coach and client. By increasing awareness of self and others, the information can be used to more effectively communicate, rather than to stereotype or categorise. Understanding learning styles can also facilitate growth. Someone with a preferred visual learning style might want to strengthen their auditory and kinaesthetic information processing capacities.

It is also useful to realise that learning styles overlap and while one style may be dominant or preferred, most people use a combination of all three styles: visual, auditory and kinaesthetic.

What Is Your Preferred Learning Style?

Being aware of how people process information can make a massive difference when presenting, coaching, interviewing, teaching, training, making a sales presentation and transmitting information to other people.

◢ When you are communicating with someone who is visual, use visual aids such as flip charts and PowerPoint presentations. Use visual words and phrases.

◢ When you are communicating with someone who is kinaesthetic, let them have a hands-on experience so they can engage in a process and feel connected to it. Sometimes when I deliver courses, I will give the kinaesthetic delegates squish balls they can clench in the hands during the my talk.

◢ When you are communicating with someone who is auditory, you can create a lecture and include a discussion process.

◢ When you are communicating with someone who is auditory-digital, make sure you are prepared with facts, figures and logical findings to support your thoughts and ideas. You can include literature they can read or take away.

Gathering Information for Presentations

When I am delivering a training programme and I don't have much information on the background of the delegates, I will email the following VAKad learning styles questionnaire so I can make the delivery of the session conducive the delegate's learning styles. It is also possible to work on the probability of the group being divided between all learning styles, though if one style is predominant and I know that ahead of time, I can adapt the presentation to more closely fit that style. For example, there might be a heavy visual preference across the group, so I would use more flip charts, power point presentations, etc.

THE VAKad QUESTIONNAIRE
Understanding Your Sensory Learning Styles

This questionnaire aims to find out something about your preferences for the way you work with information. You will have a preferred learning style and one part of that learning style is your preference for the intake and output of ideas and information.

Instructions: Read each of the scenarios. Choose the answer which best explains your preference and circle the letter next to it. You may circle more than one answer if a single one does not match your perception.

Leave blank any question that do not apply, but try to give an answer to at least 10 of the 13 questions. When you have completed the questionnaire, use the marking guide to find your score for each of the four categories: visual, auditory, auditory–digital and kinaesthetic.

Finally, calculate your preference on the scoring sheet.

1. You are about to give directions to a person who is standing with you. She is staying in a hotel and wants to visit your house later. She has a rental car. You would:
   a. draw a map on paper.
   b. tell her the directions.
   c. write down the directions (without a map).
   d. collect her from the hotel in your car.
2. You are not sure whether a word should be spelled dependent or dependant. You would:
   a. look it up in the dictionary.
   b. see the word in your mind and choose by the way it looks.

  c. sound it out in your mind.

  d. write both versions down on paper and choose one.

3. You have just received a copy of your itinerary for a world trip. This is of interest to a friend. You would:

  a. phone her immediately and tell her about it.

  b. send her a copy of the printed itinerary.

  c. show her your itinerary on a map of the world.

  d. share your feelings about what you plan to do at each place you visit.

4. You are going to cook something as a special treat for your family. You would:

  a. cook something familiar without the need for instructions.

  b. thumb through the cookbook looking for ideas from the pictures.

  c. refer to a specific cookbook in which there is a good recipe.

  d. phone somebody and ask for advice

5. You have been assigned a group of tourists who want to find out more about wildlife reserves or parks. You would:

  a. drive them to a wildlife reserve or park.

  b. show them slides and photographs.

  c. give them pamphlets or a book on wildlife reserves or parks.

  d. give them a talk on wildlife reserves or parks.

6. You are about to purchase a new sound system. Other than price, what would most influence your decision?

  a. the salesperson telling you what you want to know.

  b. reading the details about it.

  c. playing with the controls and listening to it.

  d. it looks really smart and fashionable.

7. Recall a time in your life when you learned how to do something, like playing a new board game (avoid choosing a very physical skill, such as riding a bike). You learnt best by:

  a. visual clues—pictures, diagrams, charts.

  b. written instructions.

    c. listening to somebody explaining it.

    d. doing it or trying it.

8. You have an eye problem. You would prefer the doctor to:

    a. tell you what is wrong.

    b. show you a diagram of what is wrong.

    c. use a model to show you what is wrong.

    d. explain what you think might be wrong from what you have read.

9. You are about to learn to use a new program on a computer. You would:

    a. sit down at the keyboard and begin to experiment with the
program's features.

    b. read the manual that comes with the program.

    c. telephone a friend and ask questions about it.

    d. watch a demonstration on YouTube.

10. You are staying in a hotel and have a rental car. You would like to visit friends whose address/location you do not know. You would like them to:

    a. draw a map on paper.

    b. tell you the directions.

    c. write down the directions (without a map).

    d. collect you from the hotel in their car.

11. Apart from the price, what would most influence your decision to buy a particular textbook?

    a. you have used a copy before.

    b. a friend talking about it.

    c. quickly reading parts of it.

    d. because the way it looks is appealing.

12. A new movie has arrived in town. What would most influence your decision to go (or not go)?

    a. You heard a radio review about it.

    b. You read a review about it.

    c. You saw a preview of it.

    d. It would depend on how you felt on the day.

13. Do you prefer a lecturer or teacher who likes to use:
    a. a textbook, handouts, readings?
    b. flow diagrams, charts, graphs?
    c. field trips, labs, practical sessions?
    d. discussions and guest speakers?

THE VAKad QUESTIONNAIRE SCORING CHART

Use the following scoring chart to find the VAKad category that each of your answers corresponds to. Circle the letters that correspond to your answers.

For example, if you answered b and c for question 3, circle AD and V in the question 3 row.

Question	a category	b category	c category	d category
3	A	AD	V	K

Scoring Chart

Question	a category	b category	c category	d category
1	V	A	AD	K
2	AD	V	A	K
3	A	AD	V	K
4	K	V	Ad	A
5	K	V	AD	A
6	A	R	K	V
7	V	AD	A	K
8	A	V	K	AD
9	K	AD	A	V
10	V	A	AD	K
11	K	A	AD	V
12	A	AD	V	K
13	AD	V	K	A

Calculating your Scores

Count the number of each of the VAKad letters you have circled to get your score for each VAKad category. The highest number is your preferred representational system.

Total number of V circled   =   _____

Total number of A circled   =   _____

Total number of K circled   =   _____

Total number of AD circled =   _____

If you are delivering a presentation it might be worth emailing your delegates a similar questionnaire to get an indication of their preferred representational systems. You can then adapt the session to engage the audience in the best possible way.

If you are a manager or a team leader, it might be a good idea to get your team members to do the test as a way to highlight that we all have different ways to process information.

Please note that the results of the questionnaire are not a way of labelling people. For example, if someone scores highly on visual, it doesn't necessarily mean they are solely a visual person. The score is a matter of context-based preferences on the assessment taken at time.

Tips and Ideas

If you are not familiar with the group or individual during an interview, presentation, session, or lesson, be prepared in all four representation systems. Understanding and being aware of and adapting to people's preferred representational systems can have a powerful effect. I was once coaching a women who was applying for a new job. It was an exciting opportunity and she had not been employed for a long period of time. Over 100 applicants had applied for the position and she had made the short list of people to be interviewed.

The interview process involved delivering a presentation. I helped her to prepare the presentation utilising all representation systems. She used lecture and discussion (auditory), got the interviewees to engage kinaesthetically by getting them to go through the process, and she brought in a flip chart to draw diagrams (visual).

She got the job as an accounts manager in preference to more experienced and qualified people. The interviewees commented on how excellent her presentation was.

◢ **Exercise**

In order to make the best impression during an interview or presentation, it is important to adapt your language to people's preferred learning styles.

Challenge yourself by becoming familiar with using the full range of representational systems in order to increase your flexibility in communicating. Read the four statements below and figure out which representational system the person uses. Rewrite the statement using a different representational system. For example:

◢ "That looks like a great plan"

The predicate "looks" is an example from the Visual representational system. I'm going to convert this into the Auditory representational system, replacing looks with an Auditory predicate:

◢ "That *sounds* like a great plan"

Now do the same thing using the four statements below. Don't limit yourself to just one representation system; try using a different one for each statement, or use the other 3 predicates for each statement.

◢ People don't see me in the big picture.
◢ Your boss's words gave me a bad feeling.
◢ Every day it feels like things are getting better!
◢ Things are looking pretty good.

4 Meta-Programmes

The sculptor's attitude
—Author Unknown

I woke up early today, excited about all I get to do before the clock strikes midnight. I have responsibilities to fulfil. I am important. My job is to choose what kind of day I am going to have.

- ◢ Today I can complain because the weather is rainy or I can be thankful that the grass is getting watered for free.
- ◢ Today I can feel sad that I don't have more money or I can be glad that my finances encourage me to plan my purchases wisely and guide me away from waste.
- ◢ Today I can grumble about my health or I can rejoice that I am alive.
- ◢ Today I can lament over all that my parents didn't give me when I was growing up or I can feel grateful that they allowed me to be born.
- ◢ Today I can cry because roses have thorns or I can celebrate that thorns have roses.
- ◢ Today I can mourn my lack of friends or I can excitedly embark on a quest to discover new relationships.
- ◢ Today I can whine because I have to go to work or I can shout for joy because I have a job to do.
- ◢ Today I can complain because I have to go to school or I can eagerly open my mind and fill it with rich new tidbits of knowledge.
- ◢ Today I can murmur dejectedly because I have to do housework or I can feel honoured because the Lord has provided shelter for my mind, body and soul.

Today stretches ahead of me, waiting to be shaped, and here I am, the sculptor who gets to do the shaping. What today will be like is up to me. I get to choose what kind of day I will have! What will you choose to do with today? Have a great day...unless you have other plans.

◢ META-PROGRAMMES

Have you ever delivered a presentation to a group of people and had completely different reactions from various members of the group? Or have you told the same story or a joke to different sets of people and had completely different responses? Or you might have given your clients or colleagues a set of instructions and some of them completely understood and processed what you said, while others just looked at you with blank expressions.

No doubt there are times that you're left wondering why the same message is interpreted in a completely different way. How is it possible one person reacts one way and one person reacts another way?

You may give someone a task to do and the next time you hear back from that person, it's complete. But you give the same task to another person, with the same instructions, but they keep getting in touch with you to ask for your thoughts on their progress.

When you have an idea, some people see the opportunity, get excited, happy, and enthusiastic, while others see all the pitfalls and downsides.

We can only take responsibility for what we communicate, not the other person's reaction. If the person reacts in a way that indicates the information isn't processed, this chapter will give you an insight and understanding into how to get through to these people. If you would like to be a master communicator as a coach, in business or your personal life, then read on and let's explore the power of meta-programmes.

WHAT ARE META-PROGRAMMES?

Underlying the values we have accumulated in life as a result of our experiences, are deeper-rooted values that determine the way people approach life. They are called meta-programmes—the source of people's motivations and behaviour patterns. Meta-programmes are the internal programmes, or intrinsic values, we use to decide what we pay attention to.

These intrinsic values are easily recognisable because they show themselves in patterns by what people say, how people say it and what they do. The key is not in deciding whether the behaviour is right or wrong, rather it is in making the distinction as to whether or not the behaviour is useful in the context of the circumstance.

Think of these behaviours on a scale of 1 to 10, with 10 being high. You might function at a level 1 at work but at a level 8 in your personal life. There is no right or wrong way. It is a question of whether that behaviour is serving you in that context. For example, you might be right handed and use your right hand to do many things; however, there are times when you use your left hand too.

The brain processes information pretty much the same as a computer does. The brain absorbs millions of pieces of information and organises it into a map of the world in a way that makes sense to the person. Meta-programmes are the filters we use to create this map. They run "in the background", so we usually are not consciously aware of them. They drive:

- what we pay attention to,
- what we respond to,
- what motivates us,
- how we interact with the people around us, and
- the kind of language that will influence us.

If we use an analogy that the brain is similar to a computer in the way it processes information, then the meta-programmes are the software. A computer system needs specific software to perform specific tasks, and meta-programmes are the software the brain uses to interpret information and events. One person might describe his or her job as being interesting, purposeful, and rewarding, while another may describe working in the same job as being boring, mundane and just a means to an end. To use a computer effectively, you need to be aware of and understand the software that performs specific functions. Whether you're a coach, manager, leader, or sales person, or just communicating with your spouse, partner, or kids, to get your message across powerfully and effectively, you need to understand the other person's meta-programmes.

Similar to how one computer program controls the execution of a number of other programs, selecting which ones will run at which times and sending them information they'll need in order to function properly, meta-programmes can be used to affect several aspects of a person's behaviour.

We are going to explore some of the most powerful meta-programmes in this chapter, but before we proceed, we need to identify useful information so we can recognise our own behavioural and motivation patterns as well as those of our customers, clients, and business associates.

◢ **Exercise**

1. What is important to you about your work?

2. What is important about your work to your customers, clients?

3. What is important about your work to your colleagues, people you work with and associates?

4. What is it about your work that makes all your effort worthwhile?

5. When you answer these the questions, do they come from your head or your heart?

HISTORY OF META-PROGRAMMES

The term *meta-programming* first appeared in John C Lilly's book *Programming and Meta-Programming in the Human Computer* (1968). Lilly presented the human nervous system as a biological computer, running programs either hard-wired or learned. Once we know what these meta-programmes are, we can use them to change the central control system so that we can learn more quickly and select more useful programmes.

Richard Bandler introduced meta-programmes to NLP in the late 1970s to explain the processes people used to maintain coherency in their cognitive patterns.

Leslie Cameron-Bandler and others investigated further, using the Meta Model to identify a list of meta-programme patterns for use in therapy that eventually grew to around 60 programmes. One of her students, Rodger Bailey, simplified the model into 14 patterns for use in a business context. He called these the LAB Profile (Language And Behaviour Profile patterns) These patterns were set out in Shelle Rose Charvet's excellent *Words That Change Minds* (Author's Choice, 1997).

James and Woodsmall's *Time Line Therapy and The Basis of Personality* presents a similar simplified set of patterns and links them to Jungian personality characteristics as used in the Myers-Briggs Type Indicator.

It is important to take note of what meta-programmes are not.

◢ They are not a way of putting people into boxes at the identity level! They may be influenced by context and the person's emotional state.

◢ They are not either/or programmes. Instead, each meta-programme is like a spectrum and most people will be located somewhere between the extreme ends.

◢ They are not absolutes. Each meta-programme is context-dependent. For example, people tend to be more detail-focused about subjects that interest them.

When you know someone's meta-programmes, you can more easily understand, predict and influence their behaviour. As a coach, manager or leader, we can use the meta-programme–computer program analogy. In order to use a computer software program effectively you must understand *how* to use it. In order to communicate in an efficient manner, you must understand which meta-programmes your clients, colleagues or staff use. Just like how one computer program controls the execution of a number of other programs, selecting which ones will run at which times and sending them the information they'll need in order to function properly, meta-programmes can be used to affect several aspects of a person's behaviour.

Because meta-programmes are deletion and distortion filters that adjust our generalisations (beliefs), we can predict the state of mind of virtually anyone if we know their meta-programmes. If you can predict your client's, colleague's or staff's internal states, you can easily know approximately what they are thinking and therefore how best to talk to them.

HOW YOU CAN USE META-PROGRAMMES

You can use your knowledge of meta-programmes to help you in all aspects of your life and work and facilitate your goals, such as

- ◢ **Achieving rapport:** Meta-programmes are another thing you can match and mirror to help people feel at ease with you.

- ◢ **Improving self-awareness:** If you are aware of your personal meta-programme preferences, you will have a better idea about the activities and career paths that will allow you to play to your strengths.

- ◢ **Recruiting the appropriate people for employment:** Every job has an ideal meta-programme profile. If you recruit people to match that profile, they will perform better in that role. You can even write job ads in a way that will attract the people you want and deter the people that won't be suited to the job.

- ◢ **Influencing and communicating:** You can use language that suits a person's meta-programmes in order to influence them and communicate with them in the way that it is easiest for them to understand.

- ◢ **Managing change:** Describing change in a way that is compatible with a person's meta-programme profiles will make it easier for them to accept and feel enthusiastic about changes, and avoid triggering knee-jerk resistance.

- ◢ **Improving sales:** You can help people reach a buying decision by presenting them with information in the style and sequence that works for their meta-programme filters.

HOW TO DETECT PEOPLE'S META-PROGRAMMES

Depending on the specific meta-programme, you can detect them from the words people use, the structure of their language patterns, the way they talk, the way they behave and their history; e.g., how frequently they have changed jobs.

There are several meta-programmes, but the six most powerful meta-programmes are:

- ◢ *Towards/Away From* (also known as Direction Filter or Motivation Direction)

- ◢ *General/Specific* (also known as Chunk Size Filter or Scope)

- ◢ *Proactive/Reactive* (also known as Action Filter or Motivation Level)

- ◢ *Internal/External* (also known as Frame of Reference Filter or Motivation Source)

- ◢ *Sameness/Difference* (also known as Relationship Filter and Motivation Decision Factors)

- ◢ *Options/Procedures* (also known as Reason Filter or Motivation Reason)

Towards/Away From (Direction Filter or Motivation Direction)

As human beings, we are motivated *towards* pleasure and *away from* pain. For example some people go to work to pay the lousy bills, some people go to work to buy a new car or take a holiday. Some people exercise and eat healthily because they want to move away from the health risks associated being sedentary and some people exercise because they want to go *towards* those 6-pack abs for the beach.

These are context dependent. For example, a sports person might be *away from* in his or her competitive career because the fear of failure is driving them to succeed in that area of their life. They might be very *towards* in their family life because they are happy with their spouse and children. They might be driven to take the best contract to provide a good school for their kids or a nice holiday for their family; i.e., *towards* pleasure.

There is no right or wrong meta-programme and you might be asking what that means. It means *everything* because if you're in sales, the way you promote your product might be opposite to the way that motivates your buyer. Imagine a fitness trainer promoting personal training to a perspective client. If he uses *away from* to talk about exercises and how it reduces risks of diabetes, cancer, cholesterol, etc., and the perspective client is *towards*, the information will go over the perspective client's head. The client's aim is to get into a new sexy dress or get the rippling abs for the beach. You need to use the meta-programme in each context that will resonate with the person with whom you are communicating.

I remember delivering some NLP Training at a gym where many of the trainers were very *towards*. One of the managers was very *away from*. I sat in a meeting to observe what was going on, to get to the bottom of the problem as to why there was a management–staff breakdown. I noticed that the *away from* manager was trying to use negativity to motivate the staff. He told them if they didn't pick up their game and find more clients, they would be out of a job. You can imagine the reaction of the trainers that were very *towards*. Many of them couldn't understand exactly what the manager was saying—some of them felt the message was personally targeted, some felt threatened, and I won't repeat what some trainers thought of the manager. Once I had ascertained the problem, just by changing the management style and providing more *towards* incentives, the whole atmosphere of the gym changed and so did the success of the organisation.

Working as a coach or manager, imagine how powerful it would be to understand your client's, staff's, or colleague's style of motivation. How much more powerfully you would connect and get your message across. Imagine what it could mean in your relationship to your family, kids, partner, or spouse.

I am sure you have had experiences when you attempted to deliver a message until you were blue in the face and all you got was a blank expression. It was almost like you were speaking Latin to an Eskimo. Getting your message across is just not going to happen. But, taking the time to be aware of a person's meta-programme can go a long way in effectively transmitting your message.

Whenever I deliver sales training to organisations, I always make sure they are aware of and understand the principles behind being motivated *away from* or *towards*. One of the exercises I get the staff to do is to think of a product they are looking to purchase. I have them work in pairs and one person tries to determine the other person's motivation for buying.

For example, one person (for this example her name is Anna) might say she is looking to buy a new car. The other person (for this example his name is Andrew) asks why Anna is looking to buy a new car and listens to the response to see if he can determine if Anna is a *towards* or an *away from* person. Sometimes it is worth noting the Anna may not indicate whether she is *away from* or *towards* on the first response.

For example, whenever I have worked in America, I have found that *generally* a person's first response might sounds *towards*, but when I dig deeper I realise it is actually *away from*. Suppose I asked some parents why they would like their son to go to Harvard university. The parents might answer, "Because we think it's a great university." That sounds very *towards*.

But if I asked why it was important for their child to go to a great university, the parents might say because when they were growing up their families struggled financially and couldn't afford to send their children to a great university. After they left home, these people had to settle for a less-impressive university and pay for it themselves. They had to spend years finding whatever work they could just to pay the school bills. They don't want their son to have to go through that. Now that sounds very *away from*. The reason for a statement all depends on a person's experiences and therefore their response is context dependent.

Some Tips

Extreme *towards* people will be gung-ho, and will overlook potential problems that can trip them up—think of stock market booms.

People who are very *away from* will be perceived as fault-finding and overly negative or cynical by their colleagues. They will lack direction unless given a problem to solve or a crisis to fix. They also will run out of motivation the further away they get from what they wanted to avoid (they might never lose that last 8 pounds) or as they get close to their professed goals, they may let them slide before they finally attain them.

Some of world's most powerful motivational speakers got to that pinnacle of success by being able to clearly create vivid pictures of what would happen to people if they didn't allow him or her to help them. Hundreds of the world's largest corporations have built their fortunes by pulling the mind strings of the population on the pain/pleasure meta-programme by advertising the pleasure their product will bring to you and the pain you will avoid if you buy it. Not sure about that? Just take a moment to think of some of the advertisements on TV, radio, and in magazines. (Advertisements for cleaning products often use a lot of *away from* imagery because nearly everybody wants to move away from dirt.)

◢ Exercise

Are you motivated *towards* goals, targets and what you desire, or *away from* problems and difficulties? Take a few moments to think about your responses. Remember, all meta-programmes are context-dependent. You may find that yourself to be strongly *towards* in one context and strongly *away from* in another.

How To Identify the Towards/Away From Pattern

Ask someone what they want in a job (or car, or relationship, or house). This will start to give you the person's values. For each value, you can ask, "Why is that important to you?"

The answers will be either *towards, away from,* or a mixture. Some values may be more *towards* or *away from* than others.

Keep asking, "Why is that important to you?" at least three times. The initial answer is likely to be coloured by the prevailing culture; e.g., in the US you are likely to get a *towards* answer at first so you need to go a bit deeper to find the person's real pattern.

Things To Watch For

Spoken language and body language will help you discern which meta-programme the person is using. Look out for concealed *away from* statements in language patterns. The *away from* is not explicitly mentioned, but it's there in the person's internal representations.

Towards **language:** People talking about what they want, what they would like to see, what they can get, achieve, the benefits.

Towards **body language:** Nodding, gestures indicating the vision they are moving towards, inclusive gestures.

Away from **language:** People talking about what they want to avoid, "yes, but", problems (including solving problems), pitfalls, avoiding, removing, "hang on a minute", comparative deletions, modal operators of impossibility, referring to target dates as "deadlines".

Away from **body language:** Dismissive or warding off gestures, shaking the head.

Yes, I've seen the entire spectrum of motivations. One person is motivated one way, another person the other. Obviously if someone is motivated very *towards*, then they are going to work towards certain positive outcomes. They might be working towards getting a new car, going on holiday, getting into shape. They might be working towards getting a pay raise so they can buy a new house. Ultimately the other end of the spectrum is someone who might we motivated *away from*. They work hard because they are afraid they might not be able to pay the bills and might end up living on the street. They might develop health issues if they don't exercise.

There is a wide spectrum of *towards* and *away from*. I'm not saying one is right or wrong, but I think it is really important to identify the meta-programme that people around you use, especially if you are a leader or coach. If you can understand what drives someone, then you can help motivate them.

Can you imagine someone who is very *towards* trying to motivate someone who is very *away from*? And vice versa? Suppose a *towards* senior executive of an organisation asks a staff member to deliver a report at a certain time. If the staff member is very *towards* and the executive talked about how the report could generate new business and improve the company, the staff member would be very excited and promise to get that report done in the time frame mentioned.

But what if the executive is very *away from*? He or she would talk about how if the report wasn't done, it could mean there would be dire consequences for the company and everyone would lose their job. That would cause the *towards* staff member a lot of stress and they might even walk away from the assignment.

If you want to get the most out of people you have to understand and identify with their motivational style. In that way you can talk to them in such a way that they will go the extra mile to get a report done on time or to finish any other task you have given them.

What Job Roles Suit a Towards/Away From Person

A *towards* pattern is useful in: visionary leaders, entrepreneurs, creative people and idea people. It's often found in change agents, coaches and NLP Practitioners.

An *away from* pattern is useful in: health and safety officers, process control, proof-reading, and maintenance engineers. It's often found in medicine, pharmacy, solicitors, accountants and civil service.

How to Influence and Manage the Towards/Away From Person

Towards: this is what we can achieve, this is what it will get you, benefits, results, achievement, winning, advantages, what you can have, just think about it!

If you are dealing with an extreme *towards* person, you may want to discuss the massive benefits of doing an occasional "mine sweep" to make sure the route to their goals stays clear of potential problems.

Away From: solve the problem, fix it, avoid, sort out, eliminate, this is what will happen unless we..., these will be the consequences if we don't do it.

If there are no immediate problems to motivate the *away from* person, ask them to look into the future to see the problems that they will encounter if they don't take action now.

◢ **Exercise**

On a piece of paper, write down 20 painful experiences that your customers or clients could experience if they don't own your product or use your service. Then write down 20 positive experiences your customers or clients will experience if they do use your product or service. The next time you meet with a client or potential customer, you will be prepared to connect on a level at which your client or potential customer processes information.

General/Specific (Chunk Size Filter or Scope)

Have you ever been in a conversation or a meeting with a group of people and amongst the group some of the people were very detail-oriented and specific when providing their input, while others were very straight-to-the-point and abstract?

Have you ever engaged in a telephone call with a client, colleague or staff and when you asked them a question they either gave you into a full-blown description of events or a general answer?

Have you ever gone in to work on a Monday and asked a colleague about their weekend and you got every specific detail of every event that happened? For example, "at approximately 10 am in the morning I walked to the paper shop, purchased a specific paper, and read this story. When I finished reading the paper, I took my car to the car wash and got chatting to an old friend of mine," and so forth. Or you might get an answer from another colleague, "It was a great weekend. I enjoyed it. Thanks."

Have you ever opened your emails on a Monday morning to find a reply from an email you sent the week before and it's bordering on a novel in length? Or read text on your mobile phone and it's either like a story with specific details or just a couple of words?

What level or chunk size of information are you comfortable with? The big picture or the details?

This meta-programme is about the level of the "Hierarchy of Ideas" at which the person is comfortable operating. A person at the *general* end of the spectrum will think in terms of abstract concepts and generalisations rather than specific details. When faced with too much detail they will feel overwhelmed or bored. A person at the *specific* end of the spectrum will feel more comfortable with facts, details and step-by-step sequences. Abstractions, and the big picture on its own, will feel vague and nebulous without more details and specific examples.

I was once doing some business coaching for a client. The arrangement was to see him weekly for a quick update, but as soon as I asked him how the week had gone, the session was drawing to a close by the time he had explained what had happened up to only mid-week. I realised pretty quick not to ask him how his weekend went.

Understanding he was a very specific person and time was of the essence, I asked him to fill in a diary of all the details of the week's progression. I would look at that for the details while we would focus purely on the action points in moving forward. This way the client felt he was providing me with as much detail as he thought necessary and we could still focus on the key issues in driving the business forward with the time we had.

How to Identify the General/Specific Pattern

This pattern will come out in any informal conversation. For example, you could ask a person what they are currently working on, or how their day has been. The *specific* person's answer will be in the form of a step-by-step narrative with lots of specific detail. They will use lots of qualifiers (adjectives and adverbs). If you interrupt them to ask a question, they may start at the beginning again or start where they left off after they have answered the question.

The *general* person's answer will be in the form of a summary. It may not be in a temporal sequence, but will give you what the speaker sees as the most important points first. This may seem like a random order to the listener.

What Job Roles Suit a General/Specific Person

Generally speaking, the higher the level of abstraction a person can handle, the higher they can go in an organisational hierarchy (the upper ranks of the army are even called "generals"). The ability to think strategically—in other words, to be able to work with high levels of abstraction—is usually essential for board-level roles. Having said that, people need to able to handle details to perform well at lower levels on their way up.

A *specific* focus is needed for quality control, proofreading, health and safety, and bookkeeping.

A *general* focus is needed for leadership and creative roles.

How to Influence and Manage the General/Specific Person

As with all the meta-programmes, you need to determine where the person is on the spectrum in order to communicate with them. If you need a *general* person to be more specific, or vice versa, start from where they are and use pacing and leading to help them move up or down the levels of abstraction.

General: give them the big picture, the overview, "the real issue is...", "in a nutshell". Calibrate if you notice they are getting bored or overwhelmed with detail.

Specific: use examples and sequences (first..., second...), give detail, exactly, specifically, precisely. Calibrate if you notice they are looking lost or if what you're saying is going over their head.

Proposals and reports often contain an executive summary (for *general* readers) and appendices with lots of detail and facts (for *specific* readers).

Proactive/Reactive (Action Filter or Motivation Level)

Have you ever been working in the office and a member of staff comes in and says, "we can all go home early" The *proactive* people in the office will have their coats on and are out the door before the sentence is finished. The *reactive* people will not move until they find out who has given permission and after that only when they are sure it really is OK to leave.

Have you ever given a set of instructions to a group of people or an individual? Do they take the initiative and leap into action, or do they prefer to analyse and wait for others? Any successful team has a combination of different personalities and characters. Balance is the key. For an individual it is important to be adaptable to different situations.

Proactive people are self-starters and do not wait for others before they act. They are focused on achieving results and may upset others in their single-mindedness in getting to where they want to be. If you had a business proposal and were asked to sign a contract, would you do it ASAP or would you sleep on it? If you signed it straight away, you were exhibiting a proactive pattern.

Reactive people won't act until they have analysed the situation or until other people prod them into action. Other people may get frustrated with their apparent inactivity. If you had a business proposal and were asked to sign a contract and you slept on it and discussed it with a few people, you were exhibiting a reactive pattern.

The difference is a *proactive* person does things without requiring additional information. A *reactive* person is incapable of moving until they have the right amount of information they need. Depending on the context (situation), there will be times when a balance between the two will be more useful.

For example, let's say someone phoned you up with a new job opportunity and it sounded appealing to you. If you had a high *proactive* tendency you might be sitting in the new position 6 months down the line thinking, "I am not happy in this job." However, if you were very *reactive*, you might dither until you had lost a great opportunity.

If you know this, you can make informed decisions about who would be most suited to a particular job. Never put a *proactive* person in a job that requires analysis or a lot of waiting around. They will be bored stiff and will find something to do even if it is detrimental. Don't let a *reactive* person go into sales, they would hate to be forced to "cold call" someone and will let golden opportunities pass by.

In order to achieve certain outcomes, it is beneficial for an individual or a team to function at both levels.

How to Identify the Proactive/Reactive Pattern

This pattern appears in language structure and body language.

Proactive language: Short, direct sentences, often with a "command" tonality on statements or even questions. Active verbs and verb patterns indicating an "at cause" mentality. Expects to be listened to. Needs to *act*.

Proactive body language: Generally fast. Fidgety, pencil-tapping, won't sit still for long periods (you will definitely notice this if you have a strongly *proactive* person in a meeting or training course).

Reactive language: Passive verbs, nominalisations, long sentences that tail off, verb patterns indicating an "at effect" mentality (things happen to them, others *make* them do things, lots of model operators of necessity). Conditional words like might, could, and would. May exhibit question tonality on non-question statements. A need to understand.

Reactive body language: Able to sit still for long periods. May seek lots of eye contact as if looking to others for approval or checking that they are being listened to.

What Job Roles Suit a Proactive/Reactive Person

A proactive pattern is useful for: sales people (outgoing sales), business owners, leaders.

Proactive people need to be given things to do, otherwise they become bored. If you are recruiting for a role needing a proactive pattern, you can screen out *reactive* people by requiring applicants to phone. Don't hire high *proactive* people for jobs requiring diplomacy or where consequences need thinking through

A *reactive* pattern is useful for: support desk, customer service, research and analysis, jobs which include long periods of waiting around. *Reactive* people need time to get their heads around a decision or to check how others feel about it. Don't hire them for roles requiring snap decisions.

Most job roles require a person to have a mixture of *proactive* and *reactive* abilities.

How to Influence and Manage the Proactive/Reactive Person

Proactive: use words such as "just" when talking about getting stuff done (as in "just do it"), make it happen, let's get on with it, jump in, you'll smash it. Or Richard Branson's motto: "Screw it, let's do it." Temper their belief that *they* make things happen. If you need to restrain them from jumping straight in, you can say "Just before we...", the "just" indicates that the delay will only be very short. Give *proactive* people ways to use their energy. If selling to them, give them a way of taking action or getting results straight away. If you have a strongly *proactive* person on a course or in a meeting, make sure the activities or meeting segments are short. Even one *proactive* person can disrupt things for others if they get bored and fidgety.

Reactive: use words that would indicate consideration must be taken into account; for example: as you consider, you could, we might, take as long as you need, circumstances are right, this is what you've been waiting for, everyone's doing it. Use Cialdini's "Social Proof" principle by giving examples of other people who have bought the product or are doing what you wanted them to do. If you want a *reactive* person to act, use wording that implies that they have had a period in which to consider and analyse: "Now that you've had a chance to think about it, there's no need to wait any longer."

Internal/External (Frame of Reference Filter or Motivation Source)

If you have an *internal frame of reference programme* (*internally-referenced*, you automatically know when you've done a good job and you will want to solve all your own problems. You rarely ask for advice from other people. You make decisions based on your own judgments, feelings and opinions.

If you have an *external frame of reference programme* (*externally-referenced*), you measure yourself against the feedback from other people. When faced with a challenge, you will seek facts, evidence, advice and opinions from other people and sources.

In a prior existence, I was responsible for a team of teachers who delivered home-based tutoring and learning. The job was pretty straightforward. All teachers were sent a timetable by the head teacher with the pupils' addresses and other logistical details, telling them when to go out and teach their designated lesson. The curriculum was set and agreed on at the start of the academic year.

In the afternoon, one of the teachers (let's call him Phil) would come back to the office and look for me or the head teacher, or anyone else who would listen, to check that he had done the right thing that day, even though he had been doing it for years and knew exactly what curriculum to deliver, had all the planning and a scheme of work to follow. At one time it used to frustrate me that I had to give Phil a pat on the back nearly every single day, especially when compared with John who just got on with the job and sometimes, okay, perhaps often, did not tell us about the changes that he had made during delivery of the curriculum. Occasionally we had to discuss those changes with John because they were important. The curriculum had to be right and we had to be sure that appropriate content had been delivered.

As soon as I reflected on the *internal* and *external* meta-programmes, all became clear. Phil had a very strong *externally-referenced* meta-programme; he needed feedback, he needed help in keeping on track; his way of deciding whether or not he had done a good job was to ask others.

John, on the other hand, had a strong *internally-referenced* meta-programme. He set his own standards, he was not very interested in feedback from other people, he was quite happy making decisions on his own and he was always right (even when he was wrong).

Once I knew that Phil needed daily reassurance, it took only a couple of minutes a day to keep him happy. Similarly, once we knew that John was changing parts of the curriculum, we needed to explain to him how important it was to make sure that when he made changes, the records of that change were accurate and samples taken appropriately. That kept him happy. An understanding of each man's meta-programme probably saved both of them their jobs—and me a lot of headaches.

Do you see yourself in either of these extremes? Do you see them in people you work with? Again, there is a spectrum and we can all exhibit tendencies throughout the spectrum, although we may well have an overall predisposition to operate closer to one end or the other.

Externally-referenced people need frequent feedback. If they don't get any from their boss, they will become apprehensive as the annual appraisal gets nearer, because they literally will not know how they have been doing.

How much feedback do you need? The *internally-referenced* person has internal standards that they use to assess how well they are doing, regardless of what anyone else says. The *externally-referenced* person actively needs feedback from others to stay motivated and confident that they are doing a good job.

How to Identify the Internal/External Pattern

This is a great interview question: simply ask "How do you know when you are doing a good job?"

Internal: "I just know", "I feel it", "my experience tells me", "I decide". They will refer to their own internal *evidence*.

External: "My manager/customers/colleagues tell me".

For people in between the two extremes, you will get a mixture of the two answers, plus references to objective external evidence; e.g., targets that were hit.

What Job Roles Suit a Internal/External Person

Internally-referenced people are good in back-office positions and those that require independent decision-making: leadership roles, technical specialists, the professions, creative artists.

Externally-referenced people are good in any front-line role: customer service, retail, travel, hospitality.

Usually people become more internally-referenced as they spend time in a role and build up a database of reference experiences to base their decisions on. Ideally, a person in a new role, or coming onto a training course (such as an NLP Practitioner course) will start out *externally referenced* and gradually become more *internally referenced* over time. This enables them to take on information in the early stages and become confident in applying what they have learned as they become more experienced.

How to Influence and Manage the Internal/External Person

Internal: as you know, only you can decide, you may want to think about..., this is just a suggestion, what do you want to happen?

External: people are saying, research shows, they're not happy, this is what you could do, I've noticed that the boss says.

A strongly *internally-referenced* manager in charge of a strongly *externally-referenced* person must remember to give them more feedback than they would themselves require. *Externally-referenced* people may take information or inquiries about the current state of some task as an instruction to do something about it, even if that's not what the inquirer intended.

Internally-referenced people treat instructions from their manager as just more information; they will act as and when they see fit. If you are their manager, ideally you will allow them to make their own decisions (or think they are making them, hence the use of influencing patterns such as, "only you can decide," that sets out the facts to point to a particular decision and the use of "as you know" before telling them something they don't know). Find out what motivates the *internally-referenced* person and see that they get it. Feedback will not have much impact on them.

If you have a strongly *internally-referenced* person on a training course, you may have to arrange an experience that demonstrates to them that they don't already know everything there is to know about what they are supposed to be learning.

One of my clients brought her son to do some sessions with me because he was at school and working towards getting into Eton. His mum told me that in order to get in he needed to achieve a percentile band in his subjects of 70%. In most subjects he was meeting the criteria, though in one subject he was not. He had scored 13% in a mock test, which worried the student because it brought his scores down considerably. After working out what his learning styles and meta-programmes were, I realised he was *externally-referenced* in that one subject. I set up a studying strategy which incorporated feedback. His mum said he scored 70% in a mock test only 3 weeks after I set up the new strategy.

Sameness/Difference (Relationship Filter and Motivation Decision Factors)

This pattern influences how we compare information. With *sameness* or matching, we search for what things or situations have in common. With *difference* or mismatching, we notice how things are dissimilar.

Have you ever come across the type of person who disagrees with you no matter what you say? You say a colour is purple and they insist it is lavender. Have you ever had a conversation with a client, colleague, or friend and they nod in agreement with everything you say, and tell you how they can relate to what you are saying?

Do you know the type of person who is always on the lookout for new things to do or new ways of doing current things? He or she may want to try a new restaurant every week, a new holiday destination every year, or are looking for new job opportunities. Have you ever known the type of person who will be in the same job, doing the same role, for many years? Who visits the same holiday destination every year, associates with the same friends, goes to their favourite restaurant on the same night every week and probably sits in the same spot? Whenever you suggest anything new they will probably look for similarities with previous experiences. If you suggest going to a new restaurant, they would ask how it compares to the one they attend regularly.

Let's explore how people react to change and how often they need change. There are four main groupings along the spectrum of *sameness* to *difference*. You can massively increase rapport with someone by noticing how they're making sense of the world on this spectrum.

Sameness: these people like things to stay the same and dislike or actively resist disruption. According to Rodger Bailey's LAB Profile (they will *accept* a major change every 10 years but only *initiate* change themselves, such as changing jobs, every 15 to 25 years.

Sameness with Exception: these people like things to stay the same, but with minor improvements or changes every so often. They like evolution rather than revolution. They need a major change every 5 to 7 years.

Sameness with Exception and Difference: these people are comfortable with both large and small changes, as long as the major changes are no more frequent than 3 to 4 years.

Difference: these people switch jobs, roles or assignments very frequently. They flourish in rapidly changing environments and quickly become bored in the absence of change.

How to Identify the Sameness/Difference Pattern

The classic question to identify *sameness* vs *difference* for a given context is (remember that as with any meta-programme, the degree of *sameness/difference* can change depending on the context), "What is the relationship between your work this year and last year?" or "What is the relationship between this job/house/whatever and the previous one?"

These are typical answers you might get from each of the four groupings in the pattern:

Sameness: will talk about similarities. "No change really—it's just the same as last year."

Sameness with Exception: will talk about similarities, but also mention some changes, often as comparisons. "I'm still doing pretty much the same thing, but I've been given a bit more responsibility and a new team member has joined." They will talk about how they got from there to here.

Sameness with Exception and Difference: may mention major changes and similarities, as well as using comparisons. "It's changed quite a lot since the merger. We're still expanding and we're getting better at responding to customer queries."

Difference: may not understand the question. "What do you mean, relationship?" Will talk about what's different and new. "It's completely changed—we're in a whole new ballgame." They will talk about how things are now, rather than how things got to be how they are.

What Job Roles Suit a Sameness/Difference Person

Sameness: roles that don't change are increasingly rare in the modern economy. In the past, this pattern would have suited administrative or clerical roles; now, people with a strong sameness pattern are likely to be viewed by managers as impediments to necessary change. Working with traditional crafts or in the backwaters of retail may be the last refuge for the sameness person.

Sameness with Exception: this is by far the largest category (65% according to Rodger Bailey). They will be comfortable in a role that changes gradually, where they can build on what has gone before.

Sameness with Exception and Difference: the same as for *sameness with exception*, but with the occasional major change as well, either in job role or employer/location.

Difference: the classic difference person is the management consultant, who takes on a new assignment every six months to a year. They get frustrated when people in the client organisations don't embrace change enthusiastically.

How to Influence and Manage the Sameness/Difference Person

Sameness: as usual, continuity, reliable, similar, the same, tradition, heritage.

Sameness with Exception: better, evolution, upgrade, development, improvement, the same except for...

Sameness with Difference and Exception: use a combination of elements from the *sameness with exception* (above) and the *difference* patterns (below).

Difference: revolutionary, new, paradigm shift, disruptor, unique, a whole new ballgame, totally different, new, a game-changer.

To help *sameness* and *sameness with exception* people to accept necessary changes, present the changes as small, evolutionary improvements that build on the best practice and successes of the past. The enthusiastic language of change advocates, "A revolution in how we do things! This is going to turn the whole business upside down!" will not resonate with the majority of any workforce outside the high-tech sector.

Instead, you can find similarities and parallels between the new system and the old, and present it as basically the same with a few small enhancements. This will enable *sameness* people to do what they've always done, but a bit easier and better.

Consider involving people in identifying which aspects of the current situation are working well and should be carried forward into the future to allay their fears of change (this is how the change method known as "Appreciative Inquiry" works).

When you are not able to give *difference* people the substantive change they need to stay interested, you can at least change things around by rearranging the office and moving desks every so often.

For example, John realised that he had a strong *difference* pattern and every few months he would become bored with his job and seek a change. Realising that this wasn't supporting other areas of his life, like being in a relationship, planning for holidays etc., he decided to accommodate his *difference* pattern within his personal and social life, and still stay focused on progress in his work environment. When the emotional signals of familiarity occurred he could recognise them and deal with them quickly.

Options/Procedures (Reason Filter or Motivation Reason)

Have you ever come across the type of person who can't seem to make up their mind? Whether it's buying a type of car, choosing a meal at a restaurant, or making a career choice?

Have you ever known the type of person who writes lists, ticks things off as they go along, and if any change is implemented to a process they are familiar with, they become lost?

How do you prefer to do your work? Do you look for alternatives and new ways of doing things, or do you prefer to follow the established procedures? Do you prefer to create new things or maintain existing ones?

Options people, as the name implies, prefer to keep their options open, sometimes to the point of being reluctant to commit to a decision in case they lose out. *Procedures* people like to have things settled and know where they stand. They like to complete and finish things.

Options people, when asked, "Why did you choose X,Y or Z?" will give you reasons why and their criteria for doing so. For instance, if you ask, "Why did you choose your current job?" they may answer, "I wanted to be close to my office and have to travel only 30 minutes to get to work so I could spend more time with the kids."

Procedures people, when asked, "Why did you choose X,Y or Z?" will tell you the story of how it came to be, (sort of the inevitability of the solution) rather than actually answering the why question. For instance, "I chose my new job because I was made redundant at my old one and had one month to find something new. I went to seven different interviews and the time was passing. In the end I had to take this one."

It is useful to consider these procedure filters as skills. Being able to design a procedure and then carry it out it is an effective way to operate. How much of your life do you give to routines? Where on the scale would you sit?

How to Identify the Options/Procedures Pattern

Generally the modal operators a person uses will give you a lot of their pattern. *Options* people use modal operators of possibility ("can", "could") while *procedures* people use a lot of modal operators of necessity ("must", "should", "ought", "needed to").

A good question to determine someone's *options/procedures* pattern is, "Why did you choose your current job (or house, or car, or whatever context you're eliciting the pattern for)?"

The *options* person will use a lot of values in their explanation. They will talk about what they chose to do and why it was important to them.

The *procedures* person will tell a story about *how* (rather than *why*) they came to be where they are. They talk about a sequence of events rather than choices, and don't mention their values.

Someone on the midpoint of the scale may tell you a story about how they got there, but also include references to the values or reasons why they made the choices they did.

What Job Roles Suit a Options/Procedures Person

Procedures people like to have instructions to follow and want to do things the right way, so they suit bureaucratic jobs, production environments, procedure-based areas of law like surveying, and professions like piloting where safety procedures are important.

Less obviously, sales people need a strong dose of *procedures* because success in sales is largely about following tried and tested procedures, again and again. Franchisees need to be procedures-oriented because franchises are all about following the instructions in the franchise manual.

Options people are reluctant to follow established procedures. Deep down they believe there is always a better way of doing things. They get bored before they reach completion.

They are good in roles where creativity is needed—designers and design engineers, management consultants, and entrepreneurs. They would much rather start their own business than buy a franchise.

Some jobs, such as training and teaching, need a balance of *options* and *procedures*. *Options* to be able to adapt in the moment and come up with creative ways of teaching things, and *procedures* to be able to stick to a successful format or follow statutory procedures where necessary.

Managers also need an *options/procedures* balance to be able to manage staff with either profile.

How to Influence and Manage the Options/Procedures Person

Options: improvements, possibilities, choice, reasons why, these are the options, a couple of alternatives

Find ways to allow *options* people to exercise their creativity. Get them to look at improvements to procedure or create something new.

Procedures: follow the procedure, first... then... and finally..., the right way, do it by the book, *n* steps to..., process, methodology.

Procedures people do well with clear guidelines when they get to complete the process. Procedures are not just step-by-step sequences, they can also incorporate decision points. The *procedures* person can cope with this, as long as the directions for what to do in a particular situation are clear.

If you are a salesperson trying to make a sale to this pattern, remember: *options* people are interested in alternatives, possibilities, and why they should buy something. *Procedures* people are concerned with how to use the product or service, and with going through the right steps to buy it.

USING WHAT YOU HAVE LEARNED ABOUT META-PROGRAMMES

By now you will have an understanding of how to identify people's intrinsic values and become familiar with those of your own. If you operate mainly at one end of any spectrum, you might reap the benefits in some situations and potentially feel the effects and disadvantages in others. If you can develop flexibility over all programmes, you will have the advantages with none of the disadvantages.

Meta-programmes help you understand how people sort and make sense of the world. They also help you understand your own values, beliefs and behaviours.

The mismatching of intrinsic values in business is a very common cause of misunderstanding, stress and conflict in life. When people speak of a personality clash, it is invariably a mismatch of values or misunderstanding of meta-programmes. For example, many relationships, whether it be in business or life, break down because of a mismatch of a meta-programme. A classic example is the mismatch of *in-time* and *through-time* programmes in which one person places a high priority on punctuality and the other shows no sense of urgency. The *through-time* person feels devalued and frustrated when they are late, while the *in-time* person wonders what all the fuss is about. It's repetition and interplay of various patterns that eventually causes relationship breakdowns.

Meta-programmes are unconscious, so when you're involved with activities that go against them, you feel the emotional warning signal. You probably find yourself saying things like:

- ▲ Why am I always late for meetings?
- ▲ Why is John always so organised and I leave things until the last minute?
- ▲ I hate my job; though I will stay, as I am not sure how I will find a new one.
- ▲ Why do I never get things done?
- ▲ I can never make up my mind.
- ▲ I don't feel appreciated at work. I work so hard; I don't even get a thanks.

ARE YOUR META-PROGRAMMES HOLDING YOU BACK?

When you know someone's meta-programmes, you can more easily understand, predict and influence their behaviour. In order to communicate in an efficient manner as a coach, manager or leader, you must understand what meta-programmes your clients, colleagues or staff use. Because meta-programmes are deletion and distortion filters that adjust our generalisations (beliefs), we can predict the states of mind of virtually anyone we talk to if we know their meta-programmes. If you can predict someone's internal states, you can easily know approximately what they are thinking and therefore how best to talk to them.

By understanding our own meta-programmes, we can change processes and strategies that aren't working for us. By making a conscious choice and directing awareness to what we normally delete, we can adapt to a different style.

◢ **Exercises**

Use these exercises to help you identify any patterns that may be a cause of conflict for you.

1. Identify and write down a conflict you have had that was caused by an intrinsic value.

   _____

   _____

2. From the meta-programme descriptions, choose those in which you consider yourself to be predominantly at one end of the scale. Write the name of the meta-programmes below.

   Programme: _____

   Programme: _____

   Programme: _____

3. Pick a situation in which you experienced conflict with another person or frustration with a task or responsibility.

   Situation: _____

Consider the role that you played in this situation and then ask yourself which of the meta-programmes that you identified in step 2 was responsible for the conflict. Imagine how it might change if you were to function at the opposite end of the scale.

Take your time to think this through carefully. Acting so differently may feel awkward, although this is merely a sign you have begun to develop your emotional flexibility.

ADAPTING YOUR INTRINSIC VALUES TO GIVE YOU MORE CHOICE

An awareness of your intrinsic values is very often enough to create change. Sometimes, however, awareness is not enough and circumstances may suggest that a change in behaviour could be beneficial. As the majority of behaviour is habitual, the challenge lies in breaking the old habits and developing new ones by repetition.

How you respond to experiences will depend on the nature of your values. If you once trusted someone and were let down, you may decide never to trust again, decide that any future trust will have conditions attached, or you may retain your belief in trusting and hope one day this person will also realise that. Each of these reactions has a very different underpinning intrinsic value that results from the meaning you have accrued from your life experiences.

For example, Mike had an *away from* motivation pattern and had spent many years making decisions based on what he wanted to avoid. He stayed in the same job for more than 20 years, not because he enjoyed it—he actually disliked it—but to avoid the insecurity of being jobless. He survived by avoiding any situation that he found uncomfortable, including meetings with other managers and staff.

Mike's very powerful *away from* habit of avoiding difficult situations brought with it a great deal of stress. Once he was given a little help to change the habit, he went on to pursue a more fulfilling and engaging career, feeling a lot better about himself and much happier.

If you have developed a strong habit of behaving in a certain way, it may feel strange acting in the opposite way; e.g., introducing differences when you are reluctant to change. You may not know how to act differently and find the change awkward and unnatural.

This in itself will create an emotional warning signal, a feeling something is not right, and you may want to revert to your more usual behaviour. If this happens, remind yourself why you want to change. A technique I use with my clients is having them wear an elastic band around their wrist and snapping it against their skin whenever they have an emotional warning signal to remind them to get out of a particular mindset.

Think of your emotions as a signal that you are making a transition from old habits to new ones and this will help you achieve flexibility as a person.

Listen to language patterns, particularly words such as, "must, should, need". These words can be limiting. Are the things you consider important really important? What if you were to relax your must, should, need patterns? What new possibilities might be created if you were to drop your insistence on having things a certain, familiar, comfortable way?

Developing a new habit is just a matter of repetition. The more often you act in a different way, the sooner the new habit will develop.

Remember that people use a blend of meta-programmes. It's not this or that, it's a *spectrum* of possibilities. They aren't a tool for stereo-typing or pigeon-holing. They are a tool for understanding how or why people behave the way they do and adapting your behaviour to improve communication when dealing with people whose meta-programmes are different from yours.

We have looked at individual meta-programmes and the impact they have on behavioural patterns and how we can identify specific meta-programmes in order to communicate and understand clients, colleagues, and staff. It is also possible that some people have a combination of meta-programmes, which can create extreme behaviours or balance each other out. Let's explore some combinations and the affect they can have on people's behavioural patterns.

Away From plus External Reference Combination

This combination in a given context could result in low self-esteem as the person focuses their attention on negative consequences. The *away from* meta-programme not only affects perception and thinking, it also affects *memory* and *imagination*. A person who is using this meta-programme may have difficulty remembering positive experiences, despite the fact that many good things did occur, and instead select from all their past experiences only those which were negative. This constructs a life history that presents as a very sad or unsatisfactory story. Based on this, they probably expect negative events to occur in the future. They externally focus their attention on negative feedback and ignore or make excuses for positive comments.

Towards plus General Combination

At a corporate board retreat, the participants might get creative about the company's future direction, products or organisation but do not fully vet the ideas. In such cases, the executives may return to their offices and issue directives that make little or no business sense and insist that employees execute them. If the employees make rational objections to the new plans, they may be told, somewhat ominously, that they are not "thinking positive" enough. While the ideas may be exciting, if somewhat abstract, without any concrete plan to execute them, working out the details can be a struggle.

On an NLP sales training course I delivered a few years ago, I set an exercise that asked individuals to sell an object or an idea to a partner who had previously stated that, "this was the one thing in the world that they would never buy."

"David" was completely stuck. His partner had stated adamantly that he would never buy a certain team's football jersey. No matter what David tried, he failed for 35 minutes to get anywhere near a sale.

Through a conversational elicitation, I noticed that the partner had an internal *towards* meta-programme. I suggested to David that instead of just trying to sell the jersey, he should mention to his partner that buying the jersey would ensure the donation of a substantial amount of money to his favourite charity and that there would be positive benefits from his donation. David bought the idea, although somewhat reluctantly. He said it was a fabricated, underhanded approach. He was right; it was. However it made the point, and the sale.

This is how we sell effectively. Think about the buyers' motivation and give them a reason to buy that resonates with them. Present ideas that will make them aware of the value that buying this product or service will create for them.

Even if we hate the thought of selling and cannot bear to think of ourselves as salespeople, the real truth is that selling is one of the basic skills every one of us is born with. It is something that, if we thought clearly about what we do, we would notice ourselves doing every day, every time we set about influencing or persuading someone to take on an idea we may have, or to do something with or for us!

Using More than Just One Meta-Programme

You can often communicate more effectively when you use several meta-programmes together. Imagine, for example, a *general, towards, proactive* and *internally-referenced* boss and a *specific, away from, reactive* and *externally-referenced* employee. What issues are they likely to face? Misunderstandings and strong frustration on both sides spring to mind.

The boss might feel that this employee is unable to see the bigger picture, is not proactive enough, requires too much feedback, and focuses more on fire fighting than on important priorities. The employee, on the other hand, might experience confusion as to the communication of the goal, and be concerned about their boss not evaluating potential pitfalls before acting and about their lack of follow through. They might also feel unheard when providing feedback.

One of my business clients was running several successful businesses and had a disagreement with one of the managers at a particular store. I attended the meeting between my client, the manager and other members of the staff. I talked to my client about what outcome he wanted and what proposals he could make that would be mutually beneficial to both parties as a result of the meeting. When my client put some of his proposals to the manager, she rejected them, saying she was fed up with the underperforming staff and didn't want to take responsibility for other peoples inadequacies. She said that certain members of staff needed to work harder and to stop losing customers.

My client responded that everyone was committed to finding a resolution and, as the manager was a valued member of the team, he wanted her to be happy and enjoy coming into work. The manager said she didn't give enough of a damn about whether she was wanted in the company, or about anyone else for that matter, to be happy at work. And so the meeting continued going around in circles.

It became apparent to me that the manager was very *away from, internally referenced,* and *procedure* orientated. She didn't buy into anything that was being said unless she was given time to process the information in her own way. She felt that only she had the correct procedure to manage this situation in the business.

My client was very *towards, general*, and in other ways was almost at the opposite end of the spectrum of the manager. The conflict between their meta-programmes did not foster the perfect work environment for my client and the manager.

Things got a little bit heated and I suggested a time out for everyone to gather their thoughts. It was during that time when I had a discussion with my client and suggested he change his tack. After all, this was a good, loyal, effective manager who had a hard work ethic, though she had hit a point in which she was not performing at her best. She was considering leaving the company or stepping down from her role. My client wanted to get his manager back on track, wanted to find a way to get through to her.

After giving him some pointers in regards to the manager's meta-programmes, my client changed his method of communicating. When the meeting recommenced, my client went on to say to the manager, "Think about what I am about to say. Make up your own mind (*internally referenced*) while you think of your decision. Think about what you stand to lose (*away from*) and all the hard work you have put in over time. Just think about it (*internally referenced*) before you decide what you want to do."

The manager left the meeting and went outside for a short walk. When she came back, she said, "I want to understand how to deliver the process and manage it effectively. I need a bit of help with some of the staff who have lost direction." She was enthusiastic that all this could be done.

What was the turning point? It was when my client changed his delivery to the manager's preferred meta-programmes in this context. The key was in my client becoming aware of his manager's meta-programmes and having the flexibility to adapt to them.

There are two primary ways to change meta-programmes:

1. Use SEE (significant emotional events). For example, if you were brought up in an environment in which family, friends and people continuously moved *away from*, this could influence your thinking and your behaviours to a point where you sabotaged relationship opportunities because of the fear of getting hurt, or lost a great job

opportunity because the organisation was looking for someone who was a visionary of extraordinary possibilities.

But if you were at the other end of the spectrum and you did move towards endless possibilities, you might still not get the job because you were also *proactive* and as a result did not take the time to consider the repercussions of your actions.

You may consider re-evaluating your thinking, and how it could affect your approach and see things the next time.

2. The other way is by consciously deciding to change. If you become aware of what meta-programmes you are running and a make conscious decisions to change, you might decide you have had enough of moving *away from* pain, and you want to work *towards* pleasure, or you want a combination of both so that can you have the best chance of achieving a positive outcome.

◢ KEY POINTS

Meta-programmes can be applied to participants in mediation to establish the key traits of each party before engaging in the conciliation process. Other business applications include:

◢ career selection,

◢ recruitment,

◢ development and motivation of staff,

◢ changing management,

◢ creation of powerful teams,

◢ teamwork,

◢ negotiation,

◢ target marketing,

◢ effective promotion and presentation materials,

◢ increasing customer satisfaction and conversion rates, and

◢ networking.

Meta-programmes also have a much wider relevance if they allow for increased rapport and improved communication in all areas of life, from day-to-day personal relationships to business, education, coaching, and managing. Like everything else in this book, meta-programmes should be used *towards* in any way you think applicable to assist you in achieving a positive outcome.

Wouldn't it be helpful to understand what motivates a person and how they prefer to work; i.e., what sparks their interest, how they communicate, make decisions and connect with others, and what persuades them to use your services? Meta-programmes provide an insight into a person's mental maps and can improve our interpersonal relationships at work, at home and in business.

5. Logical Levels

"The problems of today can only be solved at a
higher level of thinking than that which created them"
—Albert Einstein

I was working for a football club as a performance coach overseeing various different departments to monitor the club's performance. One department I was overseeing was in the under 9s to under 16s school of excellence in which young people develop their skills until they are offered what we call an apprenticeship. Beyond that they can get a professional contract.

The team I was working for had had mixed fortunes for a number of years. One of the areas in which I thought big changes could be implemented that would improve their fortunes was to produce young players that the organisation could apprentice to other clubs. If that happened, it would generate money for the organisation.

I knew I had to implement these new programmes and a new structure, and fast, but first I had to find out what was wrong. So I interviewed the coaches working with the under 9s and under 16s to assess the performance programme, and there I found apathy bordering on lethargy.

I asked some of the coaches what they thought about their job. To my dismay, certain coaches said that if the organisation was only going to pay them a small amount for doing their job, then the kind of work they were getting was what they could expect. I couldn't believe what I was hearing! These coaches had fantastic opportunities to work with young people, very talented young footballers, and because they felt they weren't getting paid as much as they wanted to receive, they were only going to put in so much effort and do an inadequate job.

I'm not saying the club should or shouldn't have paid these people any more or any less. I'm not saying that the pay scale was right or wrong. What I am saying there was nothing stopping these coaches from doing their job to the best of their ability. It's really important that if we take a job, we always do that job to the very best of our ability. Our job performance starts from within. I know pay is a massive incentive to some people, but going out there and giving it their best shot is probably one of the best rewards they could have for themselves and anybody else.

◢ IS YOUR PURPOSE CRYSTAL CLEAR?

In all situations, you have an intention. Often this is unconscious; you engage with other people or undertake tasks without thinking what you want to achieve. For example, what is your intention when having a conversation with someone at work? Is it to inform, gain support, satisfy your need to be heard, seek attention, boredom, or something else?

What is your intention when starting a business? Seeking a job? Choosing a new career? Is it to leave behind a stressful job? Are you seeking new aspirations? Are you bored of the position you're in? Are you looking to earn more money? Be your own boss?

If your intention is unclear, you run the risk of behaving in a way that will sabotage your best efforts and leave you feeling dissatisfied. A classic example of this is when someone is feeling bad about his or her life and decides to move to a different city or country to make a fresh start. At a deep level, the intention is to remove the bad feeling that has grown over time. The same applies to leaving or changing jobs, and many of the other things people change in life.

But, what often happens is that the new life follows exactly the same patterns of events as the previous one.

Having a clear sense of purpose will enable you to make a conscious choice about how you approach situations. It will bring your deepest intentions to surface and determine the role you play in pursuit of your purpose. For example, I know many people who like the idea of doing things, but they don't actually want to put in the work necessary to do it. They like the idea of being a pop star because they think it will bring them fame and fortune, but they don't like the idea of working hard, going on tour, learning to play an instrument, work on their singing, or start out by playing to potential audiences of only a few people.

The logical level models we are going to look at are useful for understanding change in a person, a team or a company. You can examine any problem or proposed change in terms of these different levels. Some people divide the levels into two categories: the lower levels, which are environment, behaviour, and capabilities, and the higher levels, which are beliefs and values, identity, and spirituality (purpose).

The logical levels model can assist you in making change at the higher levels or can help to ensure that your goals are aligned at all levels. Once this happens, your goals in life often become clear and are obtained effortlessly.

LOGICAL LEVELS MODEL

Have you or anyone you know made changes in life in order to make things better? Maybe by purchasing a new sports car or new clothes? By finding a new job? By socialising in a different area? By losing weight and keeping it off? By overcoming habits that were unhealthy physically or emotionally and sticking with the new behaviour? These could be thought of as long-term changes.

Have you ever watched a TV programme in which people were taught new techniques, such as dating techniques to find a partner, but they found the techniques frustrating or difficult and returned to their old behaviour? Perhaps someone was taught to cook or to eat a healthier diet but it wasn't long before they were eating fast food again. Maybe someone had cosmetic surgery and had a boost of motivation and confidence for a short period of time, but eventually went back to square one. These could be thought of as short-term changes.

I remember watching an interesting and fantastic TV programme with the famous UK chef, Jamie Oliver. He had gone to an area of deprivation, an old mining town, and the economy in that town was in transition. The rate of obesity, cardiovascular and heart disease were quite high. The idea for going there was to teach people how to cook. He showed them these weird and wonderful recipes. He helped a lot of people to cook, make better meals and eat healthier.

All the people in that town enjoyed it. Jamie Oliver was enjoying it. As long as he was there, the people followed this new programme and it was working really well. Then he went away for three months and came back. Do you think that the people of the town had carried on with this new programme? No, they did not.

I watched him have a conversation with a woman who he had taught to cook. He asked why she hadn't kept cooking? I thought he was very diplomatic. The woman said, "Well it's alright for you, Jamie. You're very well off, you can afford to buy what you want, but we can't." I thought maybe she had a point until she said that it was easier for her to give her kids £20.00 to go eat at a local chip shop than to cook for them. I was astonished. In my view £20.00 gets you a good number of bits and pieces at a store. But that's not where she wanted to spend it. Ultimately, it really came down to an issue of identity and beliefs.

As long as your identity and beliefs don't conform to a new behavioural change, regardless of your capabilities, you won't carry on doing it. You will make only a short-term change. This programme was a classic example.

As human beings we are deeply driven by our sense of identity, of who we are. "**I**" is a capital letter, denoting the importance we place on our sense of individual self. As Descartes said, "I think, therefore I am." Many social theories are based on creating or preserving our sense of identity.

If we lost our job, it would not be just the loss of money (affecting our sense of control) that hurt us, but also the loss of relationships and feelings of being outside the company with which we identified ourselves for so long.

I once worked with a recently retired director of a company. He had an issue with overeating. During the consultation he broke down in tears when he realised he was overeating to compensate for his loss of identity. He was no longer the director of a company and was struggling to find his place in the world again.

IDENTITY FORMATION

The sense of identity appears early in life as the infant begins to separate itself from the mother in what they previously viewed as an undifferentiated unit. A mirror image of themselves can provide the sudden shock of realising that they are separate beings.

Young children typically cling to a single teddy bear, toy or doll, through which they know their own identity. When this *transition object*, so called by psychoanalyst Donald Winnicott, is removed, a part of their identity is lost, causing distress and tears. This pattern continues through our lives as we identify with our possessions and the things around us and feel bad when they are changed or lost.

One of my clients, who had a successful career in modelling, was coming to the end of her career. She was suffering from anxiety, panic attacks, feeling down, uncertainty and apprehension. All her working career she had been judged on her appearance and this seemed to spill into her personal life. She said if she went out and someone made a comment about her appearance, it would stay with her for days, she would analyse it, it would affect her mind set.

After doing a couple of sessions with her, I asked the following question. "Who are you?" She looked at me with a blank expression and said she couldn't answer it. She emailed me a few days later saying she was still struggling to answer the question.

How we define who we are affects our behaviour. For example, if you're a doctor and you keep the same identity when you go home to your family after work, you will probably diagnose your family. It was the same for the model. After a few weeks she finally told me she did not know who she was anymore. She was lost and didn't know what to do. She eventually did get her life back together and went into a different career.

I told her that the key step in moving forward is to not be hung up about who you think you might or might not be. Who you *want to be* is the key.

◢ **Exercise**

Take 10 minutes to do the following exercise. Choose an area of your professional or personal life in order to answer the questions (e.g., your job or your role as a parent).

Level	Information
Spirit (Purpose)	What am I here for? What am I part of that is greater than myself?
Identity	Who am I? How do I define who I am?
Values and Beliefs	What is important to me? What do I expect (in a given situation)?
Capabilities	What do I know how to do? What skills do I have?
Behaviour	What am I doing?
Environment	Where am I?

HOW THE LEVELS WORK

To gain an appreciation of how these logical levels work, assume it is 9 am and you are at your place of work (environment). If you don't want to be there, then you need to change your behaviour. There are several possible choices. You could walk out. You could do cartwheels over to and out the door. You could start yelling and screaming (maybe in the hopes that someone will take you out of the building), etc.

The behaviour you select depends on your capabilities and strategies. If you are capable of performing cartwheels, then this is certainly a possibility. On the other hand, your strategy may be to have someone help you to leave (by you yelling and screaming). Or, if you really don't want to work there and need some source of income, your strategy might be to become ill so that you have a medical excuse and can go on long-term disability. Do you know anyone who has done this last behaviour—consciously or unconsciously?

The capability and strategy you choose will depend on your beliefs and values. If you believe that you can easily get another job to support your family, then becoming ill is not a choice for you but getting a new job is.

Your beliefs and values are determined by your identity. If you see yourself as a successful person then it is very possible that you would hold the belief that you can easily get another job or even create a business of your own.

Your identity is dependent on your purpose in life; i.e., the affect you wish to have on your community, etc.

This is a useful model for understanding change in a person, a team or a company. You can examine any problem or proposed change in terms of these different levels. Generally speaking, higher levels have more *leverage* than lower levels. In order to permanently solve a problem, you generally have to make changes at least one level higher than the level at which the symptoms show up.

UNDERSTANDING LOGICAL LEVELS IN BUSINESS

Assume it is 10 am on a Monday morning and you are with your work colleagues for a scheduled meeting in your office (environment). You have been given a new role and you feel it's a demotion because you have been stripped of certain responsibilities. Some possible response choices are: you could go up to boss and ask why, you could tell one of your work colleges how the boss has got it wrong, or you could start shouting and acting silly with the hope you will grab the boss's attention and be called into the office.

The behaviour you select depends on your capabilities and strategies. If you're confident of these, approaching the boss and asking what may have been behind decision could work for you. If you're not that confident, you could tell one of your colleagues how the boss has got it wrong or you might start screaming and acting silly to grab the boss's attention, who then calls you into the office and you ask to leave the company.

The capability and strategy you choose will depend on your beliefs and values. If you believe that you are an important part of the company, a good performer and have a lot to offer the company when you get the opportunity to adapt to your new role, then you would more than likely go up to the boss and ask him or her about the decision to change your role. If you felt you were left out because your ability or your boss's ability to understand the company strategy was inadequate (even without asking if this is so) you may tell your colleagues what a ridiculous decision it was and look for an exit strategy.

Your identity is dependent on your purpose in the company—the contribution or positive impact that you wish to have on your company—and how you define who you are.

◢ Exercises

Write down the answer to the following questions:

1. Who are you?

   In life, you have different personas, which are adaptable to different situations. For example, the way you are at work may be different from how you are with your family and your friends. You may spilt your time between being a parent, partner, the main bread winner, manager of a company, football coach, a leader, teacher, or any number of combination of roles.

   What is important is not the label for your role, it is how you define your role, because that is what has an impact on your results. The manager who defines their role as a taskmaster, a disciplinarian and controller will elicit a different response from their team than the manager who defines their role as a people developer, leader, and facilitator. How we define our role will elicit very different behavioural results from the people we associate with.

2. What values and beliefs do you hold?

   If you lead by example, you will probably have strong values relating to taking responsibility and ensuring you get the best out of your colleagues and associates around you.

   A leader who believes in getting the best out of people will have strong values concerning trust and potential of the team. A trainer creating a positive learning environment will value discovery, exploration and creativity.

These values will be supported by any number of beliefs. The nature of a belief causes you to focus on your values and proves the belief to be true. So, whatever you believe to be true, you will seek evidence to prove it and ignore the evidence to the contrary. That is why it is important to make sure your beliefs are empowering you to achieve the results you desire. For example, a manager with a belief that his team is inadequate or staff who believe the manager is inadequate, will continue to reinforce any difficulties the team is facing. On the other hand a manager who believes his staff has potential or staff who believe the manager has potential will find a way to realise it and will undoubtedly achieve better results.

3. Are you limiting your true capability?

Your values and beliefs have a direct impact on your capability. Quite simply, if you believe that you can do something, then you will find a way of doing so. If you believe that you can't do something, then you won't bother to look for a way. Empowering beliefs unlock capability and limiting beliefs act as a barrier.

Limiting beliefs stop you from putting the effort into things. It is like the kaleidoscope is stuck in the same pattern and although you have the power to change it, you refrain from doing so because you are either unaware or unsure of the consequences. Once you believe it is not possible to change something, you will find every excuse to make this true.

Think of people who stay in a job they don't like for several years and do not do anything to change other than moan, be miserable, and go through the daily motions. They use every excuse as to why they are stuck in the job: their education, upbringing, opportunities and so forth. You only have to look around you to find plenty of examples of people who use every excuse for not changing aspects of their life.

On the other end of the spectrum there are examples of many people who, against all odds, have gone on to achieve great things because of the power of their belief. Values and beliefs work together. If you value something enough, you will generate a belief that is possible to achieve it and put your energy into finding a way to do so.

For example, Mike opted out of taking a promotion at work, saying he wasn't up to the new tasks. He explained how at school his careers teacher had encouraged him to make the most of his limitations by staying in a career that he could master and therefore become valuable to the company. Mike followed this advice and took a clerical job; he worked at it for 9 years. He liked it at first though began to dislike it after a period of time.

Mike had been offered a couple of promotions and had an opportunity to become an assistant manager. While Mike was discussing his current role with me, it became apparent he was doing many of the duties of an assistant manager already because of his experience and understanding of the company. He had actually even acted as an interim assistant manager on a few occasions and received praise for his work.

Despite this praise, Mike maintained the belief he could not fulfil the role of assistant manager on a permanent basis even though he enjoyed doing it. He decided to withdraw from the opportunity to take on the new role because of Mike's acceptance of his teacher's limiting belief. Mike did not live up to his natural ability in this area for many years.

4. Is your behaviour aligned with your thinking?

Your behaviour is a result of the way you have organised your thinking at each of the preceding three levels. Once

Mike was able to change his belief about his capability to sustain the role of assistant manager, it opened up a whole new range of activities for him. He began to implement and assist in developing strategies for a more efficient work environment. He began coordinating programmes, using his initiative to generate and implement new ideas and lead by example.

Some aspects of your behaviour will be working well for you, other aspects will not. Once behaviour becomes a habit, it is almost undetectable by you, until someone points it out.

Which parts of your behaviour are no longer of use to you? What emotional warning signals are you feeling? What would happen if you changed your perspective even slightly?

5. Are you having an impact on your environment?

The way you organise your thinking on the preceding four levels will determine the impact you have on your physical environment. Limiting beliefs and unclear purpose creates stress.

The blame for stress is often placed on external factors in the environment. That moves the focus away from the self and in doing so takes away your power to influence the outcome. With empowering beliefs and a strong sense of purpose, you are likely to take responsibility for changing your environment. Even unconsciously, you are likely to have a positive impact.

Often you may believe it is the environment that is causing you some stress and is sounding your emotional warning signals. The stronger the limiting beliefs about your capability, the more likely it is that although you may recognise what is wrong, you will do nothing positive to create change. People who change things believe that they can.

The first step towards taking control is to identify the level at which the emotions are sending warning signals.

I once worked with someone who regularly changed jobs for one reason or another. Eventually he was stuck in a position for more than a couple of years. He was finding it hard to get along with his colleagues at work, was becoming desperately unhappy and feeling more and more isolated. He blamed the culture in the organisation for his not being able to fit in. Once I encouraged him to reflect on his jobs with other companies, he realised this was how he reacted to every company at which he had worked. He admitted that the way he was feeling had nothing to do with the company he was working for; he was merely shifting responsibility for how he was feeling on to the place he was working at.

The real problem was that he was not being assertive in the work environment. Fortunately we were able to identify this. He became familiar with his pattern and learned strategies to express assertiveness which led to him becoming more confident and happier.

6. Are you aligned with your purpose?

Sometimes a change in behaviour does not follow a change in thinking. Have you ever been in a position where you have done something that you didn't want to do? Perhaps you did it to please someone and then felt you had done yourself a disservice. Maybe you made a decision to start a new business or change jobs, though when it came to developing a business plan, doing market research or understanding the criteria of your new position, you let yourself down and reverted back to your old habits of going through the motions.

It's at times like these that you feel the emotional warning signals and misalignment. In NLP, this state of misalignment, or incongruence, results in behaviour that doesn't fit with other levels. Deep inside you want to act a certain way, but when the time comes you resist the inner urge. You tell yourself, "Not this time, maybe next time." That is incongruence and is not something success thrives on.

Being successful in business requires congruence, which means the alignment of all levels—from knowing who you are to being aligned with your purpose. Only then you can affect your environment in the way you really want.

One of the key aspects of a successful business is when members of the team are all congruent, focused, positive and working from a good place of mind and body. A business which is incongruent in its actions is like a rudderless ship. It fosters an insecure environment, lacking in confidence and clarity.

When you analyse all of your best work and when you have been at your most successful, chances are it has been when you were balanced and confident.

LOOK BELOW THE SURFACE

Like attracts like. In the same way that similar thoughts congregate, so do people. If you're pessimistic, you will attract pessimistic people, and positive people will avoid you. Cynical people keep each other company and strengthen their cynical attitude. Any lack of self-belief and feelings of incongruence are likely to send off signals that others may interpret as you being unreliable, irrational or uncentred. As a consequence they may judge you as ineffective.

If you decide to be negative, you will be. But, if you gain the skills to help people's lives, those who need you will find you. That's how life works—it will bring you what you express with your whole being. The key message here is that *whatever energy are you giving off will determine who and what you are attracting.*

In a work environment you often hear people being referred to as arrogant, hard to work with and useless. You also hear people being referred to as excellent, fantastic and efficient. These are all interpretations of the energy the person is giving off and how they communicate. Both may be true or not true, but as soon as you have interpreted another person's behaviour you have also chosen to relate to them with that judgement in mind. The real truth lies beneath the kaleidoscope of their thinking.

What you may pick up as a misalignment between levels is actually the result of the unconscious emotional warning signals this person is experiencing. The key to changing the way you relate to someone is to develop a curiosity about what is causing them to behave in such a way, rather than to interpret the behaviour you see. Then you reduce your chances of falling into the trap of reacting according to a misinterpretation and increase the likelihood that you will begin to understand the person and communicate more effectively.

Over years of working with many people in business who aren't making the progress they would like, I have found that what they have in common when they think about the problem they are living with is a lack of direction or incongruence. When we discuss this, what they discover is how one frustration or problem is linked to another. Cluttered thinking, lack of confidence and low self-esteem can be linked to a fear of public speaking.

In business we will encounter many different types of situations. Some managers do not make the progress they want with their team, some new businesses struggle to get off the ground, some directors are petrified at the thought of giving a presentation to the board. There are professionals who are so snowed under with tasks that they are stressed and losing sleep, workers who are not meeting their employer's expectations of performance, people with obsessions, fears, anger, frustration and lack of motivation. We meet people from all walks of life who are limiting their potential to succeed and be brilliant in all types of situations because they are experiencing incongruence.

When people are under stress because of difficulties arising at work, the mind has the ability to put any problems they are experiencing behind a veil. Doing so allows the person to fool themselves into thinking everything is okay. However, when they mask negativity, they also mask positive attributes such as energy, focus and clarity. You can create a smokescreen for your thought processes for only so long. Then, something has got to give.

What gives may be your behaviour. When you are consistently working flat out to meet deadlines, stress accumulates in your body. You may experience physiological changes due to the mind–body link. You may become tense and your breathing erratic. Your body will react to whatever changes your mind goes through and vice versa.

Your body will also give signals to other people. Even though you may be able to create a smoke screen and veil your problems in your own mind, others will intuitively know that something is incongruent. The only way to deal with this is to remove the veil of your thinking and create a change.

ALIGNING LOGICAL LEVELS FOR PERSONAL CONGRUENCE

For many of us, the logical levels operate outside of our conscious awareness. Whether we are aware of them or not, they have a significant influence over the quality of our lives. By using logical levels consciously, it can help us to identify when conflicts exist professionally or personally.

If you have a conflict in your life, the following exercise will help you to

1. Become consciously aware of what factors influence how you live your life.
2. Identify possible conflicts.
3. Recognise possible changes you can make to bring the levels more in alignment and hence achieve a higher level of personal congruence (reduced inner conflict).

Take your time doing this exercise and write down your answers based around the conflict you have. For example, you might be working for an organisation which has had a significant change of values or your values have changed since you started working there and it is causing an internal conflict.

◢ **Exercise**

◢ **Spirituality/Purpose:** For the larger system (i.e., family, workers, people needing your service/product, community), what is your purpose or the impact you wish to have?

◢ **Identity/Mission:** Who are you or what role do you play? Is it the role necessary to achieve your purpose? What do you need to change?

◢ **Beliefs and Values:** What beliefs do you have about yourself, about others, about the world in general? Do these beliefs support you in fulfilling your role?

What do you value in yourself, in others, in the world in general? Are these values in alignment with your role? Are there other beliefs and values that you could take on that would be more in alignment?

◢ **Capabilities/Strategies:** What capabilities/ strategies/action plans do you have? Do you need to develop new capabilities, strategies or action plans? Are they in alignment with each of the above logical levels? If not, what needs to be changed? Maybe you need to change your capabilities (get more training), your strategies or action plans. Or maybe, given this new information, you need to reassess your purpose, your role or your beliefs and values.

◢ **Behaviours:** What do people really see/experience in your behaviours? Are your behaviours in alignment with each of the above logical levels? Does something need to be changed?

◢ **Environment:** When, where, and with whom do you exhibit these behaviours? Are they in alignment with the above logical levels?

I was working at a football club that would hire people to give them work experience. I think a lot of the people liked the idea of being in football, but didn't understand that there was more to the job than the glamour. I remember one lad in particular that I took on board for a week. He liked the idea of football and talked about all the financial trappings of the football coach and everything else, yet he didn't suggest to me that he actually liked doing the work involved. At the end of a long week he had the realisation that football wasn't actually what he thought it would be. It was a lot of hard work. Getting into football was one thing, but staying there was another as well. What is really important to understand is what drives you and what is your purpose in a given situation. This is what can make you feel happy about who you are and what you're doing.

LOGICAL LEVEL TRANSCRIPT

The following is a transcript of a live session in which I asked a client questions relating to six logical levels of change.

Spirituality/Purpose (Your connection to a wider purpose)

Jimmy: What is your sense of purpose on a personal level?

Client: To reach my potential and provide as much as possible for myself and family.

Jimmy: Why are you here?

Client: To continue life.

Jimmy: What is your sense of purpose professionally?

Client: To achieve as much as I possibly can and be happy.

Jimmy: Why do you do what you do?

Client: Because I enjoy it and it fits with what I am interested in.

Jimmy: What is the meaning of your existence both personally and professionally?

Client: Ultimately, to provide for myself and my family.

Identity/Mission

Jimmy: Who are you as an individual?

Client: I don't know.

Jimmy: Who are you to different people?

Client: I am husband, father, son, friend and colleague.

Jimmy: Who are you professionally?

Client: I am working to become a business owner / leader.

Jimmy: Are you achieving your purpose?

Client: I don't feel as though I am at the moment.

Jimmy: How do you think of yourself on a personal level?

Client: I believe I am reasonably likeable but I would prefer to be happier with myself.

Jimmy: And professionally? For example, are you an intelligent person, an attractive person, a good person?

Client: I believe I am reasonably intelligent with a good work ethic, but I would like to be more successful.

Beliefs and Values

Jimmy: Why do you do what you do?

Client: Personally, to provide a living and a happy / successful life for me and my family.

Jimmy: And professionally?

Client: The same as above.

Jimmy: What do you believe about yourself professionally?

Client: That I could be more successful and more motivated, which in turn would hopefully make me happier.

Jimmy: On a personal level?

Client: The same as above.

Jimmy: What are your personal key values?

Client: To provide a happy, comfortable and stable life for myself and my family.

Jimmy: And professionally?

Client: Again, I would say the same as the above.

Capabilities/Strategies

Jimmy: How do you go about doing things? Personally? And professionally?

Client: I take a hands-on approach to providing my family and clients with the service they expect.

Jimmy: What are your personal and professional capabilities, skills, strategies or action plans?

Client: I believe that my approach could be adopted into a business model and the purpose of my NLP session is to provide me with the inspiration / strategy to set this in motion.

Behaviours

Jimmy: What are your personal/professional behaviours?

Client: Professionally, I believe that I start off motivated with a new idea and then when it doesn't come to fruition quickly, I lose interest and the whole thing fizzles out. I also seem to feel that I have to fit into a role to be successful in business. Personally, I believe I push those around me, maybe too hard, to make up for my failings as described above.

Environment (Where? When? With Whom?)

Jimmy: Personally and professionally, where, when and with whom do you display your behaviours?

Client: I feel that I display these behaviours most when, or my family is in, a competitive environment. I do it less when I am working with people who I am comfortable with and this is when I am most myself.

◢ **Exercises**

1. Think of a restaurant that you like to visit. You have 10 minutes to come up with one-line descriptions of what you like about this restaurant from each neuro-logical level. For example, you might write:

   Environment: "It's in a lovely area with safe parking."
   Behaviour: "Where they do it right."
   Capability: "They know how to treat people."
   Beliefs: "They put customer care before everything else."
   Identity: "The seafood restaurant."
   Spiritual: "Changing the world, one meal at a time."

   Now come up with your own statements. For which levels was it easiest to come up with something?

What would you change if you were making statements about something different, such as a car, a person, a country, or a philosophical system?

2. When people compliment you, at which level do you normally take it?

3. When people criticise you, at which level do you normally take it?

   Notice how people get into the habit of taking feedback about themselves, positive or negative, at a particular level; e.g., a criticism of something they have done (behaviour) may be taken as an attack at the identity level.

4. What are you going to do differently as a result of this exercise?

LEVELS OF CHANGE IN TEAMS

Use the questions in Table 5.1 to analyse a team's alignment with its mission statement, goals, values, skill needs, and its ability to learn from experience. This could be a team of which you were formerly a member or a team with which you are currently working (perhaps setting up a good team/bad team comparison).

I have used the logical levels process from Table 5.1 to assist organisations in their recruitment policy of hiring staff, in asking questions and sending out questionnaires.

Each level should support the one above it. If the team's behaviour contradicts the stated mission, which one are team members and customers going to believe?

GETTING TO KNOW PEOPLE THROUGH LOGICAL LEVELS

You can only physically observe two of the logical levels of another person—behaviour and environment. You can observe what they are doing and when, where and with whom. This will give you some idea as to their capabilities/strategies, beliefs and values, etc.

To be really sure about all the levels, you need to engage them in a conversation on these subjects. Having conversations with another

Table 5.1   Levels of Change in Teams

Purpose	What greater purpose (end goal) does the team or organisation contribute to?
	What larger systems is it part of and how does it contribute to them?
Identity & Mission	What is the identity of the team or organisation, and how strong is it?
	How unified is it?
	What is its stated/unstated mission?
Values & Beliefs	What stated/unstated values/norms does the team organisation subscribe to?
	What stated/unstated assumptions does it operate from in practise?
	What mechanisms allow these assumptions to be updated by experience?
Capabilities	What skills are needed to fulfil the mission and stated values of the team?
	What skill needs does it have?
	What skills do its members have that the team is not yet tapping into?
	How does the team learn?
Behaviour	How closely do the actions of the team reflect its values and mission in practise within the team and outside of the team, to customers, suppliers, other parts of the organisation?
	What should it do more/less of?
Environment	How well does the physical environment of the team enable it to fulfil its mission?
	What resource needs does it have?
	What external constraints does it face?

person at the higher logical levels provides you with a more intimate understanding of that person and why they behave the way they do. How often do you have a conversation with someone you really care about and the topic is the weather (environment) or what they are doing (behaviour) rather than who they see themselves being (identity/mission) or what their beliefs and values are. To engage in this type of conversation, you need to create a space where each of you feels safe in disclosing your inner selves.

ALIGNING YOUR GOALS WITH YOUR LOGICAL LEVELS

Many of our goals (career, family, romance, health, purpose in life, etc.) are based on the requests, desires or expectations of others: parents, spouse, teachers, religious leaders, boss, society. These goals are not ours and hence do not have the energy that propels us forward to truly achieve our goals.

When we struggle with our goals, almost always there is some hidden inner conflict that must be resolved. Often we are less then fully alive because of these inner conflicts. The following exercise will assist you in identifying these conflicts and realigning your goal with who you really are.

◢ **Exercise**

Think about your goal and answer the same questions for the logical levels as you did in Table 5.1. Notice if there is a conflict between the answers. For example you may find that achieving your goal would take time away from being with your spouse and children (assuming this is an important value for you).

If you do find a conflict, is there some way to adjust your goal or your strategies/action plan to spend time with your family and still achieve your goal? You may wish to ask those affected by your goal, as they often come up with solutions that you would never think of.

This process will allow you to become aware of the alignment (or lack of it) between your inner self and your goals. As you fine-tune your goals and align them with your inner self, you should find that your goals become clearer, more compelling and more easily achieved. You have a stronger sense of fulfilment and understanding of your life.

Having clarified your purpose, the next step is to organise your thinking within each of the five levels of alignment listed in Table 5.1.

This is a useful model for understanding change in a person, a team or a company. You can examine any problem or proposed change in terms of these different levels. Generally speaking, higher levels have more *leverage* than lower levels. To permanently solve a problem, you generally have to make changes at least one level higher than the level at which the symptoms show up.

◢ BEHAVIOURAL CHANGES

MENTAL REHEARSAL 1

Mental rehearsal puts you in the driver's seat. I once worked with a guy who was in the army and was going for a promotion. The promotion meant a lot to him, the outcome of which meant a bigger car, a nicer house, more money to take care of his wife and their new baby. He had to take a physical test that started with a 2-mile run and led to other physical activities.

His wife called me and asked if I could work with him because when he got to a certain distance in his run, he would pretty much go to pieces. He was obviously suffering from nerves, which I gathered came down to focusing so much on the outcome. If we focus too much on the outcome we put ourselves under more pressure to move forward than actually doing the activity. His wife and I booked a session over the phone and she warned me that her husband was very sceptical about NLP, psychology, etc. He came over for session on a Thursday and his test was on a Monday. We practised the New Behaviour Generator exercise found on page 221 and also on anchoring, which we will cover in chapter 6.

Because his test was on Monday, I could not take him to the track and risk injury. Instead, we focused on mental preparation and I gave him a plan to follow up with. I texted him to find out his results and he said he had smashed the required time by 47 seconds. He actually visualised to within one second the time that we rehearsed for him to run that distance. That shows how powerful visualisation can be.

MENTAL REHEARSAL 2

A woman brought her daughter to meet me. The daughter was a trampolinist who had suffered a confidence meltdown because one of her friends had had a major injury while training on a trampoline. She had gone from competing at a high level to not competing at all. She wanted to give up the sport altogether. I was her last chance in an attempt to get things back on track. I think at first she was a bit sceptical and reluctant to do some of the work, but eventually she bought into it.

We used a number of NLP techniques, including the New Behaviour Generator. The result was that she got back into competing in time for the British Championship. I was watching her on the internet, as much as I could watch on the internet. I wasn't able to view the final results of the competition, but her mum sent me a text saying that her daughter had done really well, receiving a silver medal. She had missed out by only one point of winning the gold. Both of them were really pleased, even though the daughter felt that she could have done better. We had had high expectations of moving forward, but going from not competing at all to winning a silver medal and narrowly missing out on a gold medal was a fantastic achievement.

MENTAL REHEARSAL 3

A few years ago, I was doing some work with Amelia Harris Lindsay, who at the time was a journalist at Channel M and the Manchester Evening News. She has since gone on to do some work on BBC TV as a Sports Presenter.

She told me about doing interviews with some of the highest profile managers in football and profiles in sports, which made her a little nervous and sometimes affected her ability to ask cogent questions. One of the techniques I suggested she use to overcome any problems was mental rehearsal using the New Behaviour Generator. I pointed out that mental rehearsal was a great way to refine what she wanted to say. She found that the rehearsal was extremely helpful.

MENTAL REHEARSAL 4

I was working with a radio broadcaster who had the assignment of interviewing Manchester City at a press conference. Before she would go on to interview Roberto Mancini, and any other player at the press conference, I got her to write a list of questions and visualise herself asking the questions. I had her imagine that she was watching herself on a TV screen asking the questions and then entering the screen when she had perfected the process. I stressed that it was important to visualise asking the questions as though it was the here and now.

If we can stay focused we have the biggest chance for success.

◢ NEW BEHAVIOUR GENERATOR

Choose a behaviour you would like to change, such as being nervous when delivering presentations, to feeling confident and calm when delivering presentations. Use this exercise when you want to rehearse for an upcoming event or to learn from failures and develop more effective behaviour for the future.

◢ Exercise

1. Describe a behaviour you would like to be able to do or one you would like to be able to do better. Start from a belief and create an internal dialogue of, "I am doing this".

2. Imagine creating a movie of yourself on television doing the new behaviour the way you want. Add sound so that you see and hear yourself. Adjust the movie until you are satisfied with the new behaviour.

3. Imagine stepping into the movie to check how this feels. Make any further adjustments you need to until you feel the way you want.

4. See yourself using the new behaviour in three or more opportunities in the future to solidify the new ability.

◢ KEY POINTS

Use resources from your past. If you have dealt with similar situations well in the past, see yourself doing that skill or behaviour, and then transfer that skill into the new situation.

If you can't recall a time when you displayed the desired behaviour or skill, refer back to steps 2 and 3 in the New Behaviour Generator exercise, but instead of visualising yourself, use a role model who you know can do the desired behaviour well. I once helped a women deliver more confident presentations by imaging President Obama as the role model.

Run a movie of that person performing the behaviour (step 2) but when you get to step 3, *become* that person. Finally, repeat steps 2 and 3, but this time see only yourself in the movie. Make any changes you need to.

6 Emotional State Elicitation and Anchoring

One of the key ingredients for a successful life is being able to manage your emotional state. To be in the right frame of mind, be in tune with yourself, and feeling the way you want to feel in any given situation. In the zone.

◢ IN THE ZONE

When was the last time you were in the zone? Think of a time when you were completely immersed in what you were doing and it seemed effortless to perform at your peak. Maybe you were doing a work project, delivering a presentation, attending an interview, playing sports, creating art, studying something interesting, or having a great conversation.

Imagine what it would be like if you could, right in the middle of a stressful interview, presentation or meeting when all eyes are on you, go from feeling anxious to feeling confident and absolutely focused in a moment. The idea of speaking in public can be terrifying for some people. If it is for you, just imagine that you've stepping up to the podium to deliver a presentation and you look at the audience all waiting for you to start. What happens when you imagine that?

In her initial session, one of my clients, who has since gone on to become an amazing presenter, said her palms would start to sweat and her pulse rate would shoot up. And that was when she was just thinking about it! The NLP anchoring technique we are going to cover later in this chapter made a huge difference in helping my client to present and perform with confidence and be on top of her game.

You've probably met people who believe that other people, problems, circumstances or the environment cause them to feel a certain way. They don't seem to realise that each of us can control our own state—we can, but I am not saying that it's always totally easy! How useful would it be for you to be able to change your state so that you could be relaxed when delivering a presentation or feel confident when talking to your boss or during an interview? What about having focused attention when working on a key project? What about being able to get in the zone when you needed to.

Mental preparation, another component of mental training, helps athletes tap into the zone. For several years now I have been helping athletes at the highest level mentally prepare for a game by using the NLP anchoring technique to great effect. Mentally tough athletes are at an advantage because they have the ability to tap into the zone more consistently in competition. When they are in the zone, fear of failure, worry, doubt, indecision, and other mental traps are forbidden from entering their focus.

Imagine there are two minutes left in a big championship game in which you are playing. Your team is behind by a goal and another player commits a foul against you, giving you a penalty shot. You're keenly aware of the situation and you, like everyone else in the 100,000 seat sold-out stadium and millions watching around the world, know how important it is that you score on this penalty shot.

You can feel your heart pounding and your legs are a little weak. You look with considerable anxiety at the other team's keeper standing on the goal line, poised to defend the goal. This is when mental toughness and the NLP anchoring technique could help you. If you remain anxious and shaky, there's a good chance you could miss the goal. But, if you could calm your mind and put yourself in the zone, your chances of making the goal are much higher. You take a last deep breath and kick the ball towards the goal...

Athletes talk about performing in the zone and how awesome it feels. It's a state of supreme focus when the mind is fully connected to achieving a goal that helps athletes in all sports perform at their peak potential. Many athletes view the zone as this magical, hard-to-obtain state of mind, but the zone is really not that complicated or hard to achieve, if you know how. The zone is simply a mental state of total involvement in the present moment without the mental burden of worry, doubt or fear about results. Once you have experienced the zone, you will want to return to it again.

Until you know how, entering the zone is a rarely-achieved psychological state. NLP anchoring is a technique to help anyone develop efficient game-specific strategies and game plans, to help them get in the zone and mentally prepare for competition.

It was during the premiership football season of 2006–07 when the Blackburn Rovers FC were going through a losing run of a few games. The team seemed to be suffering a lack of form. They had had only 5 wins in their first 18 games.

I was in touch with the Rovers' sports scientist, Tony Strudwick, speaking to him a few times over the phone about the team. Tony spoke to Mark Hughes, then manager of the team, about bringing me in to do some NLP. Mark agreed and I went in and demonstrated NLP Key Techniques, including anchoring, to Mark Hughes and other staff members. We discussed the application of the techniques for the club. After that, the club's form markedly improved in the second half of the season, including a semi-final appearance against Jose Mourinho, which Blackburn unfortunately lost, but only by 2.1.

I am not suggesting it was just down to my NLP delivery to the coaches, though it certainly seemed to make an impact.

Tony and I kept in touch. A few seasons later, Tony was the sports scientist for Manchester United FC and he invited me to the training ground. Tony mentioned that certain players on the team had been struggling to get to sleep because of high levels of adrenaline and cortisol after championship league matches. Practise generally started with a 7:45 pm kick off during the week. The lack of sleep was potentially affecting their game on the weekend.

I suggested to Tony that using trance and relaxation anchors to induce relaxation and release cortisol could help to break the state of stress. It helped the team's performance immensely.

◢ BUSINESS COMPETITION

Like sports, business is about competition—winning the client, attaining the largest market share or the highest stock prices. Business people often see themselves as competitors with strengths and weaknesses that affect their performance. In addition, many workplace processes require teamwork. Problems in a team can affect its productivity and effectiveness, along with damaging individual employee morale and attitudes. NLP anchoring is one tool businesses can use to improve performance, increase productivity and "win the game".

Unlike sports, businesspeople can disguise problems, make assumptions about situations, hide or even be blind to hurdles in their path. As they are careening along, executing their plan, they might find themselves knocking into things and getting perplexing or disappointing results. Without a knowledge of NLP anchoring, their performance and productivity suffer and they "lose the game".

WORKING IN THE ZONE

Being in the zone, or in a state of optimal functioning, is another sports metaphor often used in business. In this state, workers focus on the process and become so engaged in the activity that they are performing at optimal capacity. Employees working in the zone demonstrate the four Cs: concentration, confidence, control and commitment.

They are able to concentrate and maintain their focus over time. They are confident; they know they have the knowledge, skills and abilities to successfully complete the work. They are in control of their emotions and remain positive and do not let anger or anxiety interfere with their work. Finally, they are committed to the work, their team and the organisation. They manage competing and rapidly changing priorities so they can be productive and achieve individual, team and organisational goals

◢ ANCHORS

The term *NLP anchors* came about by comparing the technique to the role of a ship's anchor. What is the use of a ship anchor? It is to keep a ship in place when it is not sailing, to prevent ocean waves from pushing the ship away from where it needs to be. The anchor locks the ship in a specific location.

In the same way, NLP anchors do to us what a ship anchor does to a ship. It keeps us in a certain place (or more accurately, in a certain state). By setting up NLP anchors to different states/moods, whenever that anchor is triggered we will immediately be brought to that state.

From time to time, you may come across a certain stimulus in your environment that brings back a flood of emotions. Maybe a familiar smell took you back to a particular place and time. Or maybe it was something you saw that directed your emotion to someplace remembered. In fact, it could have been a stimulus from any of the five senses. We call a stimulus that triggers an emotional response an *anchor*. When this happens, the state is "anchored" to the stimulus.

Anchoring is extremely useful because it can assist you in gaining access to past resource states and linking those past resources to the present and the future. Anchoring is the perfect tool to help you, your staff, clients or colleagues, to each take control of his or her mind and access the zone.

EXAMPLES OF COMMON ANCHORS

Visual: Logos, celebrities, religious symbols, typefaces, facial expressions, the weather, stop signs, gestures

Auditory: Words, names, voice tonality, jingles, accents, ringtones, music, sound of familiar voices, engines, yawns

Kinaesthetic: Clothing, exercise, a certain kind of touch, warmth

Taste: Vinegar, garlic, lemon, chocolate, peppermint, cough medicine

Smell: Chip shop, newly mown grass, curry, baking bread, coffee, smoke, school, hospitals

CREATING ANCHORS

Anchors are created naturally, just as rapport and persuasion occur naturally. We have all created anchors with other people. Remember "the look" your mom or dad gave you when you were about to get in big trouble. That was a visual anchor they created that was linked to pain if you did not change your course of action. Your parents were unintentionally using the NLP anchoring technique.

Perhaps you know just the tone of voice to speak in to make your significant other feel loved? We all know of things that we can do that will sway the emotions of others or to trigger an emotion.

These things you do are stimulus you create that cause an emotional shift in others; you are using the NLP anchoring technique.

We call these stimulus an anchor because we use them to create a trigger for a particular emotion. In other words, we anchor an emotion to a certain stimulus. When a person is in a powerful emotional state, the subconscious mind will link everything that it is sensing with the emotion that is felt. This is the reason a song can take you back in time. The next time you encounter the same stimulus your mind defines what this stimulus means to you. So it replays the times when you encountered the stimulus in the past and shows preference to memories with the highest emotional impact. You may have heard a song a million times before or after the emotional event that was associated with it but you remember only one in particular. The time you remember is when the most emotion was present at the same time as the stimulus.

ADVERTISING ANCHORS

Advertising uses a lot of anchors. Marketers try to create an association between the desired product and your wants. Flipping through a magazine can have you associating nice clothes with certain brands.

Words themselves also can be powerful anchors, especially when linked with visual and/or auditory suggestions. By watching images and hearing words and music together while seeing a product, we associate one with the other. When we experience them together more than once, we get anchored. This is how advertisers convince us to buy their products.

Advertisers are driven by market research about the human behavioural responses to particular ads. Advertisers (at least in the ads I've been watching lately) are getting increasingly sophisticated with how they're reaching the public and how they implant a desire in you to buy their products later on! Have you noticed this?

Have you noticed this anchoring in your own behaviour? Let's say you're in a store and there are several major name products that you recognise. Somehow you just feel more attracted to one brand than another. (What I'm describing is different from buying one brand of soft drink over another!) Sometimes ads you've seen have caused you to attach emotional responses to a product or to the process of buying a product. Later on, you may find yourself in a situation when you're faced with that product and you just feel an urge to buy it.

A good example of that response would be a particular brand of trainer for which advertisers have done a masterful job of creating an anchor. The ads show champions wearing those trainers and engender in us those championship feelings we all want to feel. The brand has hired the best people around in influential advertising who know the value of eliciting emotional responses like championship spirit.

ADDICTIVE ANCHORS

Aside from their very real biochemical effects, food, cigarettes and alcohol are also powerful physiological and emotional anchors. We often refer to foods such as sweets (chocolate and cake) as comfort foods. Eating something sweet and/or delightful to the taste buds can be a gesture of self-nurturing, often done at a moment when we feel no one else is looking out for us. Think of how advertiser market certain types of chocolate brands, drinks etc.

I was teaching an NLP course to a group. I asked them, "If you could buy one of two brand new cars which had the same specifications, same colour, and were manufactured and designed by same company, but one of the cars was significantly cheaper, would you take the cheaper one?" They all said yes, of course. But, when I told them the branding (logo) of the two cars, one of which was a status symbol and the other not, all of them said they would take the dearer car because of the branding. Even a church pianist said he wouldn't want to turn up to work in the brand that was cheaper.

That's the power of branding association.

The smallest things can affect our behaviour. When watching a news channel, watch the tone, wording, facial motions, and hand motions of the news anchors when they are reading a story off the teleprompter with which they disagree or interviewing someone with opposing views. Their emotions about an issue aren't demonstrated by what they are reading, but in how they present the information. You may notice them speak over their guests, use hand motions to distract their viewers, ask trick questions, ignore what guests say, and continue to lie despite being disproven by what the guest says. They will discredit their guests by calling them names, cut them off, or even cut off their microphone. Even the way sentences are structured can change the real meaning behind a story and mislead the audience.

The point of having such guests on a televised interview is not to hear their viewpoint, but to disprove it as ridiculous. Viewers do not leave with an unbiased, intelligent assessment of the issues but a predetermined idea that has been implanted using neuro-linguistic programming techniques.

CONDITIONING ANCHORS

Russian physiologist and psychologist, Ivan Pavlov, is most well known for his findings on human and animal conditioning. While doing a research on dogs' digestion, he discovered a form of conditioning that eventually was termed *Pavlov's response*. When it came to meal time, Pavlov would use bells to call his dogs to the food. After repeating this numerous times, he found that even without any food, the dogs would salivate when hearing the sound of the bell.

Pavlov used the ringing sound of the bell to associate it with food. Numerous repetitions conditioned the dogs to respond to the ringing bell as they would respond to food.

This is how NLP anchoring works. By conditioning responses to unique NLP anchors, we are able to deliberately get into specific states when the anchors are triggered. Just like Pavlov's dogs.

So NLP anchors are really a stimulus for us to get into whatever states we want. Like Pavlov used the ringing bell sound to act as a stimulus, we can set certain anchors to act as the stimulus to certain states with NLP anchoring. After many repetitions, the association between the NLP anchor and the state will be conditioned.

Conditioning a Client

I worked with a client that had been made redundant in her job. She said she was struggling with anxiety, feeling stressed out and depressed. She said she faced an uncertain future and worried about providing for her family. She had a couple of interviews coming up that were big opportunities, but she was in a very negative state.

This type of negative thinking was doing her no favours because it was cranking up the stress and anxiety levels when she needed to think clearly. She told me she had seen therapists and spoken to counsellors to help her, all of which had had no effect.

It was important that she learn to focus because one of the opportunities involved a presentation to demonstrate how she would set up a new business. We did the anchoring process to help her break out of her negative state and also developed an action plan.

Within a few weeks she emailed to tell me she had delivered a successful presentation and passed with flying colours. She had a new job she was happy with.

CHOOSING STATES TO ANCHOR

If you have an interview coming up, you want to choose relaxation or confidence as the appropriate state for a presentation. Of course, the best time to anchor a state is when it's happening naturally, but that is not always possible. The second best way is to relive an actual vivid, associated memory of the state from the past. If you have neither of those, try an imagined state.

It is also possible to stack anchors to elicit several different states and anchor them with the same stimulus. The states chosen for a particular stacked anchor can be the same or different, as long as they are compatible.

Setting a Physical Anchor

1. Choose a subtle physical signal with which you are comfortable that you can repeat in any situation, such as snapping a rubber band against your wrist, squeezing your left hand twice, tapping your thumb against your forefinger, etc. This physical signal is the anchor you can fire in any real-life situation to help you achieve your desired state.

2. Think of a state that you would like to anchor; for example, confidence, determination or relaxation.

Remember any times in the past when you were able to access this state. Try to remember at least three different times when you had been in that state. It could be when you won a competition, delivered a great presentation or had some really good news. It can be anything you like, as long as it was definitely a moment which recreates the same emotions you would like to create for a future event

3. If you cannot remember a time in the past when you had been in the state that you would like to anchor, imagine yourself exactly as you would like to be in the future time—the ideal you. You could also imagine yourself being like someone—a role model—that you perceive as being confident, determined, relaxed, etc.

4. Close your eyes and relax. Imagine seeing yourself as though you are viewing a movie, either during a time when you felt your desired emotional state or by imagining yourself in that state.

5. As you are visualising this, notice where you are and what's happening around you, any colours that you can see, any noises that you can hear. Are you alone or are there others with you? Really focus on how you feel at this time. Take the good emotions and make them as strong and positive as you can.

6. Imagine stepping inside your remembered or imagined self. As you do so, take on board all of those positive, strong feelings, allowing them to flow through every part of your body. Imagine turning those feelings up to the very highest level that they will possibly go, and when they are at the very highest, fire your anchor and hold the emotional state for 5 to 10 seconds before releasing it.

7. Now, test fire the anchor. Imagine going into the future to a time when you want to feel your chosen emotional state and notice where you are and what's happening around you. See, hear and feel yourself firing your anchor and allow all of those positive strong feelings to come right back to you.

8. See the situation going exactly as you want it to unfold.

9. Notice how good you feel being able to access these resources whenever you need to.

10. Repeat steps 2 through 9 at least three times with a positive memory of the state or states you wish to anchor.

What is happening when you do this? You are psychologically associating the neural memory of your chosen physical signal—your anchor—with your chosen emotional state. Therefore it stands to reason that the more times you lay the anchor and the more clarity you have in the feeling, the better this technique will work. This is known as conditioning.

Remember the five keys to anchoring:

1. the intensity of the experience,
2. the timing of the anchor,
3. the uniqueness of the anchor,
4. the replication of the stimulus, and
5. number of times (repetition can substitute for intensity).

Setting a Visual Anchor

This is a great method for accessing resources such as confidence when you need them.

The Circle of Excellence

1. Identify an upcoming situation that you want to go really well but one in which you don't feel as confident about as you would like. Also identify how you would like to feel in that situation—your state of excellence—that will enable you to perform better. Once you have the situations fixed, set them aside for a moment.

2. Set up a *circle of excellence* on the floor. What colour is it? How big? You'll need it big enough to step into, so hula-hoop size is good.

3. Now re-access the state of excellence and associate it with the circle.

   ◢ What does it feel like when you are in that state?

◢ Relive a time when you were in that state.

◢ As soon as you start to feel that state, step into the circle.

◢ Turn the state up even more.

4. Step back out of the circle and break the state.

5. Test by stepping back into the circle. The excellent state should return.

6. You can stack more than one resource state inside the circle if necessary.

7. Future Pacing

◢ Think of a future situation in which you want to have that excellent state.

◢ What problem signs might you experience that will let you know it's time to have these resources available?

◢ Step into the circle again as soon as you start to access the "problem" state.

◢ Notice what happens. The problem state should only appear briefly and lead directly to the excellent state.

A Personal Anchoring Experience

I had been delivering weekly UK football reports for 2KY (it later became Sky Sports radio) with media personality Andy Paschalidis, the host of Sky Sports Radio's Premier League coverage. The show had been doing really well. I was due to go out to Sydney to deliver a series of seminars and while I was there I was going to do a live feature on the show. It was something I did whenever I would tour Australia.

I had been on the show a few times that week, delivering seminars. One of the things I would do prior to going on the show was to sit in a "Chair of Excellence." When I sat down on that chair, either in the studio or as a correspondent, I would focus on getting in the zone and think about what I was going to say.

I remember on one occasion I was going to give a talk at my old high school. I had been up since 3 am because the show as at 5 am. As I sat down in the principal's office, it brought back memories of when

I had been sent to that same office once or twice when I had been a student. It made me a little nervous.

I wanted to banish any nerves and instead focus clearly on delivering a positive message to the students. I sat in my Chair of Excellence and focused on the mental state I wanted to be in to do the radio show. I'm happy to say that the talk to the students went really well. All-in-all, it was a positive experience and a good day.

More Anchoring Practice

Make a list of the visual, auditory, kinaesthetic, and olfactory and gustatory anchors in your life. Use associated recall for positive resource anchors.

When could you use some of the already existing positive resource anchors in ways you haven't been doing up to now?

Notice anchors used by other people. Include anchors they are using deliberately and ones they are setting off without realising it.

When you're engaged in a conversation with someone and they appear to get into a very positive or resourceful state, either spontaneously or because you've conversationally amplified it for them, you can anchor that state with a covert visual anchor. This would be some natural seeming gesture, like adopting a particular body position, a gesture, or a facial expression. Test it when this person is back in a neutral state. When could you use that?

You can also experiment with voice-tone anchoring on someone else by using a particular word or phrase along with an appropriate kinaesthetic anchor like a mock punch on the arm or a hand on the shoulder—whatever action is appropriate to your relationship with that person. Try using this voice-tone anchor when the person is in a different state. Notice the results you get, and think about the possibilities for using these anchors.

How to Use NLP Anchoring in a Sales Setting

I used voice-tone anchoring when I was delivering a NLP telesales training for a business that sold advertising. I focused on three aspects and two anchors to put the staff in a good mental state to improve sales. The first anchor was a mantra: one sale becomes two, two becomes three and we are on the way. The second anchor involved the whole team: they could form a team huddle in the morning and repeat the manta. The third aspect was to get the customer in the right state of mind to purchase the advertising.

Throughout the training day, I had them choose a time when they were not feeling in the zone and to fire their anchor, either by individual visualising or by getting into the huddle. The improvement in sales performance was noticeable.

If you are a salesman you could use a covert auditory anchor to guide a customer to a state of desire and then anchor it to your product or service. Your product then triggers the emotion which makes it an effortless way to sell your product.

The idea is simple: get a client into a specific mental state (the stronger and more distinct the better), and create an association to it so that the state can be re-accessed (activated) at will.

There are four steps involved:

1. Access a powerful state.
2. Recognize when to set the anchor.
3. Anchor the state as specifically as possible.
4. Fire the anchor when required.

If you're trying to make a sale, then you want your customer to be in a wanting-to-buy state. The simplest way to access that state is to get the customer to remember a time when they were in that buying state by asking questions like, "Can you remember a time when you saw something and you just had to have it?" or "Have you ever felt you had to have something, your gut feeling was you had to have it, and you just brought it immediately on impulse?"

These kind of questions force the customer to remember and access a time that matches the wanting-to-buy state you're looking for. Once you recognise that the customer is in that state, anchor the state by immediately relating it to your product with a word or phrase. You can then fire the anchor to achieve the state when required during your sales pitch by using the same words. These are the keys to the success of your NLP anchoring techniques.

These technique can be incorporated into any kind of sales environment.

Other Powerful Anchors

Clothes

Clothes can be used as very powerful anchoring tools and work in a similar way to changing your physiology. You can think of clothes as costumes, which, in effect, they are. Each costume represents a different side of yourself, and each side of your personality will be more effective in some circumstances than in others. So it pays to be able to know when to wear your "different hats".

Apart from setting off your own associations, the clothes you wear also set off other people's anchors. People will evaluate you according to what they think your clothes say about you. Keep this in mind when you want to create a particular effect.

Think of how different you feel when you

- dress up for a formal dinner or wedding,
- run or work out in exercise clothes,
- put on your pyjamas or night gear,
- wear a swimsuit,
- put on your favourite baggy shirt, or
- wear something sexy.

Make sure you have clothes in your wardrobe that relate to the specific states you need in order to achieve success. If you discover you need to purchase some, look at them as an investment in your future. Purchase them consciously while aiming for a very specific result, such as

- A self-confident winner's outfit for meetings and social occasions
- Creative but comfortable outfits for working at home on your business
- Professional outfits for the office
- Comfortable clothes for relaxation

Fragrance

Scent is a very powerful anchor, particularly since it tends to be subliminal. We pay more attention to what we see and hear so the sense of smell tends to bypass our inner censors. You can make good use of this.

Did you know that scent has been shown to aid in memory and recall? Researchers at the University of Liverpool found that students who wore the same scent during exams as they wore while studying improved their recall by 15 to 20%. The researchers concluded that "you can use odour to control behaviour in all sorts of ways." The scents used in the study as an aid for recall were orange and lavender.

Here are just two ways to use scent:

1. Wear a top-quality "power" scent at meetings and important social occasions.
2. Shop for inexpensive essential oils and use them as anchors for the following situations:
    - Studying
    - Organising
    - Working
    - Networking

Jewellery

Use jewellery in the same way as clothes. You can choose one item of jewellery as an anchor for a specific state. It can also be combined with an outfit that anchors the same state.

Wearing jewellery on your hands or wrists (rings, bracelets or watches) can be doubly effective as it's more frequently in your line of vision.

Music

Keep a selection of CDs in your home, business and car and use them to anchor yourself to specific states. You will probably need to experiment to find the right piece of music for the states you desire.

Many successful business people and entrepreneurs listen to specific music before an important meeting or phone call to put themselves in the best possible state. For example, in the 1980s, the theme from the motion picture Rocky was very popular as an anchor for achieving a goal against the odds. Anthony Robbins used *Magic* by America and *I'm So Excited* by the Pointer Sisters during the breaks in his Firewalk weekend workshop to reinforce the states created by the workshop processes.

Comedy: Use comedy CDs when you need to be in a light-hearted, positive or high-energy mood.

Motivation CDs: Use these frequently. You can turn your car into a "rolling university" or an "anchoring machine".

Relaxation CDs: Use these at home or work for relaxation. Naturally, you wouldn't use these while driving.

Pictures and Photos

Any picture or photograph that inspires you in a positive way can be used as an anchor.

◢ USING NLP ANCHORING

NLP anchoring is a powerful technique to access resources, feelings and states when you want them. Replacing unwanted feelings and thoughts with desirable ones is freedom indeed.

People can make you feel good or bad, but only if you let them. Allowing yourself to be controlled by people who make you feel good is acceptable if you understand what is happening, but being in the control of people who have a negative effect on you isn't so great. Never hand over your emotional control to someone else.

NLP-style anchoring is a process that goes on around and within us all the time, whether we are aware of it or not. Most of the time we are not consciously aware of why we feel as we do. Indeed, we may not realise why we have responded the way we do in some cases, which makes it a much more powerful force in our lives.

Anchoring is used in NLP to facilitate state management. In this sense, an anchor is set up to be triggered by a consciously cho-sen stimulus deliberately linked by practice to a known useful state to provide reflexive access to that state at will. You can achieve the mental and emotional state you wish to help clients, colleagues and friends to be the best they can be.

NLP ANCHORING AT WORK

Kasper Schmeichel, son of Manchester United legend Peter Schmeichel, began his career with Manchester City. The pressure of having a father who was regarded as one of the world's best keepers was very stressful for Kasper.

At the time I was working with the Bury first team and had been brought in to help reverse the team's fortunes. We were having problems in the keeper position with injuries and loss of form. The team had been far behind on points but we had gradually clawed our way back into a position in which we could survive. Still we needed help.

Kasper arrived at Bury in February, on loan from Manchester City, to help improve the keeper position. While with Bury, he made 15 appearances in a three-month loan spell. It was a big responsibility on the shoulders of a young Kasper Schmeichel.

We had a very inexperienced keeper coach at Bury at the time who was unsure of ways of fostering confidence in his players. During my conversations with Kasper he didn't seem to have much confidence so my aim was to instil as much confidence as possible. I used every opportunity I could to get into Kasper's head. On one occasion during a training session, I challenged him to save a penalty from me. It was at that point that I saw a way to establish an auditory anchor that I would use many times during games whenever I saw his confidence drop.

Once I had done that, Kasper's contribution to the team helped to improve their fortunes.

Values and Beliefs

MEXICAN FISHERMAN MEETS HARVARD MBA

A travelling American businessman was standing on the pier of a quaint coastal fishing village in southern Mexico while he watched a small boat with just one young Mexican fisherman pull into the dock. Inside the small boat were several large yellow fin tuna. Enjoying the warmth of the early afternoon sun, the American complimented the Mexican on the quality of his fish.

"How long did it take you to catch them?" the American asked casually.

"Oh, a few hours," the Mexican fisherman replied.

"Why don't you stay out longer and catch more fish?" the American businessman asked.

The Mexican warmly replied, "With this I have more than enough to support my family's needs."

The businessman then became serious, "But what do you do with the rest of your time?"

Responding with a smile, the Mexican fisherman answered, "I sleep late, play with my children, watch ballgames, and take a siesta with my wife. Sometimes in the evenings I take a stroll into the village to see my friends, play the guitar, sing a few songs..."

The American businessman impatiently interrupted, "Look, I have an MBA from Harvard, and I can help you to be more profitable. You can start by fishing several hours longer every day. You can then sell the extra fish you catch. With the extra money, you can buy a bigger boat. With the additional income that larger boat will bring, before long you can buy a second boat, then a third one, and so on, until you have an entire fleet of fishing boats."

Proud of his own sharp thinking, he excitedly elaborated a grand scheme which he said would bring in even bigger profits, "Then, instead of selling your catch to a middleman you'll be able to sell your fish directly to the processor, or even open your own cannery. Eventually, you could control the product, processing and distribution. You could leave this tiny coastal village and move to Mexico City, or possibly even Los Angeles or New York City, where you could even further expand your enterprise."

Having never thought of such things, the Mexican fisherman asked, "But how long will all this take?"

After a rapid mental calculation, the Harvard MBA pronounced, "Probably about 15 to 20 years, maybe less if you work really hard."

"And then what, señor?" asked the fisherman.

"Why, that's the best part!" answered the businessman with a laugh. "When the time is right, you would sell your company stock to the public and become very rich. You would make millions."

"Millions? Really? What would I do with it all?" asked the young fisherman in disbelief.

The businessman boasted, "Then you could retire with all the money you've made. You could move to a quaint coastal fishing village where you could sleep late, play with your grandchildren, watch ballgames, and take a siesta with your wife. You could stroll to the village in the evenings where you could play the guitar and sing with your friends all you want."

—Author unknown.

In this chapter I will help you to decide what you want, what others want and how to motivate yourself and others. You will learn ways to discover the values of your staff, clients and colleagues. These values are unconscious to many people, yet they are the foundation people stand on that determine their happiness, well being and, potentially, building a successful career.

I was once delivering a course to a group and in this course was a very experienced man who had been in management for many years. He told the group about his career—how he had got to where he was and how long he had been in management. The man was truly amazing and the story was fascinating. When I started to ask him questions, he shared extremely valuable advice on management with the group.

I asked him, "You've been doing the role for a few years, you're a successful manager, how do you get the best out of people?"

He said, "Well, I get to know people. I people manage. And people managing is a lot more powerful when you understand people."

In essence, he took the time to understand people's values and what was important to them. He knew that if he could connect to and be aware of people's values, he had the power to motivate the person. He used an example of one great piece of management he had used with one of his employees.

The employee was a massive Liverpool football club fan and had a five-year-old son. This manager had a season ticket to Liverpool. He gave the employee his season ticket, but he also got an extra ticket for the son so both could go watch Liverpool. It was the first time the father and the son had been able to attend a live game to watch Liverpool play.

He said the employee had gone on to repay him tenfold by his unflagging loyalty to the organisation and by telling everyone what a fantastic experience it had been to go watch the club he supports and on top of that to bring his son. It was a phenomenal piece of management.

Not all management requires you to bust a bank. Sometimes it's just about considering what is really important to another person. What if one of your employees wants to go watch their child's nativity play. Do you let them go early at 2 o'clock or do you keep them on until 5 o'clock to do whatever chores and tasks they need to do and they miss the play? While you don't want to make leaving work early a frequent occurrence, because people might take liberties, making an allowance for truly important occasions will repay you tenfold because you were aware of what was important to the person you let go home early.

What is important to you in your personal and or professional life? Your career? Relationships? What makes you tick?

The importance of values cannot be overstated. Just imagine what it would be like if nothing mattered to you. Why would you want to get up in the morning and do anything? What would be the point? People who have an understanding of what is important to them usually have a real sense of purpose that acts like a propulsion system that moves them towards their goal.

Values exert a powerful effect upon your life. They determine how you relate to your family and your partner, how you perform your job, your religious convictions and who you vote for. The often-cited "generation gap" is really a statement about values.

Values also dictate your leisure time activities, your interests, what you learn, and what products you buy. Marketing companies spend millions of pounds on clearly identifying the values of its niche target groups so that they may present a product in a way to which the customer will be receptive.

◢ DETERMINING VALUES

In any particular context we tend to do the things that are important to us while we do not do the things that are not important to us. What is important to us is what we value. Sometimes we do things that we later regret because we were motivated by what we valued at the time. When our values changed, we realized our past actions were objectionable.

If one of your career values is about making a difference, then likely you will seek out employment that allows you to make a difference. If your values of making a difference aren't being met, you may not feel motivated or happy in your employment. Just think of a time when your values were not being met in your job. Reflect on what it was like. Now think about a time when your values were being met in your job. What was the difference in how you felt?

Values will affect how you spend your time and direct your focus. They will determine what is important to you and what is not important to you. Values are what you move *towards* and *away from*. They are "like a compass that directs your life". Values motivate and demotivate, and they justify behaviour.

Have you ever behaved in a certain way and either regretted it or were happier for it afterwards? These differing emotions are determined by our values. Values are an integral part of our personality and they drive our behaviours and serve to motivate us.

Values are context dependent. What is important to you in regards to your career is different from what is important to you in a personal relationship. In your career, your values might be to make a difference, but in your personal life it might be to facilitate your personal growth.

That said, most people will have core values that apply in many contexts, such as loyalty and honesty. It is essential that these traits be present in career, relationships, friendships, and other important areas of life.

WHY LEARN ABOUT VALUES?

A knowledge of values can be useful in numerous situations:

- Managing and motivating people
- Recruiting the appropriate staff
- Sales
- Understanding ourselves and others
- Improving self awareness
- Increasing personal contentment
- Making key life decisions, such as type of job, choosing a partner, developing relationships, etc.
- Aligning ourselves and others to stated goals

WHERE DO VALUES COME FROM?

What exactly are values? What impact are they having on you? In your personal life? Business? And how did you get them?

You have gathered values all your life, starting from the minute you were born. Some values you discard as you age, but others you will carry with you into adulthood. Ultimately, we choose our own values; however, there are numerous influences trying to guide us to the "correct" values.

As children, we are at the mercy of our parents. Our cognitive capacity as children is not developed enough to implement a sophisticated alternative. Even when our cognitive abilities do eventually develop, our peers and other influences enter the picture and all of them are trying to influence our values. Some of these other influences are determined by our culture and our schools, but may also be found through churches, Boy & Girl Scouts, etc.

The conditions we grow up in as children also have an important influence on our values. Inglehart's *Theory of Intergenerational Value Change* asserts that a key determinant of our values relates to the conditions of our upbringing—chiefly, how secure or insecure we felt. For instance, a child brought up in economic insecurity is likely to gravitate towards modern values, with their focus on achievement, growth and economic success. Conversely, a child brought up in conditions of great economic security is more likely to gravitate towards postmodern values, with the emphasis on self-expression, well-being, and experiences.

Determining our own values can go a long way towards helping us align our life and goals. Having the skill to determine someone else's values help us in our relationships with clients, colleagues and staff. The key ways to discover values are by listening and asking the right questions.

Some of the things we do are born out of obligation and some are born out of choice. Many people set goals and make plans, but rarely do people take the time to evaluate what's important to them and to the people around them.

Have you ever taken the time to evaluate your life and business and work out what's important to you? Do you know with absolute conviction what's important to you? In order to discover your own values, answer the following questions:

1. What is very important to you about your work?
2. What is important about your work to your customers, clients?

3. What is important about your work to your work colleagues and associates?

4. What is it about your work that's makes all your efforts worthwhile?

When you answer these questions do the answers come from your head or your heart?

These are your values, the things in life that are really important to you and you will go out of your way to protect, uphold and defend.

Common Sources of Values

- Family
- Friends
- Church or Religion
- School
- Geography
- Economics
- Media

Now consider your values. Where have they come from?

Defining Values

- Values are *abstract concepts*.
- Values are what are important to us—they motivate us.
- Values are a criteria for determining whether our actions are right or wrong.
- Values determine how we spend our time.
- Values may be different in different contexts.
- Value are related to beliefs and each other.
- Values are in a hierarchy—some are more important than others.

Our values have been gathered all our life, starting from the day we were born. In the first seven years of our lives we are the most receptive to picking up the values of those around us because our filters to make judgements are raw. During different phases of our lives we pick up and learn from different people and from other factors. For example, if you grew up in an environment in which both your parents had worked in the same job for 30 years and had a big emphasis on job security, then it's possible this could influence your decisions about how you live your life.

The Morris Massey Development Periods

According to socialist Morris Massey, there are three major periods in our life during which we develop our values. The Imprint Period, from the ages of 0 to 7, the Modelling Period, from the ages of 7 to 14, and the Socialisation Period, from the ages of 14 to 21. I would add one more: the Business Period, from the ages of 21 and beyond.

During your imprinting period, the most influential people in your life are your parents, siblings, extended family, teachers, and group leaders. This is the phase during which you pick up your most basic values: right and wrong and good and bad. If you were told to finish all of your food at dinnertime, as an adult may now find yourself saying the same thing to your own children or eating more than you need. If your parents stressed the importance of being academic, you may put a high value on acquiring a formal education when you grow up.

However, you don't always pick up the values of your parents. I remember watching a TV programme that featured Sir Alan Sugar, a rich and successful British business magnate and political advisor. He mentioned that his parents were public sector workers who believed their son should take the same employment path as they did. At the time, working for the public sector was secure a job for life. A good career choice. Obviously Sir Alan Sugar thought otherwise.

During your modelling phase, you probably started to adopt the values of your chosen heroes from the world of sports, films, and music. You may have had a favourite teacher whose values you tried out and either included in your values programme or discarded as you grew older.

When you enter your Socialisation Period, people with whom you socialise at school or home have an impact on your values.

When you enter your business period, you acquire a business persona and pick up values from business associates and your company.

You pick up values all your life. The values you experienced as you grew up had an impact on your life and the lives of others. By the time you reach adulthood, the values acquired during your formative years are a major part of your life programmes.

THE EFFECT OF VALUES

Values can have a big impact on the way people behave. Many people ignore the emotional states caused by conflicting values. People tend to drift from one emotion to the other, sometimes unconsciously feeling upset, frightened, overwhelmed, sad or uncomfortable. Our emotions act as signals telling us that there is something important that requires our attention.

I once worked with a client who had given up playing football because he was afraid of having a heart attack. He had come across a few cases of players passing away with heart problems and he was afraid the same might happen to him. Because I am not qualified in medicine, I suggested he see a GP for tests to determine if he had any problems with his heart. As it happens, he had already done that and he was given the all clear.

He was a very talented footballer and had completed a professional football apprenticeship. However, because of his concerns, he had decided to pursue a career in business. After four years of not playing and trying to make a go of it in business, he knew he wanted to get back into football.

I worked with him for three sessions. One of the sessions was instrumental in eliciting his values and understanding his motivation for wanting to get back into football. He went back to playing football at a semi-professional level and has never looked back since.

Values Inventory

Read through the list of values in Table 7.1 (adding your own, if you'd like). Place a tick next to the values that hold the most attraction for you. Then provide an example of how each ticked value is expressed in your life.

Based on the entries you checked in Table 7.1, take a moment to determine if you are living in alignment with your values. If you are, you should have ready examples of how your values manifest in your

Table 7.1 Values Inventory

☐ Achievement	☐ Learning
☐ Artistic expression	☐ Love
☐ Beauty	☐ Loyalty
☐ Commitment	☐ Material wealth
☐ Community	☐ Nature
☐ Creativity	☐ Nurture
☐ Duty	☐ Peace
☐ Empowerment	☐ Pleasure
☐ Faith	☐ Popularity
☐ Family	☐ Power
☐ Freedom	☐ Privacy/Solitude
☐ Friendship	☐ Responsibility
☐ Getting ahead	☐ Security
☐ Growth	☐ Self-actualisation
☐ Health/Fitness	☐ Service
☐ Helping others	☐ Sharing
☐ Honesty	☐ Spiritual wealth
☐ Humour	☐ Success
☐ Independence	☐ Support
☐ Integrity	☐ Tradition
☐ Interdependence	☐ Understanding
☐ Joy	☐ Wisdom
☐ Knowledge	

life. If not, brainstorm some ways that will allow you to begin working towards this alignment. You can make changes with small steps or with big leaps. You can also do this exercise for the communities to which you belong.

Compensatory Values

These values are formed when you go to an opposite extreme to compensate for something that didn't happen for you. If you had a deprived childhood, you may compensate for that by overindulging your own children. The way you perceive your own experiences will have an impact on the value you place on them. If you had a bad business experience because of the dishonesty of some associates and suffered a financial loss, you may place a high value on trust and honesty, looking for it in all future situations. This may not be appropriate in some circumstances when you may want to be more careful.

The Value of Values

On the face of it, values may seem irrelevant, but if you take the time to analyse your values, it is surprising how much they influence you and the direction of your life. When you recognise an emotional warning signal, a feeling that not all is well, examine your values to determine if what you are doing is violating a deeply held value. Understanding what's important to the people around you in business and life is a useful tool that allows you to help people achieve the outcomes that are important to them.

Many existing and new business owners focus on creating their product and figuring out how to market, sell, and finance their business. Some may even a create a mission statement, that often ends up being more of a marketing pitch than anything else.

We build our own business or go into a career for many reasons, but ultimately it is because of something that relates to our own happiness. This is why it's probably not a good idea to spend more time on your company's logo and marketing blurb than it is thinking about what your company stands for. Once you set a firm foundation for your company's values, that can function as a guideline as to how you will create a business that will make you happy.

Classic examples of that is the number of people I have come across who want to start a coaching business to escape a corporate environment, but the business they create sometimes ends up operating with the same environment they wished to escape. Or it might be a relationship coach who finds herself being more of a conflict manager than someone in the business of "relating".

ELICITING YOUR CUSTOMER'S VALUES

Remember, what is important to you may not be the same as what is important to your customers, clients, staff, colleagues, and business associates. And vice versa.

I remember working with an organisation that wanted to market a new service to existing customers. Although the script they came up with was heavily based on the benefits of the new service to the customer, they had not taken the time to find out what was actually important to the customer. The response they were receiving was not what they were expecting or wanted.

My suggestion, which seemed to have a positive impact, was to ask the existing clients if they were happy with the service they already had. Did they have a similar package elsewhere? What was that package offering? Were they happy with it. If so, what did they like or not like about the package. Then it was important to ask the customer why the service was essential to them and if they had received the information necessary to use the service intelligently.

If your values and product tie in with what is important *to the customer* and meets their criteria, it's a win–win situation. You have a good chance of making a sale. If they don't, you could lose a sale.

I once helped a friend look for a new car. She had saved up her money over a period of time to buy the car in cash. We looked at a few different car dealerships that specialised in a certain type of car. At one dealership we walked into the car yard and were greeted by a sales rep. I told the rep the budget my friend was working with and asked him if he could show us around. We explained the kind of car my friend was looking for and the rep showed us a few different cars, finally suggesting one particular model.

My friend was very interested. It was quite a nice car and it pretty much fit the criteria she was looking for. She asked whether it was possible to do a trade in for her current car in order to obtain a discount. No problem. It was when she mentioned that she wanted to pay cash that the trouble started.

The rep said that financing a car was the better way to go. My friend said she didn't want to finance, she wanted to pay cash. The rep then proceeded to tell her that she was an idiot. I couldn't believe what I heard and neither could she. He said the reason she was an idiot was because she could put that money in the bank and gain interest. He insisted she would make enough money in interest that it would offset the car repayment and that it would be a more financially-viable option than paying for the car in cash.

Now I'm not an expert in high-purchase agreements so it's possible what the rep was suggesting would have been a better arrangement. That doesn't matter. The point is, when he said she was an idiot for paying in cash, the sale was blown out the water. We walked away. There is a lesson to be learned there.

Values Utilisation

As a sales rep, you need to determine your potential customer's values by asking them what is important to them in a car. The perspective customer may answer they are interested in:

- safety,
- fuel economy,
- comfort, and
- reliability.

The sales rep might then respond with something like, "You know, this car has a great safety rating, excellent fuel economy, is reliable and is comfortable to drive". Providing the car meets these criteria, there is a good chance the buyer will be interested.

At no time should a rep tell a person they are an idiot if their values don't coincide with the rep's.

ELICITING PERSONAL VALUES

The secret to discovering and accurately eliciting true personal values is to ask intelligent questions and answer them honestly, without interpretation or rationalisation by the conscious mind.

The following exercise will help you in determining what your true personal values are.

◢ Exercise: Values Elicitation

1. Think about the last time you had an emotional warning signal. Was it to do with a relationship, your work, your family, your finances, your well being? You might have been cheated on by your partner, made redundant at work, or had a health scare. Or maybe you just got fed up with being alone.

    Let's imagine you receive a warning signal about work. Ask yourself, "What is important to me about work?" Write down the first value that comes to your mind.

    Then ask yourself, "What *else* is important to me about work?" Write down your second value. Continue asking this second question, making a list of your values until you have all the possible answers. Then summarise the list and ask the question again. The value most important to you may be very deep, so you need to dig very deep. You might list up to 10 values, if not more. The intention is not to elicit only your number one value.

2. To find out what really is important to you, you need to evaluate which is of most importance. Try asking yourself, "If I could have only one of these values, which one would I have?" After you have placed that at the top of the list, ask yourself, "If I could have one more value, which one would it be?" Do this until you have placed each value on the list in a hierarchical order. You may find that some of the values elicited in Step 1 are basically the same and have merged.

3. Now, one at a time, closely examine your top three values. If you have received a warning signal, what you are doing is either expressing or violating these values.

    For example, if you place a high value on trust in relationships with your business associates but find yourself questioning, examining and scrutinising every suggestion they make, then your behaviour is conflicting with your value. At this point you have a choice as to whether to keep the value or change the behaviour or vice versa. Other values will be driving some of your behaviour, so it is important to remember the purpose of the exercise is to gain clarity about your true values and their connection with your behaviour. This will help you to make decisions that serve you well.

Choose other areas of your life, such as career, and identify your values. Prioritise these values to create a hierarchy.

Run through this 3-step values elicitation exercise, choosing a context in which to elicit your values. For example, you might be considering joining a gym because you value your health. Ask, "Why is my health important to me?" Do you answer *away from* by pointing out the health risks if you don't join the gym, or do you answer *towards* by pointing out the fact that if you get in shape you'll be able to play sports with your grandkids?

Some personal values may no longer be valid but you are hanging onto them as a result of habit. Is it a value that works for you in some circumstances but not others? Can the value be changed? Do you know someone with different values in this area and those different values seem to work better? What would be the result if you changed your values? Asking these questions is the first step to creating change.

Ask yourself questions like:

1. Am I creating the kind of product for my company that is fully and completely in line with my values? Since you will be delivering this product on a daily basis, I suggest for your happiness that it does. Is your product of a quality that should and can be sold to your clients? You need to think about your values and your clients values.

2. How do I align my business in a way that helps me to lead a life closer to my values?

3. How can I build my company's values?

4. Am I engaging with my clients in a way that is in line with my values?

5. How about the values of the client?

6. Are the ways I market and sell my business in line with my values?

7. Are there certain clients I should not take on because they operate against my values? If I do take them on, how will I align myself in a way that doesn't go against my values?

8. You may want to consider if publically stating your values will actually help you market your business.

9. How many hours do I expect to work in order to start and maintain the business? Will I be able to live a life true to my values, given how these work hours will affect other areas of my life (e.g., my family, friends and health)?

10. How does my time and money investment to start the business affect my values? How does that affect the people around me?

11. How do I manage my employees or consultants in a way that is in line with my values? Do my values match theirs? Would I do business with them if their values were in opposition to mine? Have I communicated this clearly and set expectations?

12. If I am planning on having a business partner, does he or she have the same values as I do? Is there a values conflict? How would they answer the preceding questions? Do our values align or compliment?

I recommend doing a values check every 3 months and ask questions like these again. You may need to realign your values, make the next steps, and push forward. Most important, let go of those elements that are against your values or in conflict with them. Always keep in mind the ecology of work versus life in this process.

Eliciting Values to Assist Others in Making Decisions

Whenever one of my clients is looking for any kind of a change of direction, such as a career change, setting some goals in a specific area of their life, looking for a partner, etc., I use the values elicitation exercise to determine their values. I have included two instances where I used values elicitation to help them make decisions about the direction of their life.

In my first example, I once worked with a 36-year-old man who was trying to determine what was important to him in a career. I asked him the question, "What is important to you about a career?" After I had written down his first answer, I asked him, "What else is important to you about a career?" Eventually we had a list that included:

1. Respect
2. Helping people
3. Being a good team leader
4. Solving problems
5. Solving problems
6. Travel
7. Independence
8. Prosperity/money
9. Satisfaction
10. Working in the service industry
11. Worthwhile causes
12. Recognition
13. Belief in the product and/or service

Once we had a list, we were then able to rank them according to importance:

1. Prosperity/money
2. Satisfaction
3. Respect
4. Independence

5. Recognition
6. Helping people
7. Belief in the product and/or service
8. Being a good team leader
9. Worthwhile causes
10. Morality/ethics
11. Solving problems
12. Travel
13. Working in the service industry

You can see that the order of the list changed, which is why it is so important to not only determine the values, but also their rank.

The next step was to check for values alignment by running the entire hierarchy through a piece of content and calibrating the feedback. I wrote up a proposal for employment for this man and in it I fed back the 13 values I had elicited from him:

> *"My company has an opening for a new employee and I think you may fit the criteria. In this job you'll be able to earn a lot of money and become very prosperous. I think this may give you job satisfaction because not only will you gain respect, you'll have the independence that I know is very important to you. You'll get the recognition that comes from helping people and the service and products that we market will give you the opportunity to become a good team leader for our worthwhile cause. We require someone like you that has a sense of morality and ethics, is good at solving problems and likes the opportunity to travel while working in the service industry. Are you interested?"*

The man replied, "Yes!"

When you feed back information to someone within their value system, it becomes very attractive and difficult for them to resist.

In my second example, I had a client who was looking for a new direction in her life. However, she didn't feel she had the confidence to go back into work at the age of 62, having been out of employment for 2 years or so because of some significant life-changing events.

After doing the values elicitation exercise, it became apparent to her that it was not a question of lacking confidence about getting back into work, it was because her priorities had changed. She had financial security and really enjoyed cooking, hosting events, and spending time with her family. She loved having her children and grandchildren around. The only thing she really missed was having business-related conversations at breakfast with her husband, who was a director of a major company.

She looked at the hierarchy as to what was important to her now and how she wanted to spend her life and came to the realisation that at 62 years of age she did not want to go back into employment at any level. Spending time with her family, being there for them, was what made her happy. While at first she had thought going back to work part time was an option, after the elicitation exercise she decided it was not. She said the hour we spent on eliciting her values helped her to clarify what she really wanted.

If you are helping someone by using these exercises, it is important that you **do not** make suggestions. Give the person time to answer on their own. You want them to state their values, not yours.

Sometimes their answers will be vague. That's why it is essential to continue to drill down by asking them what else is important to them. One of my clients said having a tidy desk was important to him. When I asked him what was important about have a tidy desk, he eventually said what was really important was being organised.

Motivation

Motivation is critical for people to achieve good, consistent results in business. The art of recognising behavioural patterns in others and using language to break negative habits that limit their progress can be a very effective way of motivating clients, colleagues, staff and customers.

A good question to ask is, "What are the positive and negative consequences of your actions?" Some people are motivated *away from* pain. When you ask them why it is important for them to stop smoking, they may say, "If I don't give up smoking, it could kill me".

Some people are motivated *towards* pleasure. These people may reply, "If I give up smoking I will feel fantastic and be able to go for runs".

It is very beneficial to know which category someone falls into so you can establish how to motivate them. If you attempt to motivate someone who is very *away from* by offering them incentives, it might not resonate with them. Equally, if you tried to motivate someone who is very *towards* by pointing out the negative repercussions of their actions, it is likely to cause them a lot of stress.

It is important to respect the values of other people. You may not always agree with other people's values, but by respecting them you can adjust to their map of the world and understand if their values are being violated by your behaviour or business ethos. It works the other way too.

I've been in situations when I have been asked to do training for organisations. I found out that their values were ones with which I could agree and because of that, I took on the work. I also have been in situations when I didn't take on the work because the company's values were so different from mine that I didn't feel my skills were conducive to what they wanted.

◢ BELIEFS

Imagine you're a chairman of a football club and you are hiring a football manager. You have received a CV from one applicant and it is phenomenal. This guy played for what was the best team in the UK at the time, won loads of trophies as a player, represented his country, won European Footballer of the year, has all of the qualifications as a football coach and manager, widely received and respected. You read the CV and think, hmmm, I'm impressed.

You also receive another CV. This second guy has done some studies at university. He was never a professional player of any stature. You notice in the CV that he has a long history of being mostly self-educated. His profession was that of a translator. Which CV do you take? The one that has all the experience and background as a professional player? Or the translator?

If you had taken the first one, you'd have picked Kevin Keegan. I remember I was once watching Kevin during a TV press conference. It was after the final game at Wembley in which England had lost to Germany. During the interview, Kevin said he was not cut out for being a manager at this level. That was Kevin's belief about his identity. Regardless of how good a player he was and how knowledgeable he was about the game, if he didn't believe he could do something or feel his identity was conducive to achieving the results, then obviously he would support the belief that he wasn't up to being a manager.

If you had taken the second person, you'd have taken the most successful manager of the modern generation, Jose Mourihno. He educated himself about the game and built a powerful coaching philosophy. When he took the job of managing Chelsea, he called himself "The Special One" at a press conference. Did he genuinely believe he was The Special One? Well that was his belief. You'll support what you believe.

And that's the power of belief.

HOW BELIEF WORKED FOR JAMES BOLTON

I was working with a young talented footballer named James Bolton doing some NLP Coaching sessions. He had spent a lot of time out of the game with an Osgood Schlatter injury, an extremely painful lump below the kneecap that can be caused by sports that involve running and swift changes of direction. He was in the final year of his apprenticeship with Macclesfield, the year the team would decide whether or not to give him a contract to play professionally. Most professional teams offer, on average, 2 to 3 pro contracts to youth players.

By the time Bolton came to work with me, I found that he had lost a lot of self-belief. I took him through a series of mental NLP exercises to help him rebuild his confidence. I knew that would be key for him to believe he could still get a contract against what seemed like insurmountable odds. We had to create a bubble of belief and stay focused.

After the session, I didn't hear from Bolton or his father for a while. When they did contact me, they told me Bolton had been given a professional contract with Macclesfield Town FC and enquired about working with me during the following season. We did a lot of planning and I used techniques, like anchoring, for a peak mental state, and visualisations so he could plan his matches in his mind and practise his technique without over-training so as not to exacerbate the Osgood-Schlatter condition.

The announcement of his signing with Macclesfield is printed below and also was reprinted on Bolton's website (http://www.lfe.org.uk/news/macclesfield-town-secure-bolton-signature).

> *Macclesfield Town have handed a professional contract to young defender James Bolton. The centre-back has put pen to paper on a two-year deal with the Silkmen, who are currently battling against relegation from League Two.*
>
> *The 17-year-old, who hails from nearby Stone, has yet to make his first-team debut for the club.*
>
> *A statement on the Club's official website reads: "The Silkmen are delighted to have secured the signature of the promising centre-back, who has featured in 10 of the Club's 11 reserve games this season, and has even attracted serious interest from the Premier League."*

HOW TO MAKE BELIEF WORK FOR YOU

Just as it is important to be aware of our own learning styles and ways of thinking, it is equally important to be aware of our individual, communal, and cultural values and beliefs. A value is a culturally accepted principle or standard. For example, Western cultures generally value logical reasoning and individualism more than Eastern cultures.

Knowing your values and beliefs increases your understanding of yourself and others (thus enhancing your Emotional Intelligence), provides a firm foundation from which to pursue goals, and aids in making decisions. Once you are aware of your existing values and beliefs, you can change them if you so desire. In business, by maintaining an awareness of your own values and beliefs, you can offer unbiased, nonjudgmental support for others who may have very different values and beliefs from you.

As a coach, manager or leader in business, you have both the right and the responsibility to establish the values of the work environment. This can become tricky ground to tread—like a smoker and a nonsmoker each claiming the right to airspace. However, integrity, mutual respect, safety and honesty are relatively solid ground on which to build values.

What are your values and beliefs? Are you able to respect values and beliefs that are different from yours, without dismissing, judging, coercing, or feeling the need to defend your own values and beliefs? These are important skills for the coach, manager, or leader.

Andy Hill had played successfully for both Manchester United and Manchester City and at a number of other clubs, before he founded Provision Soccer Academy. Provision Soccer Academy helped younger players, who had been released from the game a chance to play first team football again and get back into the shop window, so to speak.

Andy called me to ask if I would work with Bacup FC because it was struggling on the brink of relegation. I had lot of experience working with other teams and helping them turn around their fortunes. I joined Andy with the first team and we kept them afloat.

We decided to continue our working relationship during the next season. We won a cup with Bacup FC, the first one in a number of years, which was fantastic. We also made it into the finals of another competition. We lost to a team that was much higher in the tier of football, though we gave a good account of ourselves. It was a great experience. Bacup FC eventually produced some really, really good players who played in the UK and abroad; a phenomenal achievement.

Bacup FC was a good experience for me because it helped to prove the worth of NLP in the professional ranks with top players and teams in the UK and the world. This was a great opportunity for me to work for a team and test my skills in a lower league level. I was happy not only to make a difference, but also to break some of my own belief barriers about working with players in a non-professional environment.

I introduced a lot of players to NLP and they embraced it. I am sure it was a positive reason in them moving forward. We developed a brand of football that caught a lot of attention and pretty much put Bacup FC on the map again in the world of football.

◢ **Exercise**

List five of your strongest beliefs. Try to recall when and how you began to form each. How have these beliefs influenced your life? What impact have these beliefs had on your life?

1. _____

2. _____

3. _____

4. _____

5. _____

8 Goals

If you don't design your own life plan, chances are you'll fall into someone else's plan? And guess what they have planned for you? Not much.

—Jim Rohn

How many people do you know who moan about their life? Not having a partner or the ideal partner, not having enough money, being overweight, not enjoying their job, they are bored, fed up, disillusioned.

And yet, they keep walking on the treadmill of life, never doing anything about their circumstances, just leaving things to chance, waking up in the morning and whatever will be, will be. The live neither here or there, fitting into a routine, plodding along, going to a job they don't enjoy or don't find the least bit rewarding and coming home to watch TV to fill in the gaps.

They drift along, leaving their life to chance, not making the most of their potential, just living in silent desperation hoping some day some miracle will happen. They might win the lottery; meet their knight in shining armour or their beautiful princess.

How many people take the time to sit down and think about how they want to live their lives, to consciously design their own destiny and set goals, decide what they want out of life, places they would like to go, things they would like to achieve, people they would like to meet, things they would like to learn. If my experience with the thousands of people I've met is any indication, not many.

Before they worked with me, I think only around 10% of my clients actually set goals or at least consciously set goals. The people who do set goals seem to be the ones who have a stronger sense of fulfilment and purpose in their life, living life the way they want to.

The majority of the people I've met say they don't set goals; they just live and take things as they come. Is that what you say? Well, you might say you don't consciously set goals, but as long as you're alive, whether you realise it or not, you have adopted a goal-setting strategy. If you're getting up for work in the morning and going to a boring job you don't like, you still have a goal. It may be to pay the lousy bills or the damned mortgage, but it is still a goal.

Maybe you're part of someone else's goals. You're paying off that damn car—that sales person sure saw you coming. You see, whether you realise it or not, goals are a fundamental part of life. The two choices you have are either to carry on leaving things to chance or to take control of your life, living in a way that brings you fulfilment, purpose and happiness.

I guess with setting goals comes the fear of not achieving them, which is understandable. Imagine setting these awesome goals only to fall flat on your face and not achieve them, what then? Well I think the most amazing thing about setting goals is the journey. Sometimes we don't achieve what we set out to achieve. Sometimes we achieve something more significant. Often, in the process of working towards and achieving goals, many other possibilities are opened before us and we accomplish so much more than we set out to achieve.

◢ GOALS

Goal setting is a powerful process for thinking about your ideal future and for motivating yourself to turn this vision of the future into reality. Goal-setting techniques are used by top-level athletes, successful businesspeople and achievers in all fields.

Goal setting gives you long-term vision and short-term motivation. Goal setting focuses your acquisition of knowledge and helps you to organise your time and your resources so that you can make the very most of your life.

However, it is possible to focus too much on one area and neglect others. I believe it is important to set goals for different parts of your life. Some people are successful in certain parts of their life and struggle in others. For example, you may spend a huge proportion of your life building a business and neglecting your family, and come home one day to find your family life is completely breaking down.

To create a life of fulfilment, growth and purpose, a life that's balanced, you shouldn't focus on only one aspect. It means consciously sitting down and making sure you prioritise your goals to determine what are the most important things in your life. Energy must be focused in those areas.

In this chapter you will find exercises you can use to determine the things you want in life. After you have listed your goals, we will then use a powerful technique to help you achieve them. Goal setting is based on you continuing to develop your life's key aspects. As Maslow suggested, we need fulfilment in different areas in order to live a well-rounded and happy life. Setting goals and outcomes can have a very strong, positive effect on our life.

What happens to the people who work 12 hours a day, 7 days a week, regardless of how much money they make? What happens to the people who are forever chasing the dream of fame and fortune, who have all the money you could imagine and are on the front cover of every magazine, and TV every night? Many profess to being unhappy, to being depressed and disillusioned. Some eventually turn to substances to enhance their feelings.

OVERCOMING A NEGATIVE PREDICTION WITH A GOAL

I remember doing a programme for BBC Greater Manchester. I was helping a 65-year-old woman called Margaret to lose weight with NLP Techniques. The programme ran for several months with Margaret and myself working together behind the scenes and then touching base on the radio to discuss how things were going.

At the start of the programme, Margaret said she didn't think she could lose weight because her GP had said her thyroid condition would make it hard, if not impossible, to do so. Well, in the space of around 4 months, Margaret had not only lost the weight, she managed to overcome a 56-year-old phobia of swimming and did some running for the first time in 30 years.

We worked on her overcoming her swimming phobia because Margaret had mentioned she would like to go swimming to help her exercise and lose weight, to swim with her friends, and to go swimming when she went on holiday.

I did *Timeline*, which is an NLP Technique, to help her remove the phobia. Margaret had booked herself for swimming lessons a few days before we were scheduled to go on air to talk about whether the technique to remove phobias worked and discuss her progress.

On the day of the first swimming lesson, she phoned me to say she hadn't gone because a friend had called and talked her out of it. The radio show was cancelled that Friday, which I guess in one sense was a relief for me. The following week Margaret had phoned to say she had decided to go through with her swimming lessons after all and she had done it! She was overjoyed with the experience and from then on never looked back.

While the original goal was to lose some weight, which she did and kept it off, the direction of her goal had literally changed the course of her life. She booked a holiday to Spain and she said it was the best she felt in years. She got her life back.

GOALS AND OUTCOMES

How many times have you heard people talk about their grand plans of what they are going to do—lose weight, stop yelling at their kids, learn to play an instrument—only to see them fail repeatedly at their attempts. The reason is because they have inadvertently programmed their brain to fail! We will see clearly how this occurs and how you can stop it if it's happening to you.

That inadvertent programming that causes failure is sometimes a fear of risk. The problem is, EVERYTHING you do requires some risk. There is a risk every time you get into a car! Successful people always acknowledge the probability of the risk occurring and the benefits of taking the risk and pursuing the goal. When in need of assistance, they enlist the aid of others, seeking input from a friend or mentor.

The other thing that prevents people from pursuing their goals is a fear of failure. If there is one thing that you take from this book and incorporate into your life from this moment forward should be this: failure equals feedback.

Failure is a signal to you that you need to learn another way to do something. In NLP, we say that if what you are doing isn't working, do anything else! Most people repeat the same behaviour over and over, expecting to obtain different results! If you do this, stop it! It's insane! Just do something else, *anything* else.

Legendary American baseball player, Babe Ruth, said he had the most strike outs *and* the most home runs of any player! He said. "Anything worth doing well is worth doing poorly at first." Think about it. When was the last time you became an expert at something after you did it once? Learn to look at fear from a new perspective and realise you will not achieve significant goals without some failures.

Do you doubt your skills? Don't believe you can do it with what you have? What will you do to increase your confidence? Well, you could learn from other people who are getting the results you want. Practise, join training programmes, get a coach and confront the situation boldly.

Establish a realistic standard for success and work towards it. When attempting something new, think about what skills or behaviours are needed. Then go out and learn them. Change is rarely easy, but if it moves you towards your goals, anything that is unfamiliar is worth doing. If change is scary, admit it, do a little at a time, try to seek out change (for a change) and begin to view yourself as one who likes and looks forward to change. Do lots of little new things—new restaurants and foods, new friends and acquaintances, new books of different genres.

Too busy to make numerous small changes? Prioritise those things of most value to you and pursue those.

Goal Setting Rules and NLP Tips

1. You must state your goals in the positive—what you *do* want, not what you *don't* want. If you state what you do want, the brain deletes any negatives.

2. You must be able to represent it to yourself by way of the five senses. How do you see it, hear it, taste it, smell it, and feel it? Where do you feel it, where do you want it, when and with whom?

3. You must be able to start or initiate your action and be able to carry it out *independently*. It is what *you* can do and not what others can do that counts. How will you start it and how will you carry it through to the end result?

4. Make sure the goal you are attempting to attain does not interfere in any negative way with your natural life state and that of others. Is there anything that you or someone else would have to give up or sacrifice when you make the change? How will you and others around you be affected?

IDENTIFYING A CLIENT'S GOALS

Identifying a client's goals is one of the most important tasks you will perform when coaching someone else. (This process also can be used if you are coaching yourself.) Focused listening and open-ended, powerful questions are very useful when assisting a client to identify their goals. For example:

- Describe your ideal life.
- If you won the lottery tomorrow, what would you do?
- What thoughts have been continually vying for your attention in recent weeks/months/years?
- What would you do if you had only one year left to live?

Another useful tool when assisting a client to identify their goals is to help them elicit their values, like in the exercise you completed in chapter 7. Goals and actions should grow out of our values. Discovering where misalignments are occurring can be quite helpful during the process of identifying and reaching goals. Alternatively, you might ask a series of open-ended questions to determine the client's values and beliefs and to decide whether their behaviours are aligned with their values and beliefs.

The range of questions you ask depends, to some degree, on the type of coaching and how much assistance the client needs to focus in on a goal. For example, a nutrition coach may focus the questioning on matters such as diet, exercise, athletic aspirations, and the like, while a life coach may focus more broadly on such matters as lifestyle, personality, career, and relationships.

When you're assisting a client to identify their goals, it's also useful to ask a few questions aimed at identifying needs. Again, your approach will vary with each individual client. The most direct approach is simply to ask, "What do you need to support you as you work towards your goal(s)?" or "What would best support you during this process?" More specifically, ask, "What do you need from yourself, from me as your coach, from your significant other, your colleagues, etc., to help you reach your goals?" As the answers to these questions may take time to emerge, consider providing clients with a written copy of key questions for goals and needs identification. Formulating answers to the questions can become homework. The following exercise is also great homework to assist with the identification of goals.

◢ Exercise: Letter to Self

Imagine it is 10 years in the future. Who are you? Where are you? What are you doing? Close your eyes and connect with who you are 10 years from now. Then, from the perspective of your future self, write a letter to yourself as you are now. Offer suggestions, perspectives, encouragement—anything that comes to you. Don't hold anything back.

The Individual Plan of Action

Once you have identified a client's primary goal or goals, it's time to get specific with an individual plan of action. Four useful questions to ask when formulating an individual plan of action are:

1. What will you do?
2. How will you do it?
3. When will you do it?
4. How will you know when it has been done?

Wrapped up in these four questions is the entire coaching agenda; that is: identifying the goal, the means of achieving that goal, when the goal will be achieved, and the means of measuring its achievement.

As a coach, your main role is to support and guide your client to answer these questions for themselves rather than imposing your own answers. Skilful inquiry is the best way to do this. To take a specific example, suppose a client's primary goal is to increase their income by 50%. Once the goal is set, next identify the specific steps, behaviours, actions, or other means, along with time frames that the client will use to reach this goal.

Milestones can be useful for some people, though not all. Milestone examples include: nine new clients by December 1st, one new client each week for the next nine weeks, spend two hours each week looking for a new position, apply to three jobs every week, etc. Support and guide your client to craft milestones that work for them, stated in their language and within their timeframes. Encourage them to identify how they'll know when the goal has been reached. At every step of the process, challenge the client to focus, narrow, refine, broaden, rethink, discover, and create toward a plan of action for meeting their goal(s).

When you have an initial plan mapped out, consider formalising it in writing, much like a contract, with the understanding that it can be modified. Some clients may wish to modify their plan every week and some may never wish to do so. This document provides a reference point for both of you as you progress through your coaching meetings. Throughout the process, it is important to remember that the client owns the goal(s), actions, solutions, and outcomes.

Long-term planning and goal setting are the essential ingredients of business success. I remember working with a client who, after a period of about 10 years or so, had built 17 different stores of a franchise. It got to a point where some of the stores were doing well and some were not. It seemed to me that the problem stemmed from there not being a clear vision, a plan. My client seemed overwhelmed with the problem and it was a case of management by crisis. I told him to take a moment to think about where he was and where he wanted to be.

My client could have taken any old job and have drawn the same wage without all the stress that went with owning these franchises. So why was he doing it? Because he wanted to retire early and he wanted financial security. It was then he realised that ultimately he had no exit strategy.

He needed a vision and a plan, and he had to do some serious planning. The two areas he looked at most seriously were whether he needed to scale back or expand, whether to bring in people to help manage the business, and if he wanted to pass on the business or sell it. Well, passing on the business didn't look like it was going to happen for various reasons. The solution we reached required a lot of restructuring. Not necessarily revolution, but evolution. Being clear about where he wanted to go helped to alleviate a great deal of stress and improve the management of his business so that eventually he could retire early with financial independence.

Building a Vision

I was working with someone who was in a finance business. You don't need me to tell you that being involved in the finance business after the great financial crisis in 2008 was a struggle. A number of finance businesses closed down. My client was in a situation where he was working long hours. He had a good staff but he was worried because a number of businesses in the same situation had fallen by the wayside. So we sat down and looked at various ways and techniques he could use to move his business forward.

The most important point was for my client to build a vision. He had to be very clear about where he wanted to go. Decide what staff he needed. How to get the best out of the staff. We deployed a number of techniques: anchoring and perceptual positions (to see a situation from someone else's point of view) for his tele-sales staff to help them to better understand the customers. We looked at different ways we could add value. Adding value is important to any business. If you can go the extra mile, you can add value and it's likely you will get more customers as a result.

In order to add value, my client knew he needed to bring in an expert tele-sales person to help train his staff. He didn't have the budget for that, but he have a lot of leads. He decided to exchange some leads for training for the tele-sales staff. We used negotiation strategies to bring in an expert to work with the tele-sales staff in exchange for the leads my client could offer.

I cautioned my client against giving this expert all the leads that were available. I suggested instead that a performance-results system be used in order to get to the desired call–sales ratio. The expert's performance would determine the number of leads he would receive. In this way we could ensure that the expert didn't just come in, do the training and then disappear.

I asked my client what his sales ratio was and he told me it was approximately 11:1. I suggested that the trade should be performance related and the tele-sales expert would be required to bring that down to 7:1. When the ratio reached 7:1, the expert would receive leads in trade. If the ratio remained at 7:1 the next month, there would be another trade, and so on. When negotiating, it's important that you are very clear about what you want and what the other party wants. Then it's a win–win situation.

My client's business, which was in its infancy, held strong when a lot of bigger, established businesses went down. I think the key aspect to his success was in starting from the end, the ultimate destination, and then building a vision towards getting there and making sure he would get the best out of the situation.

◢ Exercise: Create Your Vision Board

Get a piece of poster board and attach it to a wall in your office or home where you will see it often. Go through magazines, brochures, etc., and when you see the pictures of the things you want (e.g., a house or car you want, places you want to travel), cut them out and glue them to your vision board. In other words, make yourself a collage of the goals that excite you. Do this knowing full well that as you look at them every day, they will soon be yours.

CREATE A WELL-FORMED OUTCOME

It is important when you set clear and specific goals about what you want. In order to create a well-formed outcome, you need to visualise it in your mind, noticing all the details, and stating the outcome in the present and in positive terms. For example:

> It is July 1, 2020, and I am sitting in my 7-bedroom house in Cornwall. The house is fully paid off. The lounge is 10 metres long and

5 metres wide. The floors throughout the house are hardwood with a beautiful finish. The lounge is decorated in pastel shades of light blue, blending in perfectly with the Italian curtains and the Italian furniture. There is a spacious feel about the whole house as each room is large, allowing a sense of freedom and fresh air. Each room is decorated to my taste and I am delighted with the overall feel of the house.

Through the windows I can see the beautifully maintained gardens and the stunning Cornish coast beyond them. As I smell the scents of Spring floating in through the big windows, I reflect back to the time when I wrote this goal and recall the first step of the journey to this house when I set up my own business.

As I sit here now I have a real sense of achievement, a feeling of well being and excitement of finally achieving some of my potential.

THE BLAME FRAME VS THE OUTCOME FRAME

There are key questions you can ask to help you focus on what you want. Avoid the *Blame Frame* questions and ask the *Outcome Frame* questions:

Blame Frame

1. What's wrong?
2. Why do I have this problem?
3. What caused this problem?
4. How has this problem limited me?
5. How long have I had this problem?
6. How does this problem cause me to fail?
7. Whose fault is this problem?

Outcome Frame

1. What do I want?
2. How can I get it?
3. How will I know when I have it?
4. What resources do I have right now that will help me achieve my outcome?

5. When I get what I want, how will my life improve?

6. What will I do to begin getting what I want?

After answering the Outcome Frame questions, take a moment to breathe deeply and remember what answering them was like for you.

THE POSRE TECHNIQUE

To be successful in anything you need to have an outcome in mind. There's an old saying you might have heard, "If you don't know where you are going, you'll end up somewhere else." The POSRE techniques is a simple and excellent process you can use with your staff, colleagues, clients, and yourself to help create well formed outcomes to work towards a goal.

Choose an outcome or a goal you want to achieve and...

P State it in positive terms. Always set goals in the positive sense, what you want rather than what you don't want.

O Own it. What can you do to bring this about by your own actions? What can you do to influence the outcome? What do you need to do to achieve this goal?

S Be sensory specific. Define your goal in sensory-specific terms. By what date do you intend to reach this outcome? Put yourself in the situation of having it. What do you see/hear/feel when you have it? Make sure that your image of the goal is sensory-rich, vivid and compelling. It's much easier to work out how to get to your goal once you know where you want to go!

R Resources. What resources do you have that will help you reach your goal? What additional resources do you need?

E Ecology. This is a risk assessment on how the goal will affect every area of your life.

(a) What will happen when you have it?

What won't happen when you have it?

Are there any downsides to achieving it?

(b) How would having this outcome affect each area of your life?

Who else would be affected by you having this outcome?

How would you having this outcome affect the planet?

    (c) Congruence check: How do you feel about this goal? Do you want it 100%?

    (d) Does your energy increase when you think about it? If not, adjust the goal until you feel enthusiastic about it!

An Ecology Check is Important

I remember working with a client who told me he wanted to implement a coaching framework to deliver coaching skills in schools for young people. So we sat down and did a consultation session. During the session, I talked about long-term planning involving a period of five years or more in order to build a solid framework for his business. When I mentioned a long-term plan, he looked at me with a blank expression. At that point I noticed his dull sensory acuity. He said he wanted things sooner than that; he wanted them to work straight away. My thoughts were, "If you are looking to build a business, a solid business, a reputable business, then you want a long-term plan.

After the session something didn't quite seem right. The client sent me a message telling me he had decided to work with a different coach. This new coach had promised him the world and assured him that he would get things off the ground and make a profitable business pretty quick. So I said fair enough. Work with whomever is right for you.

I heard from this guy 7 or 8 months later . He told me that he spent a lot of money with this other coach but he felt like he had gone backwards in his energy, effort and investment. He wanted to hire me again. I told him we needed to have a talk before we did anything else. After the talk, we'd decide if we wanted to take it from there. During this consultation session we talked about his business vision, what he had been doing, where he was and what he had done with his other coach. When I asked him if he was enjoying delivering this coaching programme to young people, he said that, actually, he didn't enjoy working with young people. I thought, "Well, don't you think you might be in the wrong business?"

He finally realised he was going into coaching for financial reasons, not because he enjoyed working with young people. I was open and honest with him. I told him there were plenty of other things he was probably passionate about that he could do for financial reasons. There was no point wasting any more money and time with somebody else. If he was going to hire me it would be better if we reassessed where he was and what he wanted to do so he can move forward.

After we talked some more, he realised that his passion was elsewhere. He did go on to be very successful in the field he is in at the moment. If we had done the session earlier when he had first contacted me, rather than him going off with somebody else, it would have saved him a lot of time and money. That's life.

It is key to take the consequences of what you
want to achieve into account.

◢ **Exercise**

Write one goal you have for each of the following categories. You may think of others, but for now, use these.

1. Personal Goals

    What would you like to achieve for yourself? Travel? Swimming with dolphins? Watch a cup final live? Going to a concert to listen to your favourite musician? Learn to fly?

2. Characteristics

    Is any part of your mindset holding you back; e.g., self-belief, self-esteem, confidence? Is there any part of the way you behave that upsets you? If so, set a goal to improve your behaviour or find a solution to the problem.

3. Career

    What are you passionate about? What do you enjoy doing? What is something you have always wanted to do.

4. Education

    What do you want to learn? Go back to finish your high school education, learn how to sing, dance, get a degree, learn some new skills?

5. Family

How is your relationship with your family? How would you like it to be?

6. Financial

How much money do you want to earn a week? Month? Every year?

7. Physical

Is there an ideal weight you want to be? Do you want to run a marathon? Do a fun run?

8. Pleasure

How do you want to enjoy yourself? You should ensure that some of your life is reserved just for you!

9. Spiritual/Contribution

Do you want to make the world a better place? If so, how?

A common question many people ask is, "Can I set more than one goal?" Of course you can. You can set as many goals as you want to ensure growth, particularly for the different aspects of your life. However, for now I suggest using the strategy and the following exercise for only one goal until you develop your action plan. Then you can set different action plans for different goals.

GOAL SETTING

1. State the goal in positive terms.

    ◢ What do you want to achieve, what would you like to happen, what outcome do you want? Remember the mind cannot process a negative instruction. For example, if I say don't think of the colour red, what comes to mind? Be specific and keep it simple. If a 5-year-old can't understand it, it's too complex (in the context of health and fitness, stating you want to lose weight is vague and not specific).

    ◢ Write exactly what you want—ideal weight you want to be (e.g., 12 stone or dress size 10), the exact car you want, the type of partner you want, the kind of business you want to build. Be as specific as possible. State it in the positive (what you want to achieve).

▲ Where are you now? This is your road map, in the context of your goal (e.g., just starting up in business, 15 stone, never completed a fun run).

▲ Where do you want to be? This relates to your goal, your outcome (e.g., a successful business seeing 20 clients per week charging the market rate per session, 12 stone, completed 5 mile fun run).

2. Specify the goal in sensory-based terms.

▲ Remember we learn and build associations through our senses, which make them real. Engage all of your senses in this description process to employ more of your brain and nervous system and to build pathways in your mind to make it real.

▲ Close your eyes and imagine what it will be like when you have achieved your goal. What will you see? Hear? Feel? What steps or stages are involved in reaching this goal? Formulate a plan based on these steps. The first step might be to email or phone someone, the second step to set up a business meeting, the third step to identify your strengths and weaknesses, etc.

3. Specify the goal in a way that you find compelling.

▲ To make the goal have meaning, you need to specify it in a meaningful way. Imagine in your mind's eye the steps you have mapped out taking you to the point of having achieved your goal. See yourself achieving your goal like watching yourself on TV. Notice the screen, the clarity of the image, what you are wearing, what people around you are wearing, the surroundings, what you are saying, what people around you are saying and what it feels like to see yourself achieve the goal.

▲ What would achieving the goal mean to you? To your family? The impact it will have on the greater community? Is the goal compelling? Does it make you excited?

4. Run an ecology check on your goal (i.e., the consequences of working towards your goal or achieving it) to make sure it is what you want for yourself in all areas of your life.
   - Is the desired goal right for you in all circumstances of your life?
   - Is your goal appropriate in all your personal relationships?
   - What will having your goal give you that you do not now have?
   - What implications does it have on other parts of your life (e.g., spending time with your children, your partner, family)? Is your goal achievable?
5. The Plan: where, when, how, with whom, etc., will you get this goal?
   - Where? An office in city centre celebrating grand opening, running the New York Marathon, etc.
   - When? Set a time limit such as the exact date and even time when you will reach your goal, maybe something like by 12/10/2016 at 1:30 p.m. I will have a successful business seeing 20 clients per week at top market rate.
   - How? How do you intend to achieve your goal step-by-step: generate a plan, set up web site, business cards, meeting with key people, join gym, hire personal trainer, etc.
   - Whom? A list of the resources (family, friends, business manager) that can help you achieve your goal.
6. State the Resources needed to achieve the goal.
   - What resources will you need in order to reach this goal?
   - Who will you have to become?
   - Who else has achieved this goal?
   - Have you ever had or done this before?
   - Do you know anyone who has?
   - What is preventing you from moving toward it and attaining it now?

7.   Evidence Procedure

▲ How will you know that your goal has been realised? (How many times do we achieve a goal without even realising it? It's important to know when you have realised your goal. You wouldn't climb the highest mountain and not sit and admire the view.)

▲ What will let you know that you have attained that desired state? (How will it feel when you have achieved your goal? How many people achieve a goal and think, "is that it?" or are not sure if they're getting closer. Identify the feelings that will come with achieving your goal. Close your eyes and think about what feelings you will have, having achieved your goal.)

An Example of Goal Setting

1.   State the goal in positive terms.

▲ What do you want to achieve, what would you like to happen, what outcome do you want?

I would like to achieve fulfilment in my career, to be successful at whatever I do and to be happy. I would like to help people more, make a real difference to people's lives, I do believe that would make me feel more fulfilled, more satisfied.

I want to continue to be good at my chosen field(s). I would like to be in demand for my services and respected for the good work that I do. I want my work to be varied to keep it interesting.

I would like my career to enable me to achieve financial stability. I would like ample money in the bank to be able to afford all the material things I want. I'd like a house in Didsbury, I would like to be able to afford the nice clothes & accessories (such as a Mulberry handbag!). I'd like to be able to travel, go on more holidays, explore the world.

I'd also like to achieve financial success for other reasons too! To be able to help my family and friends. In an ideal world I'd win the lottery and then I'd be able to sort out myself, my friends, and family financially. Because there would be no financial pressure whatsoever, I could just do the things I'd really like to do. I would definitely travel more. I would spend more time working with various charities.

◢ Where do you want to be?

To begin with, I would like to bring the things I'm interested in together in some way, though later on if one area is more successful than another, I could concentrate on the more successful area.

I've been doing HR for the last ten years and I worked hard to get my masters. At this point I feel it would be a shame to give it up completely after all that work. Plus, I am good at it. Initially I would like to try other things around my full-time job and then, over time, perhaps I could go to 4 days a week. The end goal would be to work towards providing an HR consultancy service to several small businesses so that I keep my hand in HR but give up a full-time role at one particular organisation. I'd like to work more flexibly in the future rather than a set Monday through Friday type of role.

In terms of the EFT/NLP, I'd like to build this up gradually, to build my confidence and experience, and see where it takes me. I'd like to build up a good reputation and work towards building up a client base so that I see a regular amount of clients each week (even if it's only a small number to begin with). I would also like to do other things in these fields such as train or teach others.

The ideal end goal would be to have a varied, full and profitable workload (to stop me from getting bored), to be successful, happy and fulfilled in the work I am doing and knowing I was really helping people. This would also aid me in reaching my personal goals.

2. Specify the goal in sensory-based terms. Remember we learn through our senses and build an association through our senses which makes it real.

   ◢ What steps or stages are involved in reaching this goal?

   I think I'd feel that I'd made it when I felt real satisfaction, fulfilment and inner peace. I think I would be happy that I would be in a position to help the people I care about and to help other people outside of my inner circle. I think I would feel that I was making my little bit of difference to the big wide world out there! I think I would also feel more relaxed because I had achieved all that I set out to achieve. I can see me doing more work for charities because now I would have the financial freedom to do so. My steps to achieving my goal would be:

Speak to Tania about doing some EFT sessions. How I can start doing that?

Finish my NLP Practitioner's course. I'd also like to do the Master Practitioners' course in the first half of next year, if money allows for it. I'd like to build up my knowledge and skills base so I'm more confident in the service I'd be selling to others.

If I start doing some EFT sessions and, if it goes well and I like it, at some point I could get a website built and perhaps do phone EFT sessions. It's quite easy to do phone sessions. I could then build my website to sell other services as time goes on (such as the NLP/HR consultancy, etc.).

Looking at what my "niche" market could be, such as doing NLP workshops for businesses to begin with, I feel I need to build up my knowledge and experience. I could perhaps work towards putting some core training sessions together. I could try them out in my own company to begin with for practise.

3. Specify the goal in a way that you find compelling.

    ◢ What does this goal mean to you? Does it excite you? Do you find it compelling?

    It would mean a lot to me. I think if I were to achieve all the above, I would feel more like I was fulfilling my life's purpose, that I was making a difference and doing more good.

    I think as long as I'm happy, my family will be happy. I think my mum would like to see me in a position of financial freedom. I think that would relax her a lot more; she's always worried because she doesn't want us to have to go through all the things that she had to. I think, well know, that would mean a hell of a lot to her.

I'd like to think it would have a positive impact on the wider community as well because I could help more people.

Yes, it does make me excited when I think of achieving it all. Yes it is compelling.

4. Run an ecology check on your goal to make sure it is what you want in all areas of your life.

   ◢ Is the desired goal right in all circumstances of your life?

   Yes, there's nothing to stop me.

   ◢ Is your goal appropriate in all your personal relationships?

   Yes. I really only have family and friends to think about and they're pretty supportive in what I do.

   ◢ What will having your goal give you that you do not have now?

   More fulfilment, greater flexibility, more opportunity to help others, financial stability.

   ◢ What implications does it have on other parts of your life, such as spending time with your children, your partner, your family?

   Not really applicable as I don't have children or a partner. I speak to my family on the phone and see them once a month or so. I have the capacity to take on more at the moment.

   ◢ Is your goal achievable?

   I hope so! Yes.

5. The Plan: where, when, how, with whom, etc.

   ◢ How will you get to this goal?

   I'd like to continue learning, I'd like to be a sponge to experts in the field and really take it all in so I can be good at what I do. A lot of it will be down to myself to get on with it basically. I believe I have the knowledge and skills to be able to be successful.

   ◢ Where would you like to do this?

   I'd like to be based in Didsbury. I think it will be about building an online presence, or perhaps working out of other clinics to begin with.

⊿ When do you want to start work on this goal?

By the end of 2013 I would like to have made a good start towards all this. By the end of this year I definitely would like to feel more confident in my skills and have actually done some sessions or workshops (even if just within my own company). I'd like to have gotten some good feedback which will build my confidence and propel me forward.

⊿ How do you want to achieve this goal?

By using the steps already mentioned. Once I get to the stage of building a website, I would then get business cards done. I would also need at look at how to market myself and determine who would be my target audience.

⊿ Who could you contact to help you achieve your goal?

My friends. Maybe they could help to advertise my services when I get to that stage by recommending me.

People I work with like Tania and Jimmy. They could help me to increase my knowledge and guide me in the right direction.

Networking and connections.

6. State the resources needed to achieve the goal.

⊿ What resources will you need in order to get this goal?

Knowledge and skill is key for me. From those come confidence and belief in my own ability.

A bit of direction from those people who are more knowledgeable and experienced than myself. A bit of help or ideas about getting those initial clients would be helpful.

Help to build a website in time.

⊿ Who will you have to become?

Someone who is more confident in my own ability in going into a new arena.

⊿ Who else do you know who has achieved this goal?

I'd like to eventually be in the same league as people like Tania Prince and Jimmy, people who are well known and highly respected in their fields.

◢ Have you ever done this before?

No.

◢ What prevents you from moving towards it and attaining it now?

Nothing except my own feelings of nervousness and wondering if I'm ready, if I've got enough knowledge, etc.

7. Evidence Procedure.

◢ How will you know that your goal has been realised?

When my services are in demand. When I'm financially secure. When I really feel like I'm making it. When I've moved away from a full time HR role.

◢ What will let you know that you have attained that desired state?

It will feel highly satisfying that I'm meeting my life's purpose. I will feel a lot of happiness because I'm really helping people, really making a positive impact in their lives. I will have real feelings of lasting fulfilment. Being really happy with what I'm doing; not wanting to be onto the next thing, so to speak!

START WITH THE END IN MIND

When you plan out your goals, it helps to start with the final outcome in mind. I am not suggesting that every time we set goals we will go on to achieve precisely what we set out to achieve, but sometimes we go on to achieve something else in a similar direction.

Greg De Carneys, the lead sports scientist at West Ham United FC, was a student at the Liverpool John Moores University when he did some work experience at Bury FC while I was working there. His plans were to go into coaching, so I took Greg under my wing and spoke to him in regards to planning and goal setting.

A few years later Greg got in touch via email letting me know he was sports scientist at West Ham United FC. He wanted me to work with one of his players, which I did.

It occurred to me that Greg had come a long way from his days as a student. While his plans to get to the highest level of football involved hard work, they also involved a degree of planning. The actual steps Greg had taken to reach his goal were: First Team Manager at Liverpool John Moores University Academy, coach at Derby County FC, First Team Fitness Coach at Watford Football Club, and finally to Lead Sports Scientist at West Ham United FC.

When I had talked to him about goal setting and where he wanted to be, the sequence he set up wasn't in that order. What was certain was his strong desire to work at the highest tier of football, and he would eventually achieve it. Yes, of course, it is great to be specific, though it is also important to be flexible and adaptable.

PLACING GOALS ON A TIMELINE

Once you have set your goals, place them on a timeline. This allows you to note the progress you are making step-by-step.

Starting with the end in mind (at the very top of your timeline), write specifically what your goal is and the exact date of the steps you will take in order to achieve it. For example:

▲ March 2012, dress size 12, see ten clients per week part-time

▲ Jan 2012, dress size 14, see 5 clients per week part-time

▲ December 2011, complete 5 mile fun run, go part-time at work.

▲ August 2011, enter 5 mile fun run, start building web site, marketing plan.

▲ June 2011, hire personal trainer and do one session per week and two on my own, set up meeting with business manager with an eye to accumulate enough funds to go full time in business.

▲ **Exercise**

This exercise brings a sense of reality to achieving your goals and makes them manageable.

1. Write down what you envisage for yourself in 10 years.

2. Write down your goals in list form using complete sentences. Use adjectives and be specific. Instead of writing "running a business," write "I run a successful

business employing ten staff selling a product enhancing the lives of others."

3. Create tasks for each goal.

Assign each task a due date, set up steps (1, 2, 3) and so forth. Begin each task with an action verb. Instead of writing "language classes," write "Enrol in [French, Italian, German, etc.] language class at the local college."

4. Keeping track.

As a milestone to help you know if you're on track, write down what you envisage for yourself in one year (use your list from the following 10-year goals as a template).

5. Create tasks for each one-year goal.

Use your 10-year list of tasks as a template. Assign each goal at least one task per week.

6. Place your lists in a visible location.

Put your lists on your bedroom wall or somewhere else where you will see it daily.

7. Write your goals and tasks on a calendar.

Write the tasks on their corresponding due dates. Write the goals onto estimated date or dates of completion.

8. Use the lists and calendar as a template.

Write down where you expect task to be completed. Make entries for one week tasks, one-month goals, 1-year goals, 10-year goals, and other time frames.

KEEPING TRACK

It helps you to keep track of your progress if you have a written list of what you need to do and when you plan to accomplish something in order to reach your goal. Tables 8.1 through Table 8.3 are examples of how to write out your goals to keep everything in view and organised. If you have several different goals, use a different table for each goal.

Table 8.1 can be used as an outline for when you expect to achieve your goals and how you will know you have achieved them.

Table 8.1 Goal Timeline

	Goals	Timeline	When/How will I know I have achieved my goal
1.			
2.			
3.			
4.			
5.			
6.			
7.			

Table 8.2 can be used as an outline for what you aim to achieve in specific time frames. Write down where you want to be in relation to achieving your goal at each time frame. List your long-term, medium-term, and short-term goals and write the milestones you will reach along the way.

Action plans are essential if you're going to get the most out of your time. Weekly planning helps you to decide how to make effective use of your time and work proactively rather than reactively. Use Table 8.3 as an outline to write down the daily tasks you will need to accomplish in order to take you closer to achieving your goal.

GOAL-SETTING EXAMPLE

I remember sitting down in the Hilton Hotel in Manchester with Tony Basha, the founder of the Australasian Soccer Academy. It was 6 years after he first founded the academy and 5 years after I had sat down with him to discuss the direction he wanted to go. It had been an amazing journey. What started as a vision of training a few kids down at the local park in a deprived area of Sydney had grown into the realisation of a dream.

As we talked, we discovered that Tony had achieved the goals we had written down. He had two players in the Australian A league, the highest level of Australian football. He had sent a team on tour to the UK, where they had performed exceptionally well, getting excellent results against professional teams. One of the players, Alusine

Table 8.2 Time Frame Outline

10 years
5 years
3 years
2 years
1 year
3 months
1 month

Table 8.3 Weekly Action Plans

Time	Mon	Tues	Wed	Thurs	Fri	Sat	Sun
6–7am	task 1, 2, 3 (e.g., phone coach, email, go for run to build aerobic fitness)						
7–8am							
8–9am							
9–10am							
10–11am							
11–12pm							
12–1pm							
1–2pm							
2–3pm							
3–4pm							
4–5pm							
5–6pm							
6–7pm							
7–8pm							

Fofana, an African refugee in Australia, captured the attention of several UK clubs and had received an extended trial with Manchester City, in which he had excelled. He had had a very good chance of being signed, although visa restrictions had put that on ice.

In six years, the Academy had gone from a few players training at a local park to 100s of players using high-tech training equipment and cutting-edge training methods. The Academy was making an impact all the way in the UK. It was an amazing journey and a sign of bigger things to come for the Academy. It demonstrated just how powerful setting goals and planting seeds for the future can be.

STAYING FOCUSED ON THE GOAL

One of the most valuable services a coach, manager or leader can offer their clients or staff is a non-judgmental, clear-seeing, consistent perspective. How exactly you provide such a perspective will vary with each individual client and meeting. You may simply need to gently remind a client of their stated goal or ask a question such as, "How will that further your goal of XYZ?" Other clients may need a more involved form of intervention, such as help with motivation, stress reduction or time management. In helping someone, your main task is not to provide the answers but rather to hold the space, create the opportunity and provide the means for the client to realise their own answers. As they say on the playing field, always keep your eye on the ball. In coaching terms, that means staying focused on the goal.

I was working with a young athlete who had all the credentials to become an excellent footballer. My aim was to help him make the transition from playing at the amateur level of football to being taken on by Everton FC School of Excellence. When my client initially signed for Everton School of Excellence he was making steady progress; however, some of the challenges we faced were that the other players had more experience with being at that level and, by the sounds of it, many had grown up playing in the same age groups as they went up through the ranks.

When it got to the point that Everton was deciding which of the players were going to get a youth apprenticeship, I could see it added extra pressure on my client. The important thing was to find techniques to keep him focused on the process of playing. We set long-term, medium-term and short-term goals. Having an end outcome is important, but it is equally important to have the ability to focus on the process of getting there. So, the plan with my client was to set up a training schedule that would focus on taking each training session and game one step at a time.

Everton made the decision not to take him on. In a sense, it was a relief because he was not entirely happy there. However, by staying focused and playing well, he managed to catch the attention of Watford FC and eventually got a scholarship with them (www.watfordobserver.co.uk/sport/watfordfc/academy/9651479.Watford_confirm_new_scholars/).

NAVIGATING TOWARDS SOLUTIONS

From a very practical perspective, you can help your clients navigate towards solutions by helping them identify what is needed to get from point A to point B. It is also useful and helpful to introduce new perspectives. Instead of viewing or labelling a situation as a problem, consider talking in terms of opportunity and possibility. This shift in perspective can work like magic to dispel all kinds of demons that may lurk along the path to the goal and lies at the very heart of change and transformation. Instead of problem-solvers, you and your client are possibility-seekers. Edelson frames it this way: "Although the word *possibility* has been used for many years by solution-focused therapists [...] coaching goes a step further to suggest that anyone can potentially have what they want in life *by design*." Indeed, coaching is the vehicle for intentionally bringing about what we want.

Whenever possible, navigate your client towards the solutions they want and can most aptly provide for themselves and their life starting from right where they are. Ask questions such as, "What resources do you currently have that can be used to bring about what you want?" and "What if this problem was really the greatest opportunity you'd ever been given?" Like steering a ship toward shore, steer your client toward recognising the shortest path toward realising their goals. Use whatever means are most effective (again, it will be different for each client), including humour, shock, play-fulness, logic, analogy and story, or whatever else you have at your disposal. Apply these principles to your own role as coach and see the client as an opportunity of sorts, rather than a problem to solve. Just as the client's answers and solutions are within them, your answers and solutions are within you.

THE "CREATING A BRILLIANT FUTURE" TECHNIQUE

This powerful technique can be used to help clients with any goal or outcome that they want to achieve. For example, weight loss, stopping smoking, overcoming fears, phobias, passing a driving test or exam, setting up a new business or starting a new career.

1.   Take a pack of blanks cards. On five of them write one of these words on each card: "Identity", "Values & Beliefs", "Capability", "Behaviour", and "Environment".

2.   Use two blank cards to mark two spots on the floor–one to represent Today and one for a time in the Future when you will have achieved your outcome. The distance (time) between the two spots should be what *feels right*.

3.   Create an image of what your life will be like at some point in the future when you have achieved your goal/ outcome.

4.   Lay the five labelled cards at equal intervals between the Future card and the Today card. These five cards don't mark the passage of time, but instead mark the personal changes you expect to experience.

5.   Stand on the Future card and imagine what it feels like to have achieved your goal. Imagine you have a remote control like the one you use for your television. Use it to intensify the qualities of your internal imagery and sound. Turn up the brightness, increase the colour, improve the contrast, make it bigger and bring it closer. Turn up the volume and listen to the sounds. Have the sound tuned so that there is no interference. Step into the picture and notice the feelings of satisfaction and achievement of having achieved your goal.

6. Move to a spot just beyond the Future card and look back at the past you of Today who is just starting out on your journey to achieving your goal. From this position, what have you got to say to the you of Today? Have you any tips or words of advice?

7. Move your imagined self to the "Identity" card. Ask how you have changed, now that you have achieved your outcomes. What is different about you? What role are you now playing that you were not playing before?

8. Move your imagined self to the "Values & Beliefs" card. What values have you changed, if any, and how have your beliefs changed in order to achieve success?

9. Move your imagined self to the "Capability" spot. How have your capabilities changed? What did you learn along the way?

10. Move your imagined self to the "Behaviour" card. What did you do along the way? What are you doing differently now?

11. Move your imagined self to the "Environment" card. What impact has achieving your outcome(s) had on those around you? Is your environment still the same or has it changed at all? If so, how?

12. Revisit the cards in any order you wish if you feel that there is still work to do. You will know when you have true alignment because you will have a burning desire to make your first move towards achieving your goal.

Spacing the cards out on the floor can be a powerful way of programming in the changes you want to make and can sometimes give you a better concept of the time that it will take to achieve your goal.

Having the competed the "Create a Brilliant Future" technique, you should now have a clear picture of what you want, what you need to do, and what you need to change or develop to achieve your goal.

IT'S NEVER TOO YOUNG TO START PLANNING YOUR GOALS

When I work with younger children, I often use goal-setting questioning techniques to get them to think about where they want to be. I was working with a client who was doing athletic conditioning work for football. He had just signed to join with Blackpool Centre of Excellence football team and wanted to be in top shape. He would bring his 8-year-old son with him to the sessions.

To keep everything interesting for the son, when I asked my client to use the positive outcomes process along with other NLP techniques, I would also ask the son to do the same.

I remember the son saying he wanted to sign for Manchester City one day. At the time that goal seemed a long way away, but a little later his dad informed me the son had signed for Manchester City under 13s. He felt NLP was a massive help to his son's development.

BELIEF ASSESSMENT WORKSHEET

This tool allows you to assess what your beliefs are about your desired goal. Circle a number, with 1 being the least and 5 being the most.

1. My goal is achievable:
    1   2   3   4   5
2. I deserve to achieve my goal:
    1   2   3   4   5
3. My goal is appropriate and worthwhile:
    1   2   3   4   5
4. My goal is desirable:
    1   2   3   4   5
5. I know what I have to do to achieve my goal:
    1   2   3   4   5
6. I have the capabilities and skills to achieve my goal:
    1   2   3   4   5

9. Modelling

The foundation and core of NLP is modelling. NLP Modelling is a great way to figure out what someone does who is exceptional at what they do and how they organise their perceptions of the world so that you can create a simplified model of their experience. You can then teach these traits to yourself and others.

◢ MODELLING EXCELLENCE

Imagine you are an architect walking in the countryside on a nice summer day. You come across a beautiful house and you decide you would love to create a similar type of house for your family. As an architect, you realise it is not just the materials you use, it is *how* you use them. You locate the builder of the house to find out how the structure of the house was put together. When talking to the builder, you begin to take notes. You don't take down everything; at this point you only take down how the structure of the house works and stays upright.

When you go back to the office, you take your notes and begin to design your new house. You follow the same procedure the builder used, organising the structure in the same way as the house you saw. This helps to ensure you are going to build the house the same way using similar materials. This modelling gives you every opportunity to build a house equally as beautiful as the one you appreciated.

MODELLING IS INDISPENSABLE FOR BUSINESS SUCCESS

How can you apply the same modelling process to ensure essential business skills for success? Let's say you want to learn how president Obama gives such powerful presentations or how Richard Branson is such a successful, flamboyant entrepreneur. Perhaps you have a specific skill in mind, such as how the top sales rep at your organisation closes a deal.

That is the magic of NLP behavioural modelling. You can model anybody who is achieving success in any specific area in which you would also like to achieve success using the structure someone else used to create success. This helps you to produce far superior results rather than just trying to figure it out all on your own with no example to guide you.

Modelling is the heart of NLP. All the techniques of NLP applications originally came from modelling people who were *naturally* exceptional at something.

THE ROOTS OF NLP

John Grinder and Richard Bandler were primarily responsible for developing NLP. Grinder is one of the most prominent linguists in the world. Bandler is a mathematician, Gestalt therapist, and computer expert. The two men decided to pool their talents for a unique task—to go out and model the people who were the very best at what they did.

They looked at people who were achieving excellence in their field: business people, sports people, therapists, etc., in order to learn how successful people had developed successful patterns of behaviour through years of trial and error.

Throughout their research, Bandler and Grinder developed a number of behavioural-intervention patterns they had codified by modelling three of the most successful therapists of their generation: Virginia Satir, author and psychotherapist, widely regarded as the "Mother of Family Therapy" and known especially for her approach to family therapy and her work with Systemic Constellations, Fritz Pearls, psychiatrist and psychotherapist, and Milton Erikson, one of the greatest hypnotherapists that ever lived who specialised in medical hypnosis and family therapy. Satir, Pearls and Erikson were considered three of the best therapists of their generation, especially for their knowledge of verbal and non-verbal language patterns and non-verbal behaviour. Bandler and Grinder discovered how Satir was able to consistently produce results when other therapists had failed.

They had discovered what patterns of actions she produced to create results. And they taught those patterns to their students, who were able to apply them and achieve the same results, even though they did not have noted the therapist's years of experience.

The essence of NLP is "what is the difference that makes the difference?" What is the difference between a person achieving fantastic results and a person who, at best, is mediocre. What are the ingredients to being successful in business? Why is it that some people are so adept at communicating, delivering presentations, gaining rapport, leading, managing, interacting with others, and making key decisions seem effortless? What makes a Richard Branson, Anne Mulcahy, Larry Page, Warren Buffett, or Bill Gates?

Bandler and Grinder found a way of eliciting and coding the expertise of people who were really good at what they did, even the parts of their skills that the experts couldn't explain themselves because they weren't consciously aware of what they were doing. The way Bandler and Grinder did this was by becoming intensely curious about how the person got their results and reproducing it in a way similar to method acting, by *becoming* that person as closely as they could.

Instead of just thinking, "that person's a genius", they asked, "What is that person doing, consciously and unconsciously, that enables them to get their results?" How did Bandler and Grinder know when they were getting close to the way the genius did things? The results would tell them.

Once they could get similar results to the original, they started to refine their model. They would drop one piece of the behaviour at a time, to see what was the difference that made the difference. The end result of the process was a model of the skill reduced to its essentials, with everything inessential left out. This is what distinguishes a model from a carbon copy replica. This elegant, lean model was something that easily could be transferred to others to help them improve their skills quickly.

Eventually, Bandler and Grinder began to create their own patterns and teach them as well. These patterns we now know as Neuro Linguistic Programming or NLP. They provided us with a series of powerful and effective patterns to create change. More profoundly, they provided us with a system of how to duplicate any form of human excellence in a very short space of time. Over the years, many people have learnt the skills yet have had limited success in applying their effectiveness. *Knowledge is not enough. Action is what produces results.*

Success in modelling starts with finding exemplars worth modelling.

Henry Ford, famous for using the assembly line in his car factories, neither founded the world's first car company nor invented the assembly line. Borrowing an idea originally used in the meat-packing industries, Ford was able to go after a new market in his industry to great success. It goes to show that in the dog-eat-dog world of business, it's often not as much about the product as it is about the process.

Business strategy may not be a science, but using the right method with the right materials in the right place at the right time can create explosive results. What is the driving force behind companies such as Apple, Google, Amazon, Coca-Cola, Starbucks, and IBM?

Many companies, of course, never get to the top, and the few that do find it daunting to stay there. Just look at the current economic climate in which things are rapidly changing and becoming less predictable. There are businesses that haven't changed their fundamentals since their founding and now they are going bust, like Blockbuster in the UK. That store had been around for a long time and up until a few years ago, no one would have forecast they would close down, but they did. No entity is guaranteed continued success; just because they have been successful in the past does not guarantee success in the future.

Failure may come about when company leaders fixate on what made them successful and fail to notice when something new is displacing it. It may happen when a company focuses purely on the marketplace of today and fails to anticipate the future. You could say the same about individuals making their way in the business world.

Not everybody is looking to become the next Richard Branson or be a founder of a major corporation. How you define success is up to you. Some people think success is collecting things as a compensation.

They buy a more expensive car and possessions, they go for that promotion. And yet, they aren't always happy and don't always consider themselves successful. In my experience, truly successful people are people who have a degree of gratitude and purpose.

Finding your passion and purpose is an important part of success. The late Steve Jobs summed it up:

> *"Being the richest man in the cemetery doesn't matter to me.*
> *Going to bed at night saying we've done something wonderful,*
> *that's what matters to me."*

It is not just about having a lot of money. It is about doing something amazing, going to bed feeling great, and waking up knowing you are doing something wonderful. Whether you like Steve Jobs or not, appreciate his products or not, his quote is very powerful. An idea of doing something wonderful, making an impact and feeling grateful, contributing and living your dream, can make you feel more successful than being financially rich.

How can a person go from struggling to make a living to being successful in business, doing what they really love to do and having a level of financial freedom so they can provide for their family and others? In my experience, modelling someone else's successful behaviour is at the core of this transformation. Modelling will help you go beyond the cognitive mind to follow your heart and intuition.

STRATEGIES

We all have strategies for what we do, whether it is driving, operating the photocopy machine, love, happiness, etc. Strategies can be useful, because it means we don't have to learn what we do every day, or they can be destructive, because if they are not working and we keep doing things the same way, we are going to have problems, or at least not live the life we want.

Have you seen the film *50 First Dates*? It is a romantic comedy set in Hawaii that stars Adam Sandler as Henry Roth, a marine biologist, who has perfected a love 'em and leave 'em routine with countless vacationing women. That is, until he meets and falls head over heels for Lucy Whitmore (Drew Barrymore), a gorgeous, talented artist suffering from short-term memory loss. Because she can never remember meeting him, Henry must develop numerous strategies for winning Lucy's heart over and over again with every new day. He eventually helps her to remember him and their relationship by showing her a DVD of her life events and what she had done the day before.

The strategies we use work for us, up to a point, because it means we don't need to relearn the things we do, like drive a car, make a telephone call, or be reminded of who we are in love with every day. However, they also can be inhibiting to our success because if we have a specific way of conducting ourselves during a meeting or an interview and it's not working, then it might be time to change what we are doing. To accomplish this change, it might be useful to ask someone who does the process well.

Many people think that those who succeed in business have a special gift—they are lucky or are a certain character type. Yet the greatest gift people have who are successful in business is the ability to get up and go for it. To take action!

What if there was a way to accelerate the learning process? To learn to take action? What if you could learn a strategy you could implement that copied the successful mental strategies of people who are phenomenally successful? What if you could learn in 30 minutes that which may have taken someone else years to learn?

Would you be interested? If yes, then Modelling Overview is for you.

MODELLING OVERVIEW

Modelling for Business Success

Modelling focuses on the *how* of human excellence. How does the *peak performer* behave and think and feel? What do they do that is different from people who are less successful? What is the difference that makes the difference? By using our mind and body in the same way as a peak performer, we can increase the quality of our actions and our results.

Modelling is a very natural process. As toddlers and children we were unconsciously expert modellers and in this way learnt many complex skills. We had the ability to unconsciously assimilate complex patterns of behaviour or language that were available in the surrounding environment all without any understanding of the process. As adults we can apply the same processes in a conscious way, by asking the key question: "If I had to stand in for you, what would I have to do in order to think, to behave and to feel like you?"

Modelling is a different way of learning from conventional teaching and training methods. At the same time, it is something with which we are all familiar, because it's similar in many aspects to the way we learnt basic skills like walking and talking as children.

Behavioural modelling is a way to reproduce the precise excellence of others. The difference that makes the difference. What it is that successful people do that sets them apart from those who wander through life.

What is the Difference That Makes the Difference?

What is the difference between the have and the have nots? What the difference between the can and the can nots? What is the difference between the people that do and people that don't? Why do some people overcome unimaginable adversity and make their lives a triumph, while others, in spite of every advantage, turn their lives into a disaster? Why do some people take any experience and make it work for them, while others take any experience and make it work against them?

These questions have always fascinated me. Growing up I wandered what was the difference between people who had good family lives, successful jobs, happy existences and people who struggled from day to day.

The difference appeared to be the way people communicated to themselves and others, the actions they consistently took every day, their perceptions on life and how they acted and reacted. Successful people don't necessarily have fewer problems than those who fail—the only people without problems are those in cemeteries—it's just how they perceive and respond to those problems that makes the difference.

I decided many years ago to study models of excellence. If it is possible for one person to do something, I knew it was possible for another person to do the same. It was just a question of how and having the desire.

In my search I studied everyone I could find. While I managed to apply some of these models to my own life, change seemed to be only temporary. That was until I was asked to assist in delivering an NLP Behavioural Modelling course with Wyatt Woodsmall. In my extensive conversations with Wyatt, an expert in modelling behaviour who seemed to have had an influence on world-renowned motivational speaker Tony Robbins, I realised the ways and means of developing a system that could help replicate success.

When I first learnt NLP, I immediately knew it was something different to anything I experienced before. I was hooked and used my new skills to help people overcome fears and phobias in less than 30 minutes, even on live national radio. Just like the BBC Radio programme when I helped one women overcome a phobia of swimming she had had for 56 years.

I refined my process and applied it to many sports teams, participants and individuals looking to improve their life on any level and the results were astounding. It was at that point I decided to turn my attention to business and transfer the applications to create success in business. I helped many of my clients go on to produce phenomenal results in a short space of time.

The NLP modelling process I refined was exactly what I was looking for. It provided a systematic framework for directing the brain. It taught people how to direct not only their own states and behaviours, but also the states and behaviours of others. In short, NLP provided the key for unlocking the mystery of how certain people were consistently able to produce what I call *optimum results*. These people, driven by enthusiasm and motivation, were capable of setting up a successful business and produce consistent results. The next questions were: how do they produce results and what do they do?

Because actions are the source of all results, what specific mental or physical actions produced the neurophysiologic process of being enthusiastic, motivated and having the capability to structure a successful business. One of the presuppositions of NLP is that we all share the same neurology. If someone has the capability to do something, then so can anyone else if they run their nervous system in exactly the same way by the means of modelling.

If it is possible for others in the world to achieve success, it's possible for you. It's not a matter of whether you can produce the results another person produces, it's a matter of using the correct strategy. If someone can deliver fantastic presentations, there's a way to model the person so you can deliver fantastic presentations. If someone can communicate well with his clients and customers, then you can do the same thing. If someone is highly motivated, then you can be also. You simply need to model how another person directs their nervous systems.

Obviously, some tasks are more complex than others and take more time to model. However, if you have a strong enough desire and the belief that will support you while you continue to adjust and change towards your outcome of excellence, then virtually any human accomplishment can be modelled.

MODELLING EXCELLENCE

I have read many books on NLP and personal development; however, not much has been written on the subject of modelling excellence. When you consider modelling is at the heart of NLP, you realise modelling is the pathway to excellence. It means that if one person can achieve a result then so can someone else if they have the desire and are willing to put in the effort.

If you want to achieve an outcome, if you want to achieve excellence, all you need to do is find an exemplar that has already succeeded. What did they do? What actions did they take? How do they use their brain and body to achieve the results?

The process can be used in business. Whether you want to deliver better presentations, set up a new business, or revamp an existing business, find someone who has already succeeded. The people who are the best in the business are masters of learning from other people's experiences. Accelerating our learning process is key in getting us to where we want to go in the least amount of time possible. Time is precious and we only have one life.

This is an opportunity to learn a process that will allow you to duplicate success wherever you find it. It will help you to achieve success in business by learning powerful NLP models and then not just applying them, but going beyond. You have the capability to model excellence, teach it, learn it, apply it, and replicate it as often as you feel necessary to drive your business forward. So you have the freedom to manoeuvre and not be stuck to set systems or patterns. You're in the driver's seat and can consistently look for ways to produce the results you desire.

To model excellence, the key is to become curious and open minded. I learnt the skills I needed by observing and precisely modelling what people of excellence thought and did, even when those actions were a little foreign to me. I used these skills to help improve the performance of individuals and organisations.

Labels

We tend to put labels on ourselves and then conform to that label. A perfect example of that is when I have worked with people that come to see me because they have been labelled as having depression. It's almost as if they walked around every day with a label on their forehead. It became a self-fulfilling prophecy and the identity of the person to the point when experiencing any happiness went against how they thought they should feel.

The same applies in business. People have labels: directors, managers, shop floor staff, etc. But people are not their labels. Underneath a person's conformity to a label is a person who has similar needs to anyone else. You may apply these labels to yourself, even if they are negative or inaccurate. This books teaches you a methodology to break free of any negative patterns and processes and create the quality of life you deserve.

Quality Results

There are three forms of mental and physical actions that correspond most directly to the quality of the results we produce. Picture them as a series of doors labelled "Belief System", "Mental Syntax", and "Physiology".

The first door, Belief System, is what a person believes, what he or she thinks is impossible or possible. To a great extent, it determines what he or she can and can not do.

As the old saying goes, "Whether you believe you can do something or your believe you can't, you're right."

The first key step in modelling excellence is in modelling belief. Whether you believe you can or can't, you're sending constant messages to your nervous system that confirms whether or not you can achieve a result. So, modelling someone's belief system is a great place to start because when someone achieves human excellence in any area, it is always supported by a strong belief that they could achieve it.

The second door, Mental Syntax, is the way people organise their thoughts. Syntax is a code like the 11 digits in a mobile number you need to dial in the right order to reach the person you want. You use syntax when reaching the part of your brain and nervous system that could most effectively help you achieve the outcome you want.

The same is true in communication. Sometimes people don't communicate well with each other because they use different communication codes. This is particularly prevalent in business, unlock the codes and you can access the third door—modelling people's physiology.

The third door, Physiology, is the way you breathe, walk, and talk. Your posture and facial expressions affect what mental state you are in. Your mental state is crucial; the state of mind you are in will determine the way you behave and quality of behaviours you produce.

Modelling for Success

Nearly every aspect of our lives is built on modelling. How does a child learn to speak? How does a young sports person learn from an older one? How does an aspiring business person decide to structure his company? Modelling.

Modelling is useful in the business world because one way people make a lot of money is by introducing a product that's been successful in another part of the world or city. Western societies are consistent enough that if one person introduces something successful in one place, something similar will have a great chance of being successful elsewhere. Let's say you went to the USA on vacation and you noticed the latest craze. You knew it was something you could introduce in the UK, so you'd grab the idea and take it home.

Many people who succeed in business don't necessarily reinvent the wheel. A perfect example is the country of Japan. If you review business history of the last few decades you will find the Japanese have not invented new products but have taken ideas and products from the likes of the USA and Europe (cars and a variety of modern gadgets), and through modelling they retain the best elements of the products and discard the rest. They've been very successful at it.

Some of the wealthiest business people in the world have studied and learnt from other wealthy business people. They then go on and achieve their own success. I once had a client who was restructuring his business from scratch. He had modelled the beliefs and ideologies of everyone in the industry and went on to transform his business and life. I also use modelling to get immediate results for myself and others. I continue to seek out patterns of thought and action that produce excellent results in an accelerated way.

DEVELOPING STRATEGIES

Successful strategies you can implement in business are illustrated throughout this book, but it is not about just teaching you strategies that you copy exactly. You need to be able to develop some of your own strategies to achieve the excellence you deserve. One of the mains things I learnt in my journey of NLP is never to believe anything too much. If you believe something without question, there will be a time when it doesn't work. NLP is a powerful tool, but it is only a tool. You can use this tool to develop and refine your own approaches, your own strategies and your own insights because no one strategy works all the time.

When I first starting working with Bury FC Youth team, my aim was to put together a programme to help develop players to their best potential. I began a search to find a template or templates to help me achieve that goal.

My first port of call was Manchester United football club because they had been producing world-class players such as Ryan Giggs, Paul

Scholes, and David Beckham, to name a few. Manchester United was one of the biggest clubs at the time. They had resources I could only dream of. However, I believed it was possible to learn what they were doing and use some of their methods and techniques to help Bury.

A few of the other teams and organisations I would look were the Australian Institute of Sport, Ajax FC, and Crewe Football Club, which was nearer to the size and infrastructure of Bury. There was a huge variation between the teams and organisations I modelled because we didn't have the resources and infrastructure of the bigger clubs, and, in my opinion, many of the smaller clubs didn't have the psychological mindset I needed to model. Through modelling, I elicited some key strategies.

Key Strategy of Fitness

The first thing I told my players is that I was introducing a fitness test. I had been fortunate to obtain the fitness test results of a top premiership team at the time and I set my players the goal of achieving the same levels of fitness. I told them that if a top premiership player can run 20 meters in less than 3 seconds and 3500 metres in 12 minutes and less, then that is your target as a player.

Because football is a physical sport of rapid changes, each player statistically only touches the ball for approximately 3 minutes in a 90-minute game. The value of being in top shape is immense. The psychological boost for a footballer to know they are as physically fit to participate in football as the leading players in the game is a massive boost.

Key Strategy of Physiology

Physical fitness is not the be all and end all. Other key components are technique, tactics, belief, confidence and other psychological resources, which can all be modelled. When I modelled the template of excellence from several different clubs, I also looked at what they were doing technically and tactically. What were they eating? How did they walk and talk? What did they think and feel? What were their beliefs and values about themselves and football? Most important, what was going through the mind of these players at the highest level? What did they believe about themselves and their teammates?

My aim was to get into the minds of the best footballers and transfer those qualities to my players in order to improve their chances of getting signed with a professional team. The average percent of players that graduate from youth team football to play professionally is around 10%. I wanted to smash that and then some.

The fitness tests and using a measurable target to show the young players they were on par physically with some of the best players in the country was enough to build massive belief and confidence. As a result of raising the bar and replicating excellence, despite being on a tight budget and having scarce resources, the Bury FC Youth team went on to produce Colin Kazim Richards, Nicky Adams, and David Worrall; the list goes on.

SUCCESS LEAVES CLUES

I have always been interested in what makes people successful at what they do, so whenever I get an opportunity to talk to someone who is successful, I use the opportunity to learn. I am intrigued to know how they perceive themselves. What is their identity, values, beliefs, what drives them?

You might not get the opportunity to model an exemplar formally, though if an opportunity presents itself, asking certain questions can help you understand the difference that makes the difference.

I was working with the Bury FC Youth team and we had a game against Manchester United Youth. We went to play them at the Carrington training ground. While we were waiting for the game to start, I saw Roy Keane walking out to watch some of the game. I took the opportunity to approach him and ask questions about what he believed made an excellent player. I remember him saying something along the lines of that in a game of 11 against 11, you always have a chance to make a difference. That conversation stayed with me.

If you can't ask formal questions, you can always use examples. Bury FC had a young player coming through the ranks named David Buchanan. He was maybe 5 foot 7 inches. At that time, teams were looking for players who were around 6 feet tall. I talked to David

Buchanan about Roy Keane, who also wasn't very tall, and how he had made it in the league and had a successful career. I recommended Buchanan read Keane's autobiography. I don't know how much of a part that played in Buchanan going on to becoming a successful footballer, though I am sure it had a positive impact.

I have used this same principle with other athletes, business-people, sales representatives, and people looking to develop positive character traits, such as confidence, motivation, and happiness, to assist them in improving the quality of their life, get in shape, and take a positive step forward and punch above their weight.

Modelling is nothing new. The trouble is that most of us model on an utterly haphazard, unfocused level. It's possible to pick up information from people that isn't going to support your outcome, especially in the world of business, or miss out on valuable information from successful people. We become the sum of all things, some good, some bad.

This book is a phenomenal source of resources and strategies the can guide you to live a life of excellence. Use it to help you create your own templates of excellence, becoming aware of what people do to achieve excellence and how you can achieve the same result.

IT TAKES TIME

Modelling is time-consuming, so the skill you desire to have has to be something you are passionate about acquiring. Your exemplars have to be really good at what they do; there's no point modelling mediocrity.

I think it's important for you to model *in the context that you are looking for.* I was once teaching an NLP course and I was doing a modelling project in which there were a few golfers. One of the golfers said that they wanted to improve their golf swing. I suggested a few names who were the leading golfers. One of them was Tiger Woods. I thought he'd be a perfect person to model because he was very talented and was doing very well in golf at the time.

One of the delegates said he didn't feel comfortable modelling Tiger Woods. I asked, "Why? He's the leading golfer at the moment." The delegate said he didn't feel comfortable because of

Tiger's personal life. At the time there were all these allegations of personal misconduct, well documented in the media.

I told the delegate, "It's the *context* you need to model, not Tiger's personal life. I guess if it's your sex life you want to improve you might want to model his personal life, but that's not what is important here. What's really essential is that you model what is important to you in a given context."

KEY POINTS TO MODELLING

Implicit Modelling

"Become" the person you are modelling. Adopt their physiology, breathing and micro-muscle movements. Practise "being" the person until you can get similar (or much improved) results.

Explicit Modelling

Consciously duplicate each component of the skill you are modelling: physiology, breathing, micro-muscle movements.

Strategy Elicitation

Elicit the values that provide the motivation behind the skill and the beliefs that enable the exemplar to do it. Elicit relevant meta-programmes. What feedback do you look for?

You can compare the patterns common to multiple exemplars, or compare what you do and what an exemplar does, to make it easier to focus in on the essential elements. Use your comparisons to discover what makes the difference between a great exemplar and someone that's merely OK. Use the meta-model to discard any unclear areas so you can elicit the unconscious competence of the exemplar.

Deliberately drop one piece of the behaviour at a time to see which ones are essential to getting the results you want and which are idiosyncratic to the person. When the model is as simple as it can be without affecting the results, code it so you can use it or transfer it to others.

Modelling focuses on the *how* of human excellence. How does the peak performer behave and think and feel? What do they do that is different from people who are less successful? What is the difference that makes the difference? By using our mind and body in the same way as a peak performer, we can increase the quality of our actions and our results.

◢ KEY POINTS

The three phases of the modelling process:

1. Eliciting the process
    - ◢ What the model does: the behaviour and physiology
    - ◢ Why the model does it: the supporting beliefs and assumptions
    - ◢ How the model does it: the internal thinking strategies
    - ◢ The *what* you can get from direct observations. The *why* and the *how* you discover by asking questions.
2. Streamlining the Model
    - ◢ Systematically take out elements of the model's behaviour to see what makes a difference and refine the model.
3. Designing the Teaching
    - ◢ Developing a way to teach the model to others.

NLP MODELLING TECHNIQUES

◢ Identify someone who has skills or achievements that you admire and want to develop for yourself. Modelling is a strategy that requires systematic questioning and observation. If you have access to your exemplar, begin by asking them how he or she does something you would like to do. Identify each step by asking either, "what happens before that?" or "what happens after that?" Remember, many people will not be aware of their strategies so use your observation to notice changes in eye accessing, posture and breathing to help identify internal processing.

◢ If you do not have access to your exemplar, the four-step *starter brief* under "Where to Start" can be used by almost anybody. Try it a couple of times and you may find that you already have some very valuable skills in the area in which you are interested.

◢ Identify people's strategies or the sequence they go through to do something, normally by using meta-model questions.

◢ Get ideas about how someone does something by asking questions based on Robert Dilt's Logical Levels, which we covered in chapter 5.

◢ Using deep-trance identification to take on a complete skill set. This is sometimes called "True" NLP modelling. (To learn more about deep-trance identification, visit www.stephengilligan.com/interviewA.html.)

Where to Start

If this is your first attempt at modelling in an NLP context, there are a few simple rules you can follow in order to gain the most benefit from the experience.

1. Keep the modelled behaviour or skill as simple as possible.

2. Use the NLP coding system at each step to ensure you fully understand the process.

3. Use a combination of all the techniques you know as resources (e.g., Physiological Modelling, New Behaviour Generator (page 320), Strategy Elicitation, and Logical Levels).

4. Learn to be comfortable with not knowing. Accept that there will be a conscious overload of information and you may have no idea of what to pay attention to.

What to Model

When deciding what to model, it's usual to select a big project and break it down into small chunks. At some point along the way, you will discover the difference that makes the difference (an internal process or external behaviour), to model. You can focus your attention on the key point of the behaviour and have a better chance of building a structurally sound model you can use or pass on to others.

How to Gather Information

◢ First decide who you would like to model or what skills or capabilities you would like to develop. Remember NLP is about modelling the best, so set your sights high. Talking first hand to your exemplar is the best way to get this information. You'll be surprised who will see you if you come across as being genuinely interested. If your first choice won't talk to you, there are lots of others who will.

◢ Live observations of an exemplar achieving their results.

◢ Written or digital material by the exemplar which demonstrates them achieving the required results.

◢ Face-to-face interview.

◢ Questionnaires.

◢ Observations of the exemplar performing tasks, such as playing a game or closing a business deal.

Two Ways to Model

1. Imitation

   ◢ Essential to all modelling is to separate what is essential from what is idiosyncratic—the difference that makes the difference.

   ◢ Consciously start dropping pieces to find what out what is essential.

   ◢ Once you have whittled it down to the essential, imitate the action and then check yourself to see how well you did.

2. Cognitive Approach

   ◢ Analyse the action into components: physiology and strategies.

THE ART OF MODELLING

Ascertain: What are the key aspects? Ask yourself and, if you have access to them, the exemplar, "what's the difference that makes the difference so I can acquire this skill/way of being/thinking?"

Be focused: Start with the end in mind. There's a huge amount of potential information that could be gathered and if you gather it all you may not be able to separate the trees from the forest.

Contrast: Contrast analysis is crucial. Modelling can be likened to carrying out an experiment. Remember, there's no failure, just feedback. You'll often learn more when your initial assessment is incorrect; for example, whether a particular stage of the task is crucial or idiosyncratic.

Behaviour: Ask for a behavioural demonstration. If possible, it's important to hear the exemplar describe what they are doing so you can differentiate between what they remember doing or perceive they're doing and what they actually do when they're doing their excellent behaviour.

Identify: Identify each step by asking either, "what happens before that?" or "what happens after that?" Remember many people will not be aware of their strategies so use your observation to notice changes in eye accessing, posture and breathing to help identify internal processing.

Questions You Might Ask

You've chosen someone because they're good at what they do. Let them know how much you admire their skills and keep any confidences that are important to them. Don't stray off the subject into personal matters. For example, you may want to ask the exemplar questions based on the skill of delivering a presentation or closing a sale:

1. You have a reputation of being good at "communicating" (adapt to your topic). Do you mind if I ask you some questions about it?
2. **Environment:** Where and when do you do it?
3. **Behaviours:** What specifically do you do? If you were going to teach me to do it, what would you ask me to do?
4. **Capabilities:** What skills do you have that enable you to do this? How did you learn how to do this?
5. **Beliefs:** What do you believe about yourself when you do this? What do you believe about the person you're doing this to?
6. **Identity:** Do you have a personal mission or vision when you're doing this?

Other Possible Questions

1. How do you know when you're good at this?
2. What emotional and physical state are you in when you do this?
3. What happened for you to be good at this?
4. What are you trying to achieve when you do this?
5. Who else do you recommend I talk to this about?

You could compare the patterns common to multiple exemplars, or compare what you do and what the exemplar does, to make it easier to focus in on the essential elements.

MODELLING STRATEGIES

Strategies can be compared to the programs we use to run our neuro-linguistic computer. The results we get are like the outputs of those programs. Another way to look at it could be that a strategy is the person's "recipe" for achieving a particular outcome, for getting from a present state to a desired state. Change the ingredients, or the steps, and you get a different result.

If you and the exemplar are discussing the skills required for delivering a presentation or closing a sale, the following are some suggested questions you could ask. Some are in the framework of the topic, while others are just general questions you could use when you feel they are appropriate:

External Behaviour/Physiology/What?

1. Describe to me how you do what you do.
2. Because words often aren't enough, you might ask: Could you show me?
3. How would I or someone else know you were doing it?
4. How do you know it's time to start?
5. How do you start?
6. How do you stop?
7. How would I do this?
8. Internal State/Why?

9. How do you feel as you do X?

10. What do you feel as you do X?

11. Where are you feeling it?

Internal Processes/How? (note any sub modalities)

1. Elicit external rep systems—what do you see/hear/feel/taste/smell?

2. What do you say to yourself?

3. What do you see/hear/feel internally?

4. What lets you know to move onto next step?

5. Context

6. Where/when/with whom do you do it?

7. Where/when/with whom don't you do it?

8. General

9. Then what happens?

10. Then what do you do?

Meta-Programmes

1. Elicit all the meta programmes
   - Values
   - What's important to you about doing this?
   - What does this satisfy in you?
   - Why do you do this?
2. Cause and Effect
   - How do you know when to do this?
   - What makes you do X?
   - What would stop you from doing X?

Evidence Procedures

You need to know when to exit, such as when you've achieved your desired outcome.

1. Determine whether the information is specific to the task being modelled.

2. Is this necessary for the skill to happen?

3. Is it sufficient, or is more required for the skill to take place?

The questions you ask may be different depending on if you are asking the exemplar for yourself or if you are designing a model for someone else. If you are asking questions for both yourself and someone else, ask all the questions you have and then compare the answers for parallels.

THE BOTTOM LINE

Can I teach what I have learnt to other people?

◢ IN SUMMARY

1. Be curious about everything and take nothing for granted. Challenge what you would normally take for granted.
2. Get the beliefs and values behind the capabilities and behaviours.
3. Distinguish behaviours and capabilities from beliefs and identity.
4. Understand the client's motivation and determine their *towards* or *away from* balance.
5. Keep the end in mind to help you-stay on track and focussed on getting the result. Ask yourself if any step is taking you towards your outcome.
6. Shift perceptual positions. Try on the behaviours as yourself, but then try it on as though you were one or two other people.
7. Check all logical levels, including the "beyond identity" position you assume when you are using the Creating a Brilliant Future technique.
8. Motivate yourself-by believing that:
   - ◢ You can improve yourself and others.
   - ◢ You will succeed.
   - ◢ Modelling works.
   - ◢ Practise makes perfect.

WHAT ELSE DO YOU NEED TO EXPLORE?

It is interesting to find out whether the exemplar can achieve consistently excellent results at an unconscious level. If you ask a driver how they drive, they will probably respond, "I don't know. I just do it." A driver replicates the skill in a given context, but would there ever be a situation in which the driver couldn't drive? How about if the weather becomes snowy, in heavy rain, or driving abroad? Would that alter the unconscious pattern?

These are all questions you might consider when exploring the exemplar's model, and when you test the model you can see if you can break it. Sometimes you can learn a great deal when something doesn't work. You learn about the boundaries and threshold conditions that exist within the model.

When you test the model, ask the exemplar how it looks. They will know. If they acknowledge it, then you have it. If they look uncomfortable, or challenge the model, then it's back to the drawing board.

NEW BEHAVIOUR GENERATOR

⊿ Carefully watch the role model you have identified do the skill, technique or behaviour you want to duplicate. Take the time to rehearse the skill, technique or behaviour in three steps from either option below:

Step 1: Describe either the behaviour you would like to be able to do or to do better. Start from a belief and internal dialogue of, "I can do this".

Step 2: Close your eyes and create a movie of yourself performing the new behaviour just like the exemplar does. Add sound so that you see and hear yourself. Adjust the movie until you are satisfied with the new behaviour.

Step 3: Step into the movie and check how this feels. Make any further adjustments you need to until you feel the way you want.

Alternatively, you can use option 2:

Step 1: Describe either the behaviour you would like to be able to do or to do better. Start from a belief and internal dialogue of, "I can do this".

Step 2: Close your eyes and create a movie of your exemplar performing the behaviour.

Step 3: When you feel you can mimic the behaviour, remove the exemplar from the movie and insert yourself instead, making any necessary changes you need to.

◢ Learn from "failures" and develop more effective behaviours for the future.

◢ Install a new strategy.

◢ Future pace extensively. Imagine yourself using the new behaviour in the future in three or more opportunities to generalise the new ability.

◢ Chunk the behaviour down. Chunk the desired behaviour into smaller steps and run through Steps 2 and 3 with each chunk.

◢ Use a timeline. Lay out a timeline on the floor, placing the goal at the end. Walk up the timeline from the now to the goal. Stop at each step so you can associate the good feelings you will experience as each new behaviour leads up to the successful achievement of your goal.

Repeat Steps 2 and 3 of either option for each new behaviour you will learn along the timeline. Create alternatives: at Step 2 ask your unconscious mind to create at least 3 options for new behaviours. Try out each one and select the most appropriate to use in Step 3. Finally, store your goal and the new behaviours associated with it in whatever way feels right for you.

TWELVE PRINCIPLES FOR DESIGNING THE MODEL

1. **Chunking:** If the chunks are too big, people may be overwhelmed; if the chunks are too small, it could result in boredom.

2. **Patterns:** Teach the behaviour in the same sequence order in which the expert does it.

3. **Beliefs and Values:** The expert has certain supporting beliefs and values. First find out what beliefs they have that differ from yours or your client's. Remove any

disenabling belief and values you or your client may have and install supporting beliefs and values. Hypnosis, sub-modalities and double inductions are useful in doing this.

4. **Positive Suggestive Language:** Must be used by the teacher. Guard against negative internal representations. Do not use "Do not!" Be totally positive and supportive about what the student can do. Negative embedded commands create a need for permission, so make sure you have a totally positive teaching approach.

5. **Feedback:** It is the most critical component of all! Change without feedback is useless. There are two types: immediate and delayed. The conscious mind can handle delayed feedback well, but it is the unconscious mind that is the most important when using feedback! To train the unconscious, feedback must be immediate. Remember to always stay out of the correction mode and stay in the success mode.

6. **Chunk Levels:** Chunk at a level in which failure is impossible so your client can succeed at each level, at each step. However, don't make the chunks so trivial that it's too easy or else you risk boredom.

7. **Visual Rehearsal:** Successful people visually rehearse each step of their process before they do it. The mental rehearsal is a disassociated process and the actual action is an associated process. The human mind cannot tell the difference between a vivid visualisation and a real memory.

8. **Positive Internal Dialogue:** Most training involves using a positive internal dialogue or positive affirmations. (Changing the sub-modalities of the negative internal dialogue may be all that is necessary.)

9. **Positive Teaching Techniques:** Make sure to use positive language whenever you are teaching or learning a new skill.

10. **Design small wins.**

11. **While teaching, *be* a model of excellence.**
12. **Get people to laugh at themselves.**

◢ THE FINAL TEST

So now you have designed and tested the model and checked with the exemplar that all is well. The next step is to test the model in a context in which you can receive feedback from observers. Initially it might be a good idea to have this happen in a safe environment, such as with friends or NLP Groups so you will receive open, honest, and positive feedback.

Once you have made any final tweaks, it is time to use the model in a "live" context at an unconscious level and note the results. If they are similar to the exemplar then congratulate yourself on a successful project. If not? Guess what?

Just a final thought: acquiring Einstein's problem-solving strategy won't make you an Einstein overnight. However you can expect it to give you access to a different way of thinking about problems and to a wider range of solutions you had before.

10 Building Your Business

*An elderly carpenter was ready to retire. He told his employer
of his plans to leave the house-building business to live a more
leisurely life with his wife and enjoy his extended family.
He would miss the pay check each week, but he wanted to retire.
They could get by.*

*The employer was sorry to see his good worker go and asked
if he could build just one more house as a personal favour. The
carpenter said yes but as he was working on it, the employer could
see that his heart was not in his work. He resorted to shoddy
workmanship and used inferior materials. It was an unfortunate
way to end a dedicated career.*

*When the carpenter finished his work, his employer came to
inspect the house. Then he handed the front door key to the
carpenter and said, "This is your house...my gift to you."*

The carpenter was shocked!

*What a shame! If he had only known he was building his own
house, he would have done it all so differently.*

—Author Unknown

So it is with us. We build our lives, one day at a time, often putting in less than our best into the building. Then, with a shock, we realise we have to live in the house we have built. If we could do it over, we'd do it much differently.

But, you cannot go back. You are the carpenter and every day you hammer a nail, place a board, or erect a wall. Someone once said, "Life is a do-it-yourself project." Your attitude, and the choices you make today, help to build the "house" you will live in tomorrow.

◢BUILD WISELY!

I was working with a client and he had a vast amount of experience. He went from a very well paid job into setting up his own consultancy work. The consultancy work was not going well. He was taking on work at a minimal cost and after a year and a half he was spending more time working than he was before. When you calculated the hours he was putting in, he was receiving under minimum wage. Continuing the business was something he had to think long and hard about. He started the business with the intention of earning more revenue and spending more time with his family. As it happened, he was earning significantly less and seeing his family less.

He did eventually restructure his business and incorporate a new financial structure and the last time we spoke he was doing well.

On another occasion, a client had been offered some work that sounded quite lucrative. He would have to give up his full-time position to deliver a programme for a business. We sat down and had a conversation about what this new position offered financially and what the work would entail. I told my client that he needed to think about the scope of the work and how much time it was going to take to put the work together. Once we had determined that, I pointed out that once he had divided the hours put in by the money he would make, he'd barely scrape in minimum wage. He responded that taking the job would be a way to get his foot in the door.

That was true, but I reminded him that he had extensive experience in the field, he wasn't some young guy starting out. I suggested he keep in mind what he wanted to earn from the actual work itself and then return to the company with a counter offer. Obviously, if the company valued him, he would have no problem getting a fee he deserved.

He nearly ended up selling himself short. I'm not saying everything is about money, but you've got to make money to survive. If you are in a situation where you're working long hours and still not making any profit out of it, the financial pressure will be extreme and the quality of your work is going to go down. It's really important that you put a value on yourself. My client went back to the company and renegotiated his fee. They offered him a much higher contract, which he took.

I was working with another client who was exceptional at her job as a personal trainer. She was considered the best trainer in the organisation she worked for. For years she had the most clients, who held her in high regard. People would travel a considerable distances to work with her. There was even a waiting list of people wanting to work with her.

One day she decided she wanted to set up on her own business, so she booked a session to work with me. I asked her to write an action plan for this business, setting some goals and looking at some key areas that would make the business work. It was six months before I heard from her again.

She told me she had set up her business, just gone for it, and even though she still wanted to be her own boss, she was finding it tough. The vision she had had for herself had not materialised. She was starting work at 5 am, setting up her gym, cleaning the toilets, updating the web site, doing the marketing, and all the other things she hadn't envisioned. Sometimes she wouldn't stop working until she fell wearily into bed at midnight. Her personal and social life was suffering, she was working as hard as ever and yet struggling financially. She could not pinpoint where she was going wrong. She was on the verge of burn out and a break down. I did help her to turn things around, though it was a pain-staking process because of the lost six months.

The moral is: just because you are good at what you do in whatever your field of work, running a business is a completely different ball game. There are many logistics you need to take into consideration. If you don't put a plan in place for managing the process you can easily get overwhelmed.

Delegating work, working as a team, and forming good relationships is instrumental for anyone to succeed in business. Sometimes it can be hard, especially when you are starting out in a business, to get the right balance and cash flow can be tight. You need to put a value on your work–life balance and focus on your strengths. Trying to save a few pounds by doing the cleaning yourself and managing other logistics is not cost effective. You can employ someone else to do those things so you can work to your strengths. In the case of my client, the key to turning the business around was to delegate and step away from being the business.

DEFINING VALUES AND GOALS FOR YOUR BUSINESS

Just as a values inquiry is a useful starting point for you to identify what's important to you and your colleagues, clients and customers, so too is it a useful starting point for your business. Review chapter 7 on values and beliefs and then complete the Values Inventory exercise with an eye towards your business. Identify the most important values that you want your business to embody.

DEFINING GOALS AND TARGET MARKETS

Defining goals is a process that is just as important for your business as it is for your clients. Review chapter 8 on setting goals and formulate an individual action plan. Then apply these goals to your business or career.

To begin thinking broadly about your business or career, answer the following questions:

- ◢ What will I do?
- ◢ How will I do it?
- ◢ When will I do it?
- ◢ How will I know when it has been done?

Refine your thinking by defining what makes you unique as a business or profession and identify your target market. Together, these will help you find your niche and can assist with the process of identifying your goals. To define your unique qualities as a business or your profession, honestly consider not only your interests but also your existing background, schooling, experience, and talents. What makes you different from all the other people in your line of business or your profession? What unique quality or service do you have to offer? Why should your potential clientèle seek out your business or why should you be hired instead of someone else?

To define your target market, ask yourself what group or groups of people you most want to work with. Who needs what you have? Who can most benefit from it? Are you interested in working with the public or private sector, or both? How can you strike a balance between specialising and attracting enough customers to meet your goals? Investing your time, attention, focus, and energy on these matters while you are still in the planning stages will benefit you in the end.

◢ **Exercise**

Define your goals for your business or profession for 6 months, 12 months, 2 years and 5 years. Then identify your target market or markets. Put both in writing.

MISSION STATEMENT

Clarifying the values and defining your goals and target market(s) for your business or profession provides a solid foundation for formulating a mission statement. This is your next task. A mission statement is a formal statement of the objectives of your company or organisation. Values often feature centrally in mission statements. One of the best ways to learn about mission statements is to research those of your favourite organisations; mission statements are often posted on web pages. For example, the mission statement for Amnesty International is:

> *Our vision is of a world in which every person—regardless of race, religion, ethnicity, sexual orientation or gender identity—enjoys all of the human rights enshrined in the Universal Declaration of Human Rights (UDHR) and other internationally recognised human-rights standards. The UDHR states that the "the recognition of the inherent dignity and of the equal and inalienable rights" of all people is "the foundation of freedom, justice and peace in the world."*

This mission statement is a clear, succinct rendering of Amnesty International's calling as an organisation. In reading the statement, it is also possible to deduce some of Amnesty International's values.

What are some of your favourite companies or organisations and what about them do you admire? Locate and study their mission statements.

Use the Logical Levels Model in chapter 5 to assist you in developing your mission statement.

BUSINESS PLANNING, STRATEGY AND DEVELOPMENT

I think continuing your development and learning new things is very important. Some people who have thirty years of experience in a certain industry have not done any extra training after the first year. If you take one thing away from this book it would be that what is truly important is to always strive to make yourself better at what you do.

It's a good idea to draft a business plan. This document does not need to be elaborate and it can be as formal or informal as you wish. Include an overview of the business, your goals, analysis of the services offered, marketing plans, premises, management, and financials. Your strategy is essentially a plan for how you will actualise your mission statement in the real world.

How will you grow your business? Will your business be a sole proprietorship, a partnership, or a corporation? Look back at the goals you identified for your business for 6 months, 12 months, 2 years, and 5 years, as well as the mission statement you drafted. Your planning, strategy, and development should be aligned with these goals and mission.

Consider Michael, who set up a coaching practice but did not want to overload himself with clients. His main goal for each of the identified time markers was to have enough clients to live comfortably. His strategy, planning, and development was therefore geared to meeting and maintaining this goal.

His endeavour was much less complex than the one facing Fiona. She was also a coach and wanted to steadily grow her coaching practice to serve as many clients as possible. Her strategy, planning, and development needed to consider things like partnering with or hiring additional coaches and staff, finding and moving to the appropriate location(s) and office(s), funding, mass marketing campaigns, and the like.

It is important to carefully consider the context of your business—economically, financially, politically, and globally. Do as much research as you can upfront, before making any big decisions or moves, regarding risks, best practices, and best approaches. It's also a good idea to solicit ideas or advice from those who have travelled the road you want to take.

Funding, Fees, Cash Flow, and Profits

One of the most important things when you are running a business is cash flow. Speaking from my own personal experience, I think it is really important that you have clear processes and procedures to support your cash flow, particularly when dealing with big businesses. Some of the biggest challenges I faced when I started up my new business was to make sure the big businesses specified the terms of our collaboration.

I delivered some training for a big corporation and what I did for them was really, really good. After delivering the training, the corporation kept stalling the payment. Months went by but they still had not paid. I had been chasing this invoice for a long time until I got frustrated with their accounts department. They told me to send in a new invoice when I had already sent two. They told me to send a different type of invoice. This dragged on and on until eventually my fee was probably a pittance for them compared to what they had turned profit-wise. It was obviously a lot money for me, especially as I was just starting out. Someone once said to me that they thought big corporations do this deliberately because they think you as a small business are going to go bust and they won't have to pay the money. Obviously they are not supporting a smaller supplier.

So it's really important, no matter what business you run, whether you are starting out or well-established, that when you deliver a service to a big businesses that you make sure you are clear and specific about your terms. Obviously it is not easy because big businesses realise you probably would not chase them up in court because it will cost you more to take them to court than what you could get from them. What I would suggest, and what I did eventually, is to not do any work for *anyone* unless they pay you some money upfront. You have bills to pay as well and you don't want to be chasing money for nothing.

You're likely to encounter start-up expenses for your business. Look for possible funding sources as soon as possible. Make sure you have enough reserves to keep the cash flow stable and the business alive during the formative stages. As part of your business planning and goal setting, decide on your desired income. Execute a break-even analysis, which can help you determine the minimum to charge customers or clients for your service or product and still cover your expenses. Settling on a fee that works for you and your clients may take some adjusting. When deciding what to charge, research the going rate in your location for your type of service. You may need to charge less until you establish a reputation. Over time, you can increase profits by raising your rates and/or increasing the number of clients you serve.

Legalities

Check with the necessary authorities in your area regarding registering your business, obtaining permits or licenses, taxes, and similar legalities. Also find out about pertinent legal and procedural protocols that may be involved in working with a particular group of people, including sponsors and insurance.

Finding Premises

One thing to consider is premises; will you find an office to rent or buy or work out of your home? Which option you choose will depend on your business plan and, to some extent, on the type of service you will offer. Your budget and transportation are also key considerations. Can you afford office rent each month and, if so, how much? Can you find a suitable location within a reasonable distance of your home? Do you want to commute into work? These are all factors to weigh as you embark on the task of establishing your business.

Accounts

Whether you choose to work from an office or from home, you may wish to open a separate bank account for your business. Consider also setting up a means for processing credit card payments. Keep detailed records of all payments received and services rendered using a well-organised filing system. A website, a phone, and an email account are also important aspects of establishing a business. Look into setting these up as soon as possible.

Finding Customers, Advertising, and Marketing

Once you have the basics of your business in place, how do you go about finding customers? Your first customers/clients are likely to be right in front of you. Use your website, phone, and email account to help you to generate those first few leads. Networking and word of mouth are also great ways to spread the news about your business. Ask friends, family, colleagues, and existing customers and clients for referrals. Print some business cards and brochures to distribute at places where you may meet potential customers and clients. You can also post fliers and advertisements in online or print periodicals. Get creative and get motivated about finding customers and clients by advertising and marketing your services. The more creative and the more motivated you are, the more likely you are to have customers and clients. How will you make your services desirable to your target market? If you'd like to be more formal in your marketing approach, draft a detailed plan that is SMART (Specific, Measurable, Attainable, Realistic, and Time-bound).

Customer Service

What kind of customer experience do you want to provide? How does the quality of customer service you offer fit in with the values of your business and your mission statement? The answers to these questions will depend, to a certain extent, on the size of your business. If you are just starting out, *you* may be the customer service department, answering inquiries, booking appointments, and dealing with any problems that arise can be enormously educational. As your business grows and you begin to generate more money and clients, you may opt to hire someone to help you with customer service, add an additional or separate phone line, and similar adjustments.

Continuing Professional Development

Continuing your professional development is beneficial for you, your business, and your customers and clients. As you learn more skills, gain additional credentials, and broaden your reach, you will encounter opportunities to interact with greater numbers of potential clients and colleagues. It's also important to keep informed of latest developments, research, and trends so you can provide the best service possible. Be proactive about finding and taking classes and workshops and attend conferences and other professional development activities regularly. Also be aware of and meet any requirements for keeping licensures or certificates current.

Reflection

- Do I have clear values and a solid mission for my business?
- Am I committed to my goals and ready to do what is necessary to achieve them?
- Am I willing and prepared to tell others about what I do professionally?
- Am I ready for the responsibility involved in operating my own business?
- Do I have the necessary funds and, if not, am I willing to take on the necessary risk?

MEETINGS

Meetings are key when you are starting a business. You want to make sure you are very clear about the outcome. Too many people starting up a new business attend networking meetings, which are glorified social groups, and the meeting becomes more like a party. I avoid networking meetings. They are not a good use of your time.

When I started my first business, I used to get a lot of requests for meetings. As much as I wanted to help out everybody, it was very important to prioritise my time. I would often send out a questionnaire defining what I wanted from the meeting and asking what the other parties wanted. I always tried to set up meetings with people in key decision-making positions.

Meeting Strategies

Determine if the Meeting is Really Necessary

- Meetings, preparing for meetings, and travelling to and from meetings, take up a lot of time that often could be spent more productively elsewhere. You need to establish your outcome or where you want to be by the end of the meeting. If you have previously been unconfident in meetings, this helps to switch the focus from you to your desired outcome. You need to determine:

1. Is the meeting necessary?
2. What will happen by the end of this meeting?
3. What will be measurably different?
4. What you will do for each contingency?
5. What could happen that might disrupt the meeting and establish "if–then" options for what you will do if it does?
6. Who needs to be there and agree on the agenda?
7. What are their outcomes?

Meeting Environment

◢ When setting up the meeting place, make the environment conducive to the outcome you want and ensure there will be no interruptions.

◢ As people come in, greet them and establish rapport. Notice body language. You want alert, responsive people, so if someone appears to be in the grip of a strong, negative emotion this could disrupt their concentration or even the whole meeting if you don't deal with it. You can ask them if there is a problem; they might have left their car in a place that has limited parking or something else that is dividing their attention.

◢ You need to state the outcome and have everyone agree to it by saying something like: "This is where we want to get to by the end of the meeting, and we will know when we've got there because..."

◢ Make sure everyone knows the time the meeting has to end. Leave enough time that everyone has a chance to say what they need to.

⊿ With team meetings, always start with the positives. A good way to get people into a better (and therefore more capable and creative) state is to ask, "What successes and achievements have you had since we last met?" This should be in the spirit of an invitation to contribute, rather than picking on individuals: "You! What have you achieved?"

⊿ Keep the meeting at the right level of detail. Discuss ideas, objectives and responsibilities rather than every little detail of how someone is going to achieve them. If details need to be discussed, it can be done outside the meeting. Remember, the more you drill down into detail, the less interesting it gets for people not directly involved in that topic, and the more opportunities there are for people to disagree.

⊿ Keep the meeting relevant by staying on track. Make the agenda and desired outcome explicit and write it up and put it where people can see it. If any participant goes off on a tangent, you can respectfully challenge them by saying, "Excuse me. How is this relevant to the agenda/outcome we agreed on?" Pretty soon, just a nod or gesture to the agenda should be enough to bring people back on track.

Dealing with Unproductive Participants

⊿ If the person appears to have switched off, you need to establish what's going on with them. Are they worried about something outside the meeting? Consider allowing them to leave and deal with it.

⊿ Are they thinking they shouldn't be there? (Ideally, this is something you would find out beforehand.) If their responsibilities and actions have already been established and they don't need to be there for the rest of the meeting, consider letting them leave.

⊿ If this happens regularly with more than one person, take it as evidence that your meetings are too long or that you are inviting the wrong people.

Dealing with A Participant Who is Objecting or Nitpicking

◢ If the person is constantly raising objections, give them the job of "devil's advocate". Ask them to make notes of any flaws or objections they notice and allocate them some time at the end of the meeting to report back on these.

◢ If there's a major disagreement or objection at any stage, interrupt and summarise what has been agreed on up to that time, starting from the beginning of the meeting and continuing up to the last point of agreement. Match the tonality of the objector to help lead them towards a calmer state.

Ending the Meeting

◢ At the end of the meeting, summarise what has been agreed on, who is going to carry out each action and the completion date. You could also do a mini-summary at the end of each stage.

◢ Confirm the date for the next meeting and thank the participants.

Conclusion

Business can be a highly pressurised environment in which many people seek to get that extra edge over the competition. The cutting edge techniques and skills you have learned by reading this book will assist you with your ability to motivate yourself and others, and stay focused and confident in increasingly competitive fields, whether you're a coach, manager, sales person, or running you own business.

NLP has played a big part in helping businesses to succeed over the past 10 years. Several of the world's leading corporations use the latest NLP techniques to assist with their success, as do many small-to medium-sized business. All are aiming to thrive in ever more competitive fields.

NLP has grown and will continue to grow because of its user-friendly practically in business.

Success in business is a matter of turning over every stone and looking for every advantage possible. What separates a leading business from a mediocre one is the use of a forward thinking mentality.

It all comes down to focus, confidence, motivation, and direction. Ultimately the measure of every successful business is fulfilling its potential, flourishing and evolving. Whether your aspirations are to build or continue the evolution of a major corporation or to be a part of a successful enterprise or organisation, you can fulfil your dreams and live your passion. This book has given you invaluable information to help you on your journey.

Jimmy Petruzzi, January 2014

# Glossary

Accessing Cues: External signs that give us information about how we think.

Analogue: Analogue distinctions have discrete variations, as in an analogue watch. This is as opposed to digital.

Analogue Marking: Using a verbal or non-verbal cue to mark out words in a sentence.

Anchoring: The process by which any representation, internal or external (the stimulus), gets connected and linked to and triggers a subsequent string of representations and responses (the response). Anchors can be naturally occurring or set up deliberately.

As-If Frame: This is "acting as if" something were true, such as pretending that you are competent at something you are not.

Associated: The relationship you have with the memory of an experience as if seen through your own eyes.

Auditory (A): The representational system dealing with hearing. It can be internal or external. Also known as Auditory Tonal (At).

Auditory Digital (Ad): The representational system dealing with logic and the way we talk to ourselves.

Backtrack: To go back and summarize, review or contemplate what was previously covered (as in a recent meeting, etc.).

Behaviour: An external, verifiable activity we produce or engage in.

Being At Cause Beliefs: Taking responsibility for the results of one's actions. Generalizations we make about the world and our opinions about it. They form the rules about what we can and cannot do.

Break State: Using a movement or distance to change an emotional state.

Calibration: The ability to notice and measure changes with respect to a standard. Usually involves the comparison between two different sets of external, non-verbal cues. By comparing, we can notice the difference between persons, places, things, states and behaviours. Calibrating depends on refined sensory acuity.

Chaining: Sequencing a series of states.

Chunking: Changing a perception by moving a "chunk", or a group of bits of information, in the direction of a deductive or inductive conclusion through the use of language.

Circle of Excellence: Using an imaginary circle on the floor as a spatial anchor to install new or additional resources relative to a situation where different behaviour or thinking is wished.

Complex Equivalence: This occurs when (1) you attach meaning to something specific and (2) when two statements, one behavioural and one capability, are considered to mean the same (*see* meta-programmes, chapter 4 or page 341).

Confusion to Understanding: Original pattern developed by Richard Bandler using submodalities to change the meaning of your internal representations and is the basis of "Like to Dislike."

Congruence: When behaviour (words, tonality, physiology, etc.) matches the words a person says.

Conscious: That of which we are currently aware.

Integration: When our thoughts and behaviours are integrated at the conscious and unconscious levels.

Content: The details of a story. The history of the client.

Content Reframe: Giving another meaning to a statement by recovering more content, which changes the focus (also called a meaning reframe).

Context: The particular setting or situation in which the content occurs.

Context Reframing: Giving another meaning to a statement by changing the context.

Contrastive Analysis: This is a process of analyzing two sets of submodalities to discover the critical submodalities. What makes the two sets different.

Convincer: Something that convinces the client's conscious mind that their unconscious mind can do something.

Convincer Strategy: The filter used in becoming certain or confident that something is okay.

Criteria: The NLP word for value. Values are what is important to you and determine how you spend your time.

Critical Submodality: In submodalities, critical submodalities are the difference that makes the difference. Discovered through the process of contrastive analysis, critical submodalities account for the difference between two different internal representations. When submodalities are compared through contrastive analysis, the critical submodalities are the submodalities that are different.

Cross-Over Matching: Matching one aspect of a person's external behaviour or physiology with a different physiological movement.

Deductive: Reasoning from the general to the specific. To chunk down.

Deep Structure: The unconscious basis for the surface structure of a statement. Much of the deep structure is out of awareness. The deeper underlying root cause, or meaning of a spoken word.

Deletion: One of the three major processes (including distortion and generalisation) on which the meta-model is based. Deletion occurs when we leave out a portion of our experience as we make our internal representations.

Derivation: Obtain from the deep structure to create the spoken word.

Digital: Digital distinctions have distinct variations of meaning as in a digital watch, or an on/off switch. This is as opposed to analogue.

Dissociated: The relationship you have with the memory of an experience. As if seeing your whole body in the picture.

Distortion: One of the three major processes (including deletion and generalisation) on which the meta-model is based. Distortion occurs when something is mistaken for that which it is not, when things are incorrectly included in our internal representations.

Double Binds: Questions that give a client a "free choice" among two or more comparable alternatives. They are based on the notion of multilevel communication.

Downtime: Having all sensory inputs focused inward. Therefore, there will be no attention available for outward attention.

Drivers: The submodality that makes the most difference in our meaning of an experience. It is so important that it carries all the other submodality differences, the critical submodalities, when we change it.

Ecology: The study of the consequences or results or impact of any change that occurs on the wider system.

Elicitation: Inducing a state in a client, or gathering information by asking questions or observing the client's behaviour (*see* Accessing Cues).

Embedded Command: A command that is inside a longer sentence marked out by voice tone or gesture.

Embedded Question: A question that is inside a longer sentence marked out by voice tone or gesture.

Eye Accessing Cues: Movements of the eyes in certain directions that indicate visual, auditory or kinaesthetic thinking.

Feedback: The results of your actions to influence your next step.

First Position: This is one of the perceptual positions. First Position is when you are associated, looking through your own eyes, and in touch with only your own inner model of the world.

Fractionation: Repeating the induction of trance which deepens trance.

Frame: The context or particular point of view around a specific experience.

Future Pace: Mentally rehearsing a future result so that the desired outcome automatically occurs.

Generalisation: One of the three major processes (including distortion and deletion) on which the meta-model is based. Generalisation occurs when one specific experience represents a whole class of experiences. Generalisation also occurs when one experience is generalized to the whole.

Gestalt: A collection of memories around a certain topic.

Gustatory (G): The representational system dealing with taste.

Hallucination: Sensory experience of something that does not exist.

Hypnotism: A relaxed state induced in a person so change work can be done at the subconscious or unconscious level.

Incongruence: When the external, verifiable behaviour of a person does not match the words the person says.

Inductive: Drawing a general conclusion (abstract) from specific facts. Chunking up.

Intent: The desired outcome of a behaviour.

Internal Representations: The content of our thinking or the confirmation of information which includes pictures, sounds, feelings, tastes, smells, and self talk.

In Time: An In Time person will prefer to code their memories from front to back, up to down, in a 'V' or any arrangement where part of the past, present of future is behind or inside the memories.

Kinaesthetic (K): The representational system dealing with feelings and sensations. It can be internal or external.

Law of Dominant Effect: A suggestion is more effective when it is experienced simultaneously with a strong emotion.

Law of Requisite Variety: In a given physical system, that part of the system with the greatest flexibility of behaviour will control the system.

Leading: Changing your own behaviour will provide enough rapport so another person will follow.

Lead System: The representational system used to access stored information and lead it from the unconscious mind to the conscious mind. Watching eye accessing cues (page 110) discovers the lead system. We look where the eyes go when someone accesses information.

Limiting Belief: Beliefs or decisions we make about ourselves and/or our model of the world that limit the way we live.

Limiting Decision: The decision that preceded the adoption of limiting belief.

Logical Level: The level of specificity or abstraction. Think of logical levels as going up or down from abstract at the top to specific at the bottom.

Mapping Across: Following contrastive analysis, mapping across is the submodality process of actually changing the set of submodalities of a certain internal representation to change its meaning.

Matching: Doing the same, copying or adopting the behaviour of the client or replicating exactly some aspect of a person's physiology.

Meaning Reframe: Giving another meaning to a statement by recovering more content, which changes the focus (sometimes called a content reframe).

Meta: Something is meta to another if it is at a higher level.

Meta-Model: A model of language, derived from Virginia Satir that gives us an "over" view of language. It allows us to recognize deletions, generalisations and distortions in our language, and gives us questions to clarify imprecise language and gain specificity.

Metaphor: A story which is symbolic and which allows us to bypass the conscious resistance of the client and to have the client make connections at a deeper level.

Meta-Position: A location outside a situation enabling you to view the situation in a more objective way. A dissociated position not involved with the content of the event or the person. Very similar to third position.

Meta-Programs: These are unconscious, content-free programs we run which filter our experiences.

Milton Model: The Milton Model is designed to produce trance or agreement. It is a series of abstract language patterns, which are ambiguous so as to match the client's experience and assist in accessing unconscious resources. The Milton Model has the opposite intent of the meta-model.

Mirroring: Reflecting the behaviour or physiology of another person as if looking into a mirror.

Mismatching: Using different patterns or contradictory responses regarding behaviour or words to interrupt communication.

Modalities: Refers to our internal representations, which relate to the five senses (visual, auditory, kinaesthetic, olfactory, gustatory) plus our internal dialogue.

Model of the World: A person's value, beliefs and attitudes as well as their internal representations, states and physiology, that all relate to and create their belief system of how the world operates.

Model Operators: Modal Operator of Necessity relates to words, which form the rules in our lives (should, must, have to, etc.) Modal Operator of Possibility relates to words (will, may, would, could, etc.) that reflect an optimistic model in which we view various options and alternatives as possible. "Another day, another dollar."

Model: In NLP, a Model is a description of a concept or behaviour, which can be adopted easily.

Modelling: Modelling is the process by which all of NLP was created. In modelling we elicit the strategies, filter patterns (beliefs and values) and the physiology that allows someone to produce a certain behaviour. Then we codify these in a series of steps designed to make the behaviour easy to reproduce.

Neuro Linguistic Programming: NLP is the study of excellence, which describes how the language of our mind produces our behaviour, and allows us to model excellence and to reproduce that excellent behaviour.

Nominalization: A noun describing a state of being which exists in name only. Not a tangible item. Can be a verb or another process word that has been formed into an abstract noun.

Olfactory (O): The representational system dealing with smell.

Outcome Orientation: Having a specific, sensory-based, desired result for the client. Having an end and an aim in mind.

Overlapping: Moving from the preferred representational system representational system to another representational system.

Pacing: Gaining and maintaining rapport with another person over a period of time by joining them in their model of the world by matching or mirroring their external behaviour.

Parts: Parts are a portion of the unconscious mind, often having conflicting beliefs and values that are different from the whole of the system.

Parts Integration: A technique, which allows us to integrate parts at the unconscious level by chunking up and to go beyond the boundaries of each to find a higher level of intention and wholeness.

Pattern Interrupt: Changing a person's state. Can be abrupt (*see* Break State).

Perceptual Position: Describes our point of view in a specific situation. First Position is our own point of view. Second Position is usually someone else's point of view. Third position is the point of view of a dissociated observer, much like an overview or meta-position.

Personal Edit: *see* Self Edit.

Phobia: A severe, associated, unwanted response of fear regarding some person or event in the past.

Phonological Ambiguity: This occurs when there are two words which sound the same but have different meanings.

Physiology of Excellence: Modelling excellence in others and utilising it in yourself and others.

Post-Hypnotic Suggestion: A hypnotic suggestion that activates and operates at a time after the induction of trance.

Precision Model: Derived by John Grinder from the meta-model as a series of five pointers to greater understanding.

Predicates: Words and phrases (primarily verbs, adverbs and adjectives) that often presuppose one of the representational systems.

Preferred Rep System: This is the representational system that someone most often uses to think, and to organize his or her experiences. This is the representational system

Presuppositions: The assumptions that a client makes to support their model of the world. Presuppositions are what are necessarily true for the client's belief systems of make sense and have meaning to the client.

Primary Rep System: This is how we represent our internal processing externally. Most people tend to favour one representational system over another and process most communication in that manner.

Presuppositions on NLP: Assumptions or convenient beliefs, which are not necessarily "true", but which, if accepted and believed, will change our thinking and improve our results.

Projection: To attribute one's ideas or feelings to other people or to another model of the world.

Punctuation Ambiguity: An ambiguity which is created by changing the punctuation of a sentence, by pausing in the wrong place, or by running on two sentences.

Quotes: This is a Linguistic Pattern in which your message is expressed as if by someone else.

Rapport: The process of responsiveness, at the unconscious level. The ability to relate to others in a way that creates a climate of trust and understanding.

Reference System: The base against what we calibrate. How we organize information so that we know what we know.

Referential Index Shift: Finding someone else who has a way of thinking or a resource you wish to model by entering their model of the world and noting from their perspective and in all modalities the process and results of their thinking and/or action. Also making a change in the referential index (subject) of a sentence to create overload at the conscious level.

Reframing: The process of making a shift in the nature of a problem or changing the structure or context of a statement to give it another meaning.

Representation: A thought in the mind which can be comprised of visual, auditory, kinaesthetic, olfactory, gustatory, and auditory digital (self talk).

Representational System: This is the way we code sensory information and experience our world. There is a representational system for each of our senses.

Resources: Resources are the means to create change within oneself or to accomplish an outcome. Resources may include certain states, adopting specific physiology, new strategies, beliefs, values or attitudes, even specific behaviour.

Resourceful State: This refers to any state where a person has positive, helpful emotions and strategies available to him or her and is operating from them behaviourally. Obviously the state implies a successful outcome.

Search Anchor: An anchor used to identify the source of a problem or issue.

Secondary Gain: The reason/reward the client has or receives for not changing from a presenting problem or outside source.

Second Position: Relating to a perceptual position. Second position is usually someone else's point of view.

Self Edit: Accessing your personal resources & making a change.

Self Inventory: A sensory-based internal scan.

Sensory Acuity: The ability to notice and gain awareness of another person's conscious and unconscious responses through their physiology.

Sensory-Based Description: Is describing someone's verifiable external behaviour in a way that does not include any evaluations or assumptions, but in a way that just relates the specific physiology.

State: Relates to our internal emotional condition. In NLP we believe that the state determines our results, and so we are careful to be in states of excellence. In NLP, our internal representations, plus our State, and our physiology results in our behaviour.

Strategy: A specific repeatable and anchored sequence of internal and external representations that leads to a particular outcome.

Submodalities: These are fine distinctions (or the subsets of the modalities) that are part of each representational system that encode and give meaning to our experiences.

Surface Structure: This is a linguistic term relating to the organization of the spoken level of our communication, which generally leaves out the totality of the Deep Structure. The way we leave out the deep structure is by deletion, generalisation and distortion.

Synaesthesia: A two-step strategy, between modalities, where the two steps are linked together with one usually out of awareness.

Syntactic Ambiguity: Where it is impossible to tell from the syntax of a sentence the meaning of a certain word.

Third Position: Relating to perceptual positions. Third position, or meta-position, is the point of view of a dissociated observer, an overview.

Through Time: Through Time people will store their memories left to right or right to left or in any other way so that all time is in front of them. Time is a conscious and uninterrupted line. These people generally like to write list and will always aim to be on time.

Time Code: The way we store our memories into the past, present and future.

Time Line: A way in which we store our memories of the past, the present and the future making each person's time line metaphorically unique to them.

Trance: Any altered state. In hypnosis it is usually characterised by inward, one-pointed focus.

Transderivational Search: Part of eye accessing cues. Looking through several or all of the representational systems for the same piece of information.

Transformation: A series of derivations which connect the deep structure to the surface structure.

Trigger: The external event or internal belief that starts a behaviour or response.

Unconscious: That of which you are not conscious, or which is out of conscious awareness.

Unconscious Mind: The part of your mind that you are not conscious of.

Universal: An experience that is so well known that it is assumed.

Universal Quantifiers: Words that are universal generalizations and have no referential index. Includes words such as "all", "every", and "never".

Uptime: Having all sensory inputs focused outward, leaving no attention available for inward attention.

Utilisation: Pacing someone's reality by simply describing their ongoing sensory experience of what they must be feeling, hearing, or seeing.

Values: High-level generalizations that describe that which is important to you. In NLP sometimes called criteria.

Visual (V): The representational system dealing with the sense of sight. It can be internal or external.

Visual Squash: An NLP technique which allows us to integrate parts at the unconscious level by assisting each one to traverse logical levels (by chunking up) and to go beyond the boundaries of each to find a higher level of wholeness. Now called Parts Integration.

Well-Formedness Conditions: The well-formedness conditions allow us to specify outcomes that are more achievable, because the language conforms to certain rules.

About the Author

Jimmy Petruzzi is a world-renowned performance coach and NLP, CBT and Hypnotherapy expert. For more than 15 years he has worked and continues to work with many top professional soccer teams and soccer individuals at the national and international level in the English premiership and worldwide. He also works with international and Olympic athletes, top professional sports people, and is a consultant to sports organisations, businesses and associations, helping them to achieve peak performance in all aspects of their lives. Jimmy has worked with thousands of people worldwide during the past 15 years and is a sought after and highly regarded speaker for international conferences and seminars.

Jimmy is a regular columnist for several leading publications, including *Peak Performance* and *Mens' Fitness*, and appears regularly on television news and sports-related documentaries, on radio and in the press. He won the highly commended "Coaching Award for International and Domestic Work" in 2006. He was nominated for Britain's top coach in 2008.

Jimmy is the author of the best-selling book *Excel at Sports*.

ther Books from Dragon Rising

Excel at Sports—Jimmy Petruzzi
Be the Best at Sports, Business & Life with
NLP Neuro Linguistic Programming

Elite athletes know that there is as little as 1% difference between being the best, and being at the back of the field.

Excel at Sports by Jimmy Petruzzi is a simple, concise and ground-breaking guide to NLP Neuro Linguistic Programming and other techniques that can give you that extra 1%, whether in sports, business or life in general.

Everything in life is better if you tackle it head on, with a clear, focused mind and the right attitude.

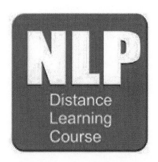

The Neuro Linguistic Programming Distance Learning Course—Jimmy Petruzzi

Includes Full Tutor Support & Certification

DragonRising, in conjunction with the NLP Centre of Excellence, invite you to study to become a fully qualified NLP Practitioner Coach from the comfort of your own home.

The NLP Practitioner Distance Learning Course is tutored by DragonRising author Jimmy Petruzzi and is fully certified by the Institute of Leadership & Management (ILM) and The International Association of Neuro Linguistic Programming and Coaching (IANLPC).

The Hypnotherapy Practitioner Distance Learning Course—Sara Lou-Ann Jones & Jimmy Petruzzi

Includes Full Tutor Support & Certification

DragonRising Publishing and the Hypnotherapy Centre of Excellence invite you to study to become a fully certified Hypnotherapy Practitioner.

The course is tutored by Hypnotherapy Trainer and Master Practitioner Sara Lou-Ann Jones and DragonRising author Jimmy Petruzzi, and is fully certified by the Hypnotherapy Centre of Excellence and the IANLPC, as well as being approved by the Institute of Leadership & Management (ILM).

The Perfect Fit—Ed Grimshaw
Advanced Skills For Finding And Hiring The Ideal Candidate

Here is a thorough approach to making good recruitment decisions and to avoid costly mistakes.

This book will show you how to attract, interview and test candidates without incurring extra profiling costs, and to discover if the candidate matches your organisation's culture to be "The Perfect Fit".

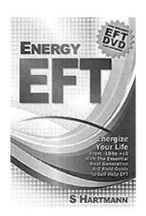

Energy EFT—Silvia Hartmann
Next Generation Tapping & Emotional Freedom Techniques

Silvia Hartmann, chair of The AMT, takes Gary Craig's classic EFT to the next level with this wonderfully comprehensive book that is an absolute must-buy for anyone interested in energy and its use in turning negative emotions into positive ones. All emotions can be worked with, including Stress, Anxiety, Fear & PTSD. Energy EFT is suitable for both beginners, energy workers in different modalities and also top-level EFT master practitioners & trainers wanting to know more.

Positive EFT—Silvia Hartmann
Stronger, Faster, Smarter but Most of All, Happier

Positive EFT is the antidote to depression, anxiety, stress, temper tantrums, low energy, misery, impatience, indecision, confusion and feeling helpless, hopeless, powerless and alone. Positive EFT makes introducing EFT an easy and thoroughly enjoyable, uplifting experience. It is perfect for self help and an absolute "must have!" resource for the modern practitioner.

BIG Ted's Guide to Tapping—Alex Kent, Illustrated by Jen Smith
Turn Negative Emotions Into Positive Ones with BIG Ted

Join the loveable BIG Ted as he guides you and your child through the near miraculous Emotional Freedom Techniques (EFT). You'll both discover how your emotions are transformed by tapping with your magic finger on points around your face, body and hands.

BIG Ted is suitable for children of all ages and adults will also benefit from joining in with the fun.

◢ THE EFT MASTER PRACTITIONER DISTANCE LEARNING COURSE—SILVIA HARTMANN & KELLY BURCH

Includes Full Tutor Support,
Certification & 12-DVD Set

The AMT EFT Master Practitioner Course takes the developments from the last 14 years of EFT worldwide and brings them together so that the student can experience a clear, logical, direct and powerful way to resolve problems with EFT Emotional Freedom Techniques.

The successful student will gain the AMT EFT Master Practitioner Certification and become a full member of The Association for Meridan & Energy Therapies (The AMT).